Theses From Natural Theology

William J. Brosnan, S.J.

GOD AND REASON

GOD INFINITE AND REASON

GOD INFINITE, THE WORLD, AND REASON

GOD INFINITE
THE
WORLD
AND
REASON

Some Theses From Natural Theology

by WILLIAM J. BROSNAN, S.J., PH.D.

Professor of Natural Theology

Woodstock College, Woodstock, Maryland

NEW YORK

FORDHAM UNIVERSITY PRESS

1943

60513

CONTENTS

The different classes of objects which include all things knowable. The knowability of these objects from all eternity. — God's knowledge considered in itself and in comparison with man's knowledge.

Adversaries. — Proofs.

Can the possibles be said to constitute, in any way, an actual infinite multitude? — Some points to be noted concerning the futuribles. — Is there any objective medium in which God can know man's free acts? True and false answers to this question.

The formal object of God's knowledge, or the objective medium in which God knows all things knowable, is the Divine Essence. How the different objects of God's knowledge co-exist, as knowable objects, with that knowledge, from all eternity.

Divisions of God's knowledge: Simple Intelligence, Vision; Necessary and Free Knowledge; Scientia Media.

Modern philosophy and God's infinite knowledge.

Difficulties.

The world: its meaning. Was brought into existence by creation: its meaning. Creation: its definitions.

Adversaries. — Proofs.

Unaided reason and the notion of creation. — The creative power belongs to God alone. — It is impossible for any creature to have existed from eternity.

Difficulties.

Conservation: its divisions; definitions.
Sense of the thesis.
Adversaries. — Proof. — Confirmatory proof.
God's action and its effects in the production and conservation of various classes of beings. God has the absolute power to annihilate creatures. This power He will not exercise.
Difficulties.

Scope of the thesis.
Divine Concursus: its divisions; definitions, with explanations.
Adversaries. — Proofs.
Some notes on the opinion concerning the nature of God's physical concursus, which appears to be the true one (to be more fully explained in *Thesis V*.) — Saint Thomas and the necessity of God's immediate, physical concursus.
Difficulties.

Scope of the thesis.
The previo-simultaneous concursus of the Thomists. Physical predetermination: defined; definition explained. — Some historical data. *Congregatio de Auxiliis.*
Aim of the Thomists in advancing their theory. Aim of the Jesuits in opposing it. — God physically predetermines man not only when his act is morally good but also when it is morally bad—sinful. — The simultaneous concursus as commonly explained by the Jesuits. Some historical data. Bañez; the Bannesians. Molina; the Molinists.
The physical immediate concursus of God looked at in itself. The concursus as it affects the will and its actions.
The offered concursus. The conferred concursus. In what sense God's conferred concursus is simultaneous with the action of the creature. In what sense the conferred concursus of God must be given precedence over the action of the creature. In what sense the free action of the creature may be said to take precedence over the conferred concursus of God. God, then, so concurs with the free act of the creature that

viii CONTENTS

GOD INFINITE, THE WORLD, AND REASON

INTRODUCTION

In the Introductions to *God and Reason* * and *God Infinite and Reason*,* former works which the present one complements, to stress the importance, especially the present-day importance, of clear, reasoned thinking concerning God—the Fundamental Truth, we showed, through numerous quotations from the writings of not a few of its current representative exponents, the utter confusion into which Modern Philosophy has been led in this matter most vital to man, by its all but universal rejection of Reason as a safe guide in solving any of the deeper problems of life.

We shall follow the same plan here, directing our attention more particularly to the errors of Modern Philosophy touching upon the matter treated of in our present work, namely, the relations which must necessarily exist between God, the infinite and freely-willing source of all reality distinct from Himself, and that reality.

It may be well, however, to note that though the word *World*, as we use it in the title of our book, is, consequently, to be understood as embracing all reality other than God, still, in Thesis VI and Thesis VII of this book, which consider God's providential government of the world, though the principles used in them are universal, still their application is restricted to the World in which we live, with all its evils, moral and physical—the only World, namely, which is known to us as philosophers, that is, through the light of Reason.

Of the authors whom we shall cite, some are professedly philosophers; the others, men more or less eminent in other sciences, for example, mathematics, physics, biology, who, perhaps because of that eminence, have considered themselves fully equipped to dogmatize on matters philosophic, including even God, Religion, and Morality.

Though all of those authors agree in degrading reason,

* *God and Reason,* Fordham University Press; *God Infinite and Reason,* America Press.

3

they differ widely, as might be expected, in their positive teaching. They present their views, for the most part, as personal theories, and, in some cases, in such vague language, that it is hard to tell of what philosophic complexion they severally may be, Idealist or Realist, Pantheist or Monist, or non-Theistic Pluralist.

A rather general trend, however, will be found among the Scientists, away from a mechanistic explanation of the Universe. In increasing numbers, they now admit that the final solution of the World-problem must be found in a ruling intelligence of some kind. The intelligence they speak of, though, is not the Creator-God of Theism, the physical and moral Governor of a world utterly distinct from, yet utterly depending on Himself.

Our first witness is a biologist, Julian S. Huxley, a grandson of the famous Agnostic, Thomas Huxley. He definitively rejects the God of Theism. His God, if indeed he believes in one, may be man or may be an ideal. We quote from his contribution to a symposium of modern scientific opinion published in 1931 under the title, *Has Science Discovered God?* (edited by Edward Cotton). Huxley's paper is entitled, "Religion: Its Persistence and Human Character."

He begins by confessing quite humbly that he is an Agnostic. "The first, and in a way, most important ingredient of any religion congruous with science must be a reverent agnosticism concerning ultimates. . . . Man is a limited and partial creature, a product of material evolution. . . . We have no grounds for supposing that his construction is adapted to understand the ultimate nature or cause or purpose of the universe, and indeed, every reason for supposing the contrary." With this humble confession of ignorance "concerning ultimates," he then goes on, quite illogically assuming the role of a dogmatizing Atheist, to reject the only possible "Ultimate" who explains the riddle of the Universe —its Creator, the God of Theism. Huxley writes:

Where then does the solution of the religious problem lie? It would seem to lie in dismantling the theistic edifice, which will no longer bear the weight of the universe as enlarged by recent science; and in attempting to find new outlets for the religious spirit. God, in any but a philosophical, and, one is almost

tempted to say, a Pickwickian sense, turns out to be a product of
the human mind. As an independent or unitary being, active in
the affairs of the universe, He does not exist. . . .

To imagine, as many people do, that religion will cease to
exist [if the idea of God or gods is done away with] is to be
lamentably illogical. The religious emotions are the product of
man's nature. Robbed of the outlet of deity, they will find other
outlets. No longer moulded by the idea of God, they will be
moulded by other concepts, and will manifest a fresh evolution
into new forms. . . . It is obvious that with the abandonment
of the idea of God as a single independent power, with a nature
akin to personality, many current religious practices will become
meaningless. There will be no room for services of intercession,
of prayer in the ordinary sense, for fear of incomprehensible
punishment, for propitiatory sacrifices, or for the worship that is
regarded as agreeable for its recipient. Providence turns out to
be wrongly named, and the Will of God resolves itself into a
combination of the driving forces of nature with the spiritual
pressure of abstract ideas and certain of the conscious and sub-
conscious desires of man.

[And the end of it all, as Huxley sees it, is this:] I see the
human race engaged in the tremendous experiment of living on
the planet called earth. From the point of view of humanity as
a whole, the great aim of this experiment must be to make life
[on this earth] more truly and more fully worth living; the religious man might prefer to say that the aim was to realize the
Kingdom of God upon earth, but that is only another way of
saying the same thing. (Pp. 105-117, *passim*.)

Ernest Haeckel, another biologist, a pure Materialist,
though he claims that he is not (cf. *Riddle of the Universe,*
Translated by McCabe, p. 16) explains the world riddle
without any appeal to God or creation. He rejects both.
Eternal matter in motion from eternity explains everything.
Though he calls himself a Pantheist he admits farther on
that Pantheism is really Atheism. And rightly so, for according to the common consent of mankind, the word, God, in
its least true signification, stands for a real and actual being
distinct from the world, superior to it, its ruler. Pantheism
denies the existence of such a being. The name, Pantheism,
it is to be noted, is given frequently only to Spiritualistic
Monism, whilst Materialistic Monism, the system defended

by Haeckel, is called simply Monism. The following passages
from *The Riddle of the Universe* make Haeckel's position
sufficiently clear.

The extent of the universe is infinite and unbounded; it is
empty in no part, but everywhere filled with substance. The duration of the world is equally infinite and unbounded; it has no
beginning and no end; it is eternity. Substance is everywhere
and always in uninterrupted movement and transformation; . . .
yet the infinite quantity of matter and of eternally changing
force remains constant; . . . Our own "human nature," which
exalted itself into the image of God in its anthropistic illusion,
sinks to the level of a placental mammal, which has no more
value for the universe at large than the ant . . . or the smallest
bacillus. Humanity is but a transitory phase of the evolution of
an eternal substance, a particular phenomenal form of matter
and energy. . . .
Pantheism teaches that God and the world are one. . . .
There is always this fundamental contradition between them,
that in Theism God is opposed to nature as an *extramundane*
being, as *creating* and *sustaining the world,* and acting upon it
from without, while in Pantheism God, as an intramundane being, is everywhere identified with nature itself, and is operative
within the world as "force" or "energy."
The latter view alone is compatible with our supreme law—
the law of substance. (Pp. 198f., 236.)

In the last passage, Haeckel, the self-styled Pantheist,
speaks of God; in the following one, he admits that the
word *God* stands for nothing. There is no God. "Schopen-
hauer justly remarks: 'Pantheism is only a polite form of
Atheism. The truth of Pantheism lies in its destruction of
the dualist antithesis of God and the world, in its recognition
that the world exists in virtue of its own inherent forces.
The maxim of the Pantheist, "God and the world are one,"
is merely a polite way of giving the Lord God his congé.'"

The two authors we next cite are Idealistic Pantheists.
Not matter but spirit is the substance of the one being they
call God. All things that are, are but mental or ideal manifestations of this one being, produced by a necessary and
intrinsic evolution of itself. These manifestations, therefore,
have no real physical existence. God is, in no sense, an

efficient physical cause of a really existing physical world distinct from Himself. He is not a Creator.

Josiah Royce, in *The Religious Aspect of Philosophy*, writes in this wise of creation.

Creation, for the popular conception, certainly involves producing a thing of some kind by a creative act, the thing produced existing forthwith outside of the creator. To give up this separation of Creator and product is to become Pantheistic. And with Monism we are not here concerned. But now the idea of an infinite creative power outside of his products involves more than one difficulty. We shall not dwell on the old difficulty that this infinite power would become finite as soon as there was in existence something outside of itself. We shall proceed at once to a more fruitful and serious difficulty, which we find in the fact that the concept of producing an external thing involves, of necessity, a relation to a Law, above both producer and product, which determines the conditions under which there can be a product at all. The creative power must then work under conditions, however magical and mysterious its acts may be. And working under conditions, it must be finite. No device for minimizing the meaning of this separation of creative power and created thing will really escape the difficulty resulting. And this difficulty will appear in all cases of supposed creation. It may be summed up once more in the statement that any creative power in act, just as much needs explanation in some higher law and power as does the thing created itself, so that whatever creates a product external to itself becomes thereby as truly dependent a power as we ourselves are. . . . Mysterious as creation may be, we may be sure that if creation is of such a nature as to involve an external power and an external law, outside of God's creative power itself, then God is himself not infinite. And we can be equally sure that unless God as a creator is identical with his products, the idea of a creative act does involve just such a power preceding the act and outside of God himself. . . . Hence the deepest assertion of idealism is not that above all the evil powers in the world there is at work some good power mightier than they, but rather that through all the powers, good and evil, and in them all, dwells the higher spirit that does not so much create as constitute them what they are, and so include them all. (Pp. 274f., 279, 335.)

Again, in the *Spirit of Modern Philosophy*, Professor Royce, emphatically rejects our Creator-God:

I know nothing of any first cause in the world of appearances yonder. . . . I imagine no world-maker far back in the ages, beginning the course of evolution. . . . The living God, whom Idealism knows, is not the first cause in any physical sense at all. No possible experience could find him as a thing amongst things or show any outer fact that would prove his existence. . . . He makes from without no worlds. . . . The absolute self simply doesn't cause the world. The very idea of causation belongs to things of finite experience, and is only a mythological term when applied to the truth of things. (P. 348.)

Friedrich Paulsen, another Idealistic Pantheist, in his *Introduction to Philosophy,* though he speaks of God as a Creator, clearly rejects our Creator-God, a God, namely, who by His omnipotent power brings into existence from nothingness a real world which, though in being and action ever dependent on Him, is, nevertheless, utterly really distinct from Him. Professor Paulsen writes:

Reality is unity. The individual objects do not possess absolute independence; their reality and essence is contained in the All-One, in the *ens realissimum et perfectissimum,* of which they are the more or less independent members. Or, in Spinoza's proposition: Reality is one substance, objects are modifications of its essence posited in it. The essence of the All-One reveals itself to us, in so far as it reveals itself at all, in the two aspects of existence, in *nature* and *history.* In Spinoza's proposition: The substance is developed and conceived under two attributes, *extension* and *consciousness.* This proposition is then modified by epistemological reflections to mean that the mental world is the true reality, the corporeal world, however, its phenomenon and representation in our sensibility. The universal reciprocal action in the corporeal world is the manifestation of the *inner, aesthetico-teleological* necessity, with which the All-One unfolds its essence in a variety of harmonious modifications, in a cosmos of concrete ideas. . . . Is there any foundation for this view? After what has gone before, I can not be expected to establish it by proofs that bind the understanding. All that can be done is to show that whoever attentively and candidly inquires into the meaning of things and impartially observes reality, finally accepts such thoughts. (P. 232f.)

Professor S. Alexander, whose rather perplexing (not to say unintelligible) theory of reality, advanced and developed in *Space, Time, and Deity,* and which was explained and criticized in the Introduction to *God Infinite and Reason,* offers us a concept of God which makes of Him a mockery. He uses the word creation to mean the bringing into existence, through the emergent evolution of Space-Time, of the ascending grades of perfection of being found in this world of ours. Space-Time, therefore, is their creator; and Professor Alexander's God, in so far as it is real at all, is one of its creatures. Professor Alexander claims that his theory is not pantheistic. What answer is to be made to that claim will appear in the following brief account of his theory, which we take from parts of our previous review of it in *God Infinite and Reason.* Quotation marks are used only for Professor Alexander's own words.

According to this theory, the original reality is not God, but a "single vast entity" (I, p. 66), Motion or Space-Time, that is, pure motion, motion without anything moved; pure space and pure time, that is, space and time devoid of existing things. Motion or Space-Time is infinite, eternal. It "does not exist, but it is existence, taken in the whole" (I, p. 338); uncaused existence, for "there is no cause which is not itself a part of it" (I, p. 338). "It is not a substance" (I, p. 339) but "the stuff of substances" (I, p. 341), "the stuff out of which all existents are made" (I, p. 342). It is "their creator," "their parent" (I, p. 342), creating through the active principle Time. Professor Alexander's god, therefore, "like all things in the universe . . . is in the strictest sense not a creator but a creature. . . . He is an infinite creature of the universe of Space-Time" (II, p. 398). He is a complexity of motion, and motion is his creator, for his "deity owes its being to the pre-existing finites, with their empirical qualities, and is their outcome" (II, p. 398); and pre-existing finites are only complexities of motion. He is "not first but last in the order of generation. The notion of a Creator-God is a hybrid blending of the creative Space-Time with the created deity" (II, p. 399). "For any level, deity is the next higher empirical quality. It is, therefore, a variable quality, and as the world grows in time, deity changes with it. . . . For creatures who possessed only the primary qualities . . . deity was what afterwards appeared as materialty, and their God was matter" (II, p. 348).

"As actual, God does not possess the quality of deity, but is the universe as tending to that quality. . . . Only in this sense of straining towards deity can there be an infinite actual God . . . and this is the God of the religious consciousness, though that consciousness habitually forecasts the divinity of its objects as actually realized in an individual form" (II, p. 361f.). Professor Alexander, finally asserts, "In respect of his deity the conception of God is theistic, and since his deity is what is distinctive of him, this notion of God remains predominantly theistic" (II, p. 394). This means that "in respect of his deity" he transcends the world. But he never possesses, nor can he ever possess, his deity. Therefore, he does not transcend the world, he is a purely pantheistic god, if he is a god at all. It is difficult to see how such a concept of God could be put together by anyone.

Another Pantheist, who, as such, quite consistently rejects explicitly and emphatically our Creator-God, is Clarence A. Beckwith (Illinois Professor of Christian Theology, Chicago Theological Seminary). *In God and Reason* we gave many quotations from Professor Beckwith's work, *The Idea of God*, all of which warranted our classification of him as a *Sentimentalist, a Pragmatist, and a Pantheist*. After rejecting the Nicene God as "not being acceptable to the scientific temper and intelligence of today," and admitting the right each one has to make his god to suit himself, Professor Beckwith presents us with his god, who is immanent in the world which he also transcends; immanent, as its ever-changing Energy, Purposive Will, Creative Good Will; transcendent, not at all, however, as a real being, but only as an ideal, a goal, towards which the Purposive Will, which at no time is fully realized in the world, is ever pushing, onward and upward. Referring the reader to the above-mentioned quotations for a fuller knowledge of Professor Beckwith's views, we add here others from the same work, which reject our doctrine of a Creator-God, and make evident, at the same time, that Professor Beckwith has not a clear knowledge of the true nature either of that doctrine and its necessary implications, or of others commonly defended by Scholastic Philosophers. He writes:

A doctrine such as the idea of God, which originated in modes of thought alien to the modern scientific spirit and world-view, requires restatement, in order to become acceptable to the scientific temper and intelligence of today. A changed view of the world cannot fail to influence our idea of God. The traditional idea was connected with the certain conceptions of the world which are no longer possible to us. The world, for example, originated in an absolute creative act, due to an instantaneous *fiat*. . . . God was free to create or not to create, and free at any moment to withdraw his sustaining power, in which contingency the world would sink into nothingness; his power was also unlimited in respect to every single thing, to allow it to exist as it is or arbitrarily change it. While, therefore, the world was utterly dependent on God, he was in no sense dependent on the world. His inner (Trinitarian) life remained wholly unaffected by the creation. . . .

In view of the fact, on the one hand, that in the nature of the world as we know it, there is not a single thing which argues for an absolute beginning of its existence—and "revelation" is silent concerning this—and, on the other hand, there is the same reason for assuming that the ultimate constituents of being are eternal as there is for holding that anything exists now, the idea of God begins to take on a very different character. There are also certain realities which lie wholly beyond the region of possible creation, which are by their very nature changeless and eternal, as, for example, time and space, number, the principles of logic, and also the principles of change. Nor must we here overlook the evolutionary doctrine of the world, which holds that the entire process of development is to be referred to resident forces, operating according to ascertainable fixed laws, implying, if at all, a vastly different divine activity from that which tradition alleges. Moreover, there is evil in the world which is no less inherent and indestructible in it than is goodness; this which does not arise by divine permission is not to be overcome by divine power. Furthermore, when we consider personality and the social aspect of the world, we become aware of the serious limitations set by these to the power of God. (Pp. 6-8, *passim*.)

Professor A. Seth Pringle-Pattison (Professor of Metaphysics, University of Edinburgh), in the *Idea of God in the Light of Recent Philosophy* (the *Gifford Lectures*, 1912 and

1913), is just as explicit as Professor Beckwith in denying that God is a Creator, who brought by His efficient action from nothingness into existence a world, utterly distinct from, yet utterly depending on Himself. Professor Pringle-Pattison is a Personal Idealist. He admits the existence of an Absolute, God, who is a Supreme Intelligence, a Person. Finite intelligences derive whatever being they have from God, by some kind of ideal communication, in no sense transient, which Professor Pringle-Pattison calls creation, and which leaves God immanent in His creatures, whilst at the same time, as the Absolute Supreme Intelligence, He transcends them. Is Professor Pringle-Pattison, then, in his theory of being, i.e., as an Idealist, a Pantheist? Does creation for him mean some kind of a communication of the divine nature to other consciousnesses, which, though finite, are, nevertheless, immanent manifestations of that nature, and, hence, themselves divine?

A negative answer to these questions is given by Shailer Matthews, (Dean of the Divinity School, Chicago University), who writes, in the *Growth of the Idea of God:*

> Pringle-Pattison holds that "man is organic to nature and that nature is organic to man." He thinks of God as no "Absolute existing in solitary bliss and perfection, but a God who lives in the perpetual giving of himself, who shares the life of his finite creatures," who is "the eternal Redeemer of the world." God exists as a self-communicating life. "In theological language creation is an eternal act or process—which must be ultimately understood not as the making of something out of nothing, but as the self-revelation of the divine in and to finite spirits." Such a view of course approaches the view that a cosmic self-consciousness or the Absolute finds expression in centers of finite consciousness, but this is not Pringle-Pattison's conception of the divine consciousness. He would hold neither to pantheism nor to panpsychism. For while the human consciousness is the outcome of the universe, it is objective to the cosmic consciousness. (P. 205.)

Innumerable passages, however, in Professor Pringle-Pattison's book show that he is as an Idealist, a Pantheist, and that creation, as he understands it, is an immanental communication of God's reality to his creatures which can be explained only pantheistically. It is true, however, that Professor Pringle-Pattison rejects what he calls "the lower Pantheism," a theory which "by ascribing everything that happens to the direct immediate agency of God, is a virtual denial of the existence of reflective self-conscious, spiritual centres, such as we know them in our experience." (P. 253.)

The insistence, however, on the existence of finite "reflective self-conscious, spiritual centres," in no way changes the nature of the creative act, as understood by Professor Pringle-Pattison, namely, an immanental communication of God's reality to his creatures which makes them divine, and which therefore, can be explained only pantheistically. Professor Pringle-Pattison may not be a lower Pantheist, but he is a Pantheist nevertheless.

The passages which follow, taken from the *Idea of God*, will show clearly Professor Pringle-Pattison's pantheistic understanding of God as Creator. It may be well, however, before citing them to note that the charge, at times veiled and at times open, made by many modern philosophers—and Professor Pringle-Pattison is one of them—that our doctrine on creation necessarily implies not only Deism but also change in God, is in every sense false. We are not Deists; our God, free in creating the world, is not mutable. Professor Pringle-Pattison writes:

The process of such a life [i.e., man's with its "lower and higher self, with the discord and struggle thence resulting"] is explicable only through the actual presence within it, or to it, of the Perfection to which it aspires. Theories of the sheer transcendence of the divine, defeat their own object, because the very exaltation of the divine into an inaccessible Beyond confers a spurious independence or self-existence on the finite. It is treated as existing in its own right. But as soon as we begin to treat God and man as two independent facts, we lose our hold upon the experienced fact, which is the *existence* of the one in the other and through the other. Most people would probably be willing to admit this mediated existence in the case of man, but they might feel it akin to sacrilege to make the same assertion of God. And yet, if our metaphysics, as it professes to be, is an analysis of experience, the implication is strictly reciprocal. God has no meaning to us out of relation to our own lives or to spirits resembling ourselves in their finite grasp and infinite reach; and, in the nature of the case, we have absolutely no grounds for positing his existence out of that reference. . . . The Productive Reason [i.e., God] remains at once the sustaining element of the dependent life, and *the living content,* continually offering itself to the soul which it has awakened to the knowledge and quest of itself. (Pp. 254f.)

Hence as Professor Bosanquet rightly, more than once insists, "the finite self, like everything else in the universe, is now and here, beyond escape, an *element in the absolute.*" Or, if we use the more concrete terms of religion, we may say that no act of creation is conceivable or possible which should extrude us from the life of God and place, us as solitary units, outside the courses of his being. . . . How should we explain the fact of progress, if not by this indwelling in a larger life—this continuity with what is more and greater than ourselves? (P. 259.)

It is hard to understand how any philosopher, be he Realist or Idealist, can escape the charge of being a Pantheist, within the system he holds, if, whilst admitting that God is an absolutely supreme being from whom all other beings derive whatever existence they have, he denies that those beings are distinct from Him. Professor Royce, an Idealist, expresses the same view in *The Religious Aspect of Philosophy.* "Creation, for the popular conception," he writes, "certainly involves producing a thing of some kind by a creative act, the thing produced existing forthwith outside the creator. To give up this separation of creator and product is to become a pantheist." (P. 274.) And farther on in the same work, after stating that God is "Universal thought," and claiming that his God is "the God of the idealistic tradition from Plato downwards," he adds, "we are quite indifferent whether anybody calls all this, Theism or Pantheism." (Pp. 475, 477.)

In the light of this statement, it appears to be true that Professor James Ward (Professor of Metaphysics, University of Cambridge), who claims to be a Theistic Pluralist, in reality defends a pantheistical view of creation. Professor Ward is an Idealist. He rejects our proofs of the existence of God. He denies that God is a First Cause through whose efficient creative action the world came into being. Creation, as he understands it (he uses the term, and calls God a creator), "is not to be brought under the category of transient causation," it is rather an "intellective intuition" which contains "only what is ultimately posited by it," its object being "not phenomenal but noumenal, not independent manifestations of an Other but the creation of itself," i.e., of "the Being to whom this intellective intuition belongs." By creation God is not the cause but the "ground of the world's being," and creation is not free to God but essential to Him, so that "God is God only as being creative," "if the world should cease to be, it would be because God had ceased to be."

The following passages from Professor Ward's *Pluralism and Theism* (*Gifford Lectures,* 1907 to 1910), will show quite clearly the truth of this brief summary of his views concerning the nature of divine creation.

There are but few thoughtful people nowadays who regard the world as somehow made at a certain point of time by the transient activity of a so-called First Cause. (P. 458.)

Theism is not simply the possible crown and completion of pluralism. . . . It introduces one essential modification, at any rate, viz., the idea of creation. It does not, that is to say, assume merely that one transcendent Being exists above and beyond the whole series of many, however extended; but it assumes further that this one Being is related to them in a way in which none of them is related to the rest; they do not simply co-exist along with it, they exist somehow *in it* and through it. . . . It can not be said that the world as we know it involved the idea of creation as a fact. If it did, we should have direct and tangible evidence of God's existence. "The heavens declare the glory of God and the firmament showeth his handiwork," sang the Psalmist long ago. Possibly it is so, but there is nothing in all our physical experience that *compels* us to admit it; on the other hand, there is nothing that would justify us in denying it. Further, the metaphor of making, of handiwork, which is the sole empirical content of the term "creation," is inadequate; making out of nothing, in short, is a contradiction. But then this is not the meaning of creation, it is not a making or shaping at all. The idea is, in fact, like the idea of God, altogether transcendent. It is impossible, therefore, that experience should directly give rise to it at all.

But, it has been urged, the universe can not have existed forever, since in that case, at any assigned moment, an infinite time would be completed, and that is impossible. The universe must, then, have had a First Cause. Well, if this argument were valid, it would apply equally to God. . . . Keeping within experience, we can only endlessly regress, with no prospect of ever reaching the beginning or of forming any concept of what it was like. . . .

There is equally little to support the view of creation as an event that occurred at a finite date in the past, when we attempt to consider it from the side of God as Creator. Whatever the reason or motive for creation may have been—and some motive or reason the Theist must assume—it seems "absolutely inconceivable," as Von Hartmann put it, "that a conscious God should wait half an eternity, content without a good that ought to be." If creation means anything it means something so far involved in the divine essence, that we are entitled to say, as Hegel was fond of saying, that "without the world God is not God." In calling God the creator, then, it is simply the world's dependence on God that we mean to express. If so, it seems that this dependence is not, as commonly maintained, a causal dependence strictly understood. . . . Creation, in other words, is not to be brought under the category of transient causation. Nor can we, regarding it from the side of God, bring it under the category of immanent causation, as being a change in Him, unless indeed we abandon the position that God is God only as being creative. To say that the world depends on God is tantamount to saying that could God cease to be, the world would also cease to be; or that if the world should cease to be, it would be because God ceased to be. In other words, God is the ground of the world's being, its *ratio essendi*. The notion of ground, it will, I assume, be conceded, is wider than that of cause, which is only one of its special forms. (Pp. 231ff., *passim*.)

A thesis which we shall shortly develop and which demonstrates that God freely brought the world into existence through His creative act, presupposes that we have already proved—as we have already proved—that our concept of God represents a definite personal being, existing from all eternity, who is absolutely changeless, who is in perfection infinite, and, hence, infinitely above and absolutely distinct from the world of His creation. Fundamentally opposed to this thesis, then, because of his utter rejection of this true concept of God, is Dr. Shailer Matthews, (Dean of the Divinity School, University of Chicago). His views on God will be found in his work, *The Growth of the Idea of God*. He appears to be some kind of real, partial Pantheist, whose God —the Christian Contemporary God—not a person, is represented under the pattern of a universal formality; "our conception, born of social experience, of the personality-evolving and personally responsive elements of our cosmic environment with which we are organically related." (P. 226.) If Doctor Matthews admitted the concept of soul to have any value, we think he would call the vague something he conceives to be God, in some sense, the soul of the world. As his views are fairly typical of those of many of the modern God-makers, it will be worth while to present them more fully, with added quotations to justify our presentation of them.

According to Dr. Matthews, then, there is in man a natural urge to get help from the environment on which he depends—the cosmic environment. This urge, when it leads us to seek that help by establishing personal relations with the universe, is the religious urge. Religion, consequently, is "a phase of the life process which seeks by control or co-operation to get help from those elements of its cosmic environment upon which men feel themselves dependent, by setting up social, that is, personal relations with them." (P. 6.)

The word *God*, then, as might be surmised, stands for that something in the world's environment from which man gets help; from those world activities, namely, which produce personality and foster it. The personal relations, which man, in his religious efforts, sets up with these activities, i.e., with God, are, as we said above, social relations, and as these social relations change with our advancing knowledge especially of the world's activities, so man's concept of God will change.

The concept of God has ever been used to represent some objective reality. In less critical times, men thought that there was something physical exactly corresponding to that concept. Now, however, we know that "there is no existence exactly corresponding to the patterns with which the deity has been conceived." Our idea of God, then, gives us, as it were, a pattern according to which we strive to represent the personality-producing activities of the world as we individually know them, and under the aspect under which we judge them to be helpful for the fostering of our own individual personal relations with them. Though no concept of God is supposed to represent any definite being or person, still the cosmic activities which it does represent are always conceived under the symbol of personality, and "as variously personal as the concept-making persons."

The pattern, then, which our present-day knowledge of the universe offers us, does not represent God as a super-human person, from whom the personality-building activities proceed, and who is man's sovereign and moral ruler. It attributes these activities to the world itself, representing them as though proceeding from a personality—"in a personal pattern," but not an individual personality but a universal one.

At this point theological theism must be abandoned and a new theism organized. Such adjustment [with the cosmic personality-producing activities] is not with a super-individual. A man becomes more individual in personal relations, but the idea of God becomes less individual. The God of the primitive person is thoroughly individual. He can be pictured as imagined. But man came to think of God as universal. So God was thought of in the pattern of a spirit, which is an early attempt to rise above the concrete conception of individuality. . . . It is impossible to extend the concept of spirit into the universe when it no longer has a place in our psychology. In its place comes a new pattern which is personal without individuality. (P. 222.)

If, then, the moral and religious life of man is measured by his efforts to adjust himself to the world's personality-producing activities, it will be seen from the following paragraph that Dr. Matthews, following the lead of other modern philosophers, acknowledges Evolution to be his God. He writes:

The mysterious process which we call evolution brought man into being. But if that be the case, then there must be activities within the cosmos sufficient to account for the evolution of the human species with its personal qualities. There must be personality-evolving activities in the cosmos. Furthermore, these personality-evolving activities of the cosmos must be continued as elements within the total environment in the midst of which men must live and to which they must be adjusted. (P. 214.)

Nature, however, is not alone in supplying Dr. Matthews

with his God; man has his share in the work. Man helps to make his own God, for man's efforts combined with nature's activities integrate the cosmic environment.

Society is included in this cosmic environment in which men live. . . . The growth of the idea of God is due to this man-made environment, subject to the influence of the cosmic. As social order has developed, new personal needs have affected both society and the individual. In meeting such needs we adjust society and ourselves organically to the cosmic personality-evolving activities expressed in the integrating process from which society results. Social relations are mediating disciplines for a bio-mystical adjustment with the activities themselves. Love is the social expression of cosmic co-ordination on the personal plane. (Pp. 221f.)

Nor need we wonder at the power given by Dr. Matthews to man, the power, namely, to aid in the developing of his God, for, according to Dr. Matthews, man is one with God. "For we are not comrades in doom but children of hope. We are organically one with the cosmic activities we know as God." (P. 234.) This is Pantheism.

It may be well, now, to present the views of some of our modern scientists concerning our Creator-God. The modern scientist, who dabbles in philosophy and who quite generally is an out-and-out evolutionist, is beginning to see what nature itself has been proclaiming to man down through the ages, what the man in the street has long since discovered, and what a sane philosophy has ever insisted on, namely, that this ordered world of ours demands as its cause a governing intelligence. Modern Science calls this intelligence, which it claims to have discovered, God. It is somewhat boastful of its achievement, as we may gather from a recent work already referred to, *Has Science Discovered God? A Symposium of Modern Scientific Opinion,* edited by Dr. Cotton. Heartened, no doubt, by the views expressed by the scientists contributing to his symposium, and with a naïve presumption springing from ignorance, Doctor Cotton in his introduction to the work, has not feared or hesitated to make, among other statements, those following, all of them more or less startling and more than questionable.

We see leading scientists centering their efforts on a solution of the puzzle of the ages ("the precise problem with which re-

ligion and philosophy so long have been struggling"); the creative force back of phenomena, and the destiny of man's spirit.
. . . It is probably true . . . that the entire endeavor of research
from the beginning until now has been to find God. But not
until the present time has science left its traditional seclusion,
come out into the open, and declared—or at all events not denied
—that its true objective is the Eternal Reality, creating and sustaining in this mysterious universe. Consciously or unconsciously,
research has set itself to prove that the universe is more than a
fortuitous concourse of atoms—it has a soul. . . . The ecclesiastics of his [Jesus'] day feared what ecclesiastics of all times have
feared—that their philosophy of life, built up with extreme care
and system, would be found wanting. . . . Somehow the methods
and deductions of established religion do not inspire confidence;
and the cry of despair is heard in the land, the quality of which
no observing mind will mistake.

The question, then before us is—and it is exceeded in importance by no question of our time—Can Science find God? And,
equally important, Can it prove to us that we survive the event
of death? . . . Opinions included in this book have been gathered for the purpose of proving to everyday men and women that
men of research are beginning to find evidence of God and of
continuance of active life in spheres beyond that of earth.

If God is found, research will find Him and not traditional
religion. . . . We are inclined to think that the sooner religion
in the orthodox and traditional sense surrenders the quest for
Cosmic Reality, and concentrates on serving men in their personal needs, the better for religion and the better for humanity.
Religion has been given a considerable chance. But has it found
any but a nebulous, uncertain, unsatisfactory God? . . . Until it
broadens its horizons considerably, it never can comprehend the
light, the glory and the majesty of this tremendous "Cosmic
Force." . . . Probably the conceptions of God in the minds of
men of research and those in the minds of sectarians [Dr. Cotton
includes Catholics under the unacceptable word *sectarians*] are
as far apart as the antipodes; so that when the two talk of Eternal
Reality and of religion also, they mean entirely different values.
(Pp. xl-xlv, *passim.*)

All of which goes to show that, though modern science is
to be praised for having rejected a purely material, mechanistic explanation of the universe, we shall find, nevertheless,
in many instances that the God it offers—the God of Dr.

Cotton's Introduction—who is frequently called the world's Creator, is, in no sense of the word, the Creator we speak of in our philosophy, and whose perfections we have clearly defined. On the contrary, he is a vague, changeable something, in evolutionary fashion energizing the world from within, not its Lord and Master, either in the physical or moral sense, and hence, though made the object of a groping, creedless cult, altogether unworthy of man's reverence or service. In a word, it will be found that the God of Modern Science, though it may seek to deny it, is none other than the old god of the Pantheists, and frequently even with its name unchanged—"Cosmic Realty," "Cosmic Force," "The Universal-All" of which "human nature is one of the most important manifestations."

Among the modern scientists of Dr. Cotton's *Symposium* are Professor Robert A. Millikan and Professor Albert Einstein. We shall let these two speak for what Dr. Cotton calls *Modern Science,* and tell us something of the God it has discovered.

Professor Millikan is rated rather highly as a physicist by his fellow scientists, and, no doubt, deservedly. His views, however, on God, religion, and morality which are scattered plentifully through his book, *Science and the New Civilization,* must be rejected as utterly false. And the danger is, that, owing to his reputation as a scientist, to the fact that he professes to be a Christian, believing in the "essentials" of Christianity, and to the rather self-confident way in which he expresses his opinions on religious matters, many of his readers may be led not only far from the religion of Christ, but far from any religion worthy of the name, and, what is worse, far from the belief in the true God. These are hard sayings: nevertheless, they will be found to be true.

Professor Millikan, playing the role of philosopher, tells us in *Science and the New Civilization,* from which work our quotations will be taken, that there are three great ideas which, above all others, have helped the upward development of the human race.

The first great idea—the Idea of the Golden Rule—after probably "millenniums" of evolution was given to man by religion. "The greatest, most consistent, most influential pro-

ponent of this idea who has ever lived was Jesus of Nazareth."
This idea has made Christianity what it is; it is the essence of
the Christian religion; its "significance," Professor Millikan,
with the supreme, unwarranted confidence of a pseudo-phi-
losopher, continues, "is completely independent even of the
historicity of Jesus. The service of the Christian religion, my
own faith in essential Christianity, would not be diminished
one iota if it should be in some way discovered that no such
individual as Jesus ever existed," rather, in that event "the result would be even more wonderful and more inspiring than
it is now." And he adds: "In making this statement, I am en-
deavoring to say just as positively and as emphatically as I
can, that the credentials of Jesus are found wholly in his
teachings, and in his character as recorded by his teachings,
and *not at all in any real or alleged historical facts.*"

Jesus made it [the golden rule] the sum and substance of his
whole philosophy of life. When he said, "All things whatsoever ye
would that I should do unto you, even so do ye also unto them,
for this is the law and the prophets," I take it that he meant by
that last phrase that this precept epitomized in his mind all that
had been commanded and foretold—that it embodied the sum-
mation of duty and of aspiration. (P. 168.)
My conception then of the essentials of religion, at least of
the Christian religion and no other need here be considered, is
that those essentials consist in just two things: first, in inspiring
man with the Christ-like, i.e., the altruistic *ideal,* and that means
specifically, *concern for the common good* as contrasted with
one's own individual impulses and interests, wherever in one's
own judgment the two come in conflict, and second, in inspiring
mankind, to *do,* rather than merely to think about, its duty, the
definition of duty for each individual being what he himself conceives to be for the common good. . . . It is very important to
notice that in the definitions I have given, duty has nothing to
do with what somebody else conceives to be for the common
good, i.e., with morality in the derivative sense of the mores of
the people. (Pp. 169f.)

Professor Millikan's religion, then, which he calls Christianity, has for its end the group-welfare of man; and man's
duty is to further that welfare. There is not a word in the
essentials of his Christianity about God. However, there
need be no wonder that God is not the center of Professor

Millikan's religion, when one realizes that the God he believes in, is worthy neither of praise, nor of reverence, nor of service. Professor Millikan is a Pantheist, and his God is "Nature or the Universe, whatever name you prefer." These words, and others to follow, tell us and show most clearly that, in his opinion, one of the greatest gifts that science has given to man is the light to realize that the God of our fathers, the world's Creator and Ruler, has seen His day, that the new God, Nature, is a God of order, and the new duty is to make this world a better place for man to live in, an end "quite independent of the ultimate destination of the individual and also much more alluring to some sorts of minds than singing hosannas forever around the throne." (P. 179, *note*).

The idea of God, or Nature, or the Universe, whatever term you prefer, is not a being of caprice or whim, as had been the case in all the main body of thinking of the ancient world, but is, instead, a God who rules through law, or a Nature capable of being depended upon, or a Universe of consistency of orderliness and the beauty that goes with order—that idea has *made* modern science . . . it has changed the philosophic and religious conceptions of mankind. It has laid the foundations for a new and stupendous advance in man's conception of God, for a sublimer view of the world and of man's place and destiny in it. The anthropomorphic God of the ancient world, the God of human passions, frailties, caprices, and whims is gone, and with it the old duty, namely, merely or chiefly the duty to propitiate him, so that he may be induced to treat you, either in this world or the next or both, better than he treats your neighbor. Can any one question the advance that has been made in the diminishing prevalence of these medieval, essentially childish, and essentially selfish ideas? The new God is the God of law and order, the new duty to know that order and to get into harmony with it, to know how to make the world a better place for man to live in, not merely how to save your individual soul. . . . The emphasis upon making this world a better place is certainly the dominant and characteristic element in the religion of today. (Pp. 177-179, *with note*.)

[What is more], because of the growth of this evolutionary idea in human thinking ["The youngest—*sic*—of the two great ideas born of modern science"], we have come to see that an institution like religion, in so far as it deals with the conceptions of God, *the integrating factor in this Universe of atoms and of ether, and of mind, and of ideas, and of duties, and of intelligence,* has not been and cannot be a fixed thing, that it has been continually changing with the growth of human knowledge, and that it will continue to expand as knowledge continues to grow. . . . The world of science dominated by the reign of law has necessitated the increasing association of men into co-operating groups, but the effectiveness of these groups, indeed the whole group life, becomes at once impossible unless the altruistic ideals of religion, the sense of social responsibility, permeates the whole, while the evolutionary concept, the last contribution of science, is absolutely essential to an understanding of the development both of religion and of science. (Pp. 185-186.)

In a previous passage Professor Millikan had cited with approval the following verse in which Evolution is hailed as God: •

A fire mist and a planet, a crystal and a cell,
A jellyfish and a saurian, and caves where cavemen dwell.
Then a sense of law and duty, and a face turned from the clod.
Some call it Evolution and others call it God.

But enough and more than enough has been said to show that Professor Millikan's God, whom he calls *Creator,* is not the Creator-God we reverence, serve, adore.

What Professor Einstein thinks of God and religion may be told in a few words. His God appears to be the Cosmos; his religion, that founded on the cosmic religious sense. Only those especially gifted rise to this religious level, at which the anthropomorphic idea of God, that is, as modern philosophers usually mean, the idea of God as a person, is excluded. The Cosmos, therefore, or the world, experienced under some vague concept of the cosmic religious sense as the mysterious, rational principle of order, is Professor Einstein's God; and a devoted study of it, his religion. It is this devotion, as a religion, which urges on the scientist in his work. In fact, Professor Einstein holds that the only deeply religious men are the scientists—the earnest men of research. As Professor Einstein's God is the order-evolving Cosmos, it is quite evident why a God who could interfere with Nature's laws, is rejected by him as absolutely impossible. It may be well to add that Professor Einstein does not believe in a future life for man. He denies, also, that man is free, and hence, rejects the notion of a God by whom man is to be rewarded or punished for his actions.

Professor Einstein is a Pantheist. Quite evidently his God is not in any sense our Creator-God.

I do not believe we can have any freedom at all in the philosophical sense, for we act not only under external compulsion, but also by inner necessity. (P. 93.*)

To ponder interminably over the reason for one's own existence, or the meaning of life in general, seems to me, from an objective point of view, to be sheer folly. (P. 94.)

The most beautiful thing we can express is the mysterious. It is the source of all true art and science. . . . To know that what is impenetrable to us really exists, manifesting itself as the highest wisdom and the most radiant beauty which our dull faculties can comprehend only in their most primitive forms—the knowledge, this feeling, is at the center of the true religiousness. In this sense, and in this sense only, I belong to the ranks of the devoutly religious men.

I cannot imagine a God who rewards and punishes the objects of his creation. . . . Neither can I believe that the individual survives after the death of his body, although feeble souls harbor such thoughts through fear or religious egotism. It is enough for me to contemplate the mystery of conscious life perpetuating itself through all eternity, to reflect upon the marvelous structure of the Universe which we can dimly perceive, and to try humbly to comprehend even an infinitesimal part of the intelligence manifested in nature. (P. 96f.)

In primitive peoples, it is, first of all, fear that awakens religious ideas. . . . I call this the religion of fear. . . . The longing for guidance, for love and succor, provides the stimulus for growth of a moral or social conception of God. This is the God of Providence, who protects, decides, rewards, punishes. . . . Common to all these types is the anthropomorphic character of the idea of God.

Only exceptionally gifted individuals or especially noble communities rise essentially above this level. In these there is found a third level of religious experience, even if it is seldom found in a pure form. I will call it the cosmic religious sense. This is hard to make clear to those who do not experience it, since it

* This and the extracts following, are cited from Einstein's, "The Meeting Place of Science and Religion," in *Has Science Discovered God? A Symposium of Modern Scientific Opinion*, ed. Cotton. This essay appeared originally as two articles, one in the *Forum*, the other in the *New York Times*.

does not involve an anthropomorphic idea of God. . . . The religious geniuses of all times have been distinguished by this cosmic religious sense, which recognizes neither dogmas nor God made in man's image. Consequently there can not be a Church whose chief doctrines are based on the cosmic religious experience. It comes about therefore, that we find precisely among the heretics of all ages men who were inspired by this highest religious experience. Often they appeared to their contemporaries as atheists, but sometimes also as saints. . . .

It seems to me that the most important function of art and of science is to arouse and to keep alive this feeling in those who are receptive. . . . From the study of history one is inclined to regard religion and science as irreconcilable antagonists; and this for a reason that is very easily seen. For anyone who is pervaded with a sense of causal law in all that happens, who accepts in real earnest the assumption of causality, the idea of a Being who interferes with the sequence of events in the world, is absolutely impossible. Neither the religion of fear, nor the social-moral religion can have any hold on him. A God who rewards and punishes is for him unthinkable because man acts in accordance with an inner and outer necessity, and would, in the eyes of God, be as little responsible as an inanimate object is for the movements it makes.

Science, in consequence, has been accused of undermining morals—but wrongly. The ethical behavior is better based on sympathy, education, and social relationships, and requires no support from religion. Man's plight would indeed be sad if he had to be kept in order through fear of punishment or hope of rewards after death.

It is, therefore, quite natural that the churches have always fought against science, and have persecuted its supporters. But, on the other hand, I assert that the cosmic religious experience is the strongest and noblest force behind scientific research. . . . A contemporary has rightly said that the only deeply religious people of our largely materialistic age are the earnest men of research. (Pp. 98-102, *passim.*)

After reading the passages just cited, one is forced to conclude that not only Professor Einstein's philosophy of religion and morality, but also not a few of his statements of facts, are far removed from truth. As a mathematician he may be held in honor, but certainly not as a philosopher.

The last witness we shall call is the well-known modern

philosopher, Professor William James. He rejects the idea of God as Creator, as a Being existing apart from the world. God dwells in the world, but not in a world which is one being only, but in a world composed of many beings, all of the same nature as God Himself. Professor James, then, is a Pluralist, who may be called a Pantheist or a Polytheist. Both names have been used to describe his world-philosophy. With a certain amount of flippancy, shown not infrequently in his handling of matters calling at least for reverent treatment, Professor James rejects the idea of a Creator-God, though, with a duplicity unworthy of a true philosopher, he admits that belief in a Creator, for form's sake, may be confessed in Church. In *A Pluralistic Universe,* Professor James writes:

The theistic conception picturing God and his creation as entities distinct from each other, still leaves the human subject outside of the deepest reality in the universe. God is from eternity complete, it says, and sufficient unto himself; he throws off the world by a free act and as an extraneous substance, and he throws off man as a third substance, extraneous both to the world and himself. . . .

This essential dualism of the theistic view has all sorts of collateral consequences. Man being an outsider and a mere subject of God, not his intimate partner, a character of externality invades the field. God is not heart of our heart and reason of our reason, but our magistrate, rather; and mechanically to obey his commands, however strange they may be, remains our only moral duty. Conceptions of criminal law have, in fact, played a great part in defining our relations with him. . . . It has to be confessed that this dualism and lack of intimacy has always acted as a drag and handicap on Christian thought. . . . God as intimate soul and reason of the universe has always seemed to some people a more worthy conception than God as external creator. So conceived, he appeared to unify the world more perfectly, he made it less finite and mechanical, and in comparison with such a God an external creator seemed more like the product of a childish fancy. I have been told by the Hindoos that the great obstacle to the spread of Christianity in their country is the puerility of our dogma of creation. It has not sweep and infinity enough to meet the requirements of even the illiterate natives of India.

Assuredly most of the members of this audience [at Manchester College, England, listening to this Hibbert Lecture] are ready to side with Hindooism in this matter. Those of us who are sexagenarians have witnessed in our own persons one of those gradual mutations of intellectual climate, due to innumerable influences, that make the thought of a past generation seem as foreign to its successors as if it were the expression of a different race of men. The Theological machinery that spoke so livingly to our ancestors, with its finite age of the world, its creation out of nothing, its juridical morality and eschatology, its relish for rewards and punishments, its treatment of God as an external contriver, an "intelligent moral governor," sounds as odd to most of us as if it were some outlandish savage religion. The vaster vistas which scientific evolutionism has opened, and the rising tide of social democratic ideals, have changed the type of our imagination, and the older monarchical theism is obsolete or obsolescent. An external creator and his institutions may still be verbally confessed at Church in formulas that linger by their mere inertia, but the life is out of them, we avoid dwelling on them, the sincere heart of us is elsewhere.

I shall leave cynical materialism entirely out of our discussion, as not calling for treatment before this present audience, and I shall ignore old-fashioned dualistic theism for the same reason. Our contemporary mind having once for all grasped the possibility of a more intimate *weltanshauung*, the only opinions quite worthy of arresting our attention will fall within the general scope of what may roughly be called the pantheistic field of vision, the vision of God as the indwelling divine rather than the external creator, and of human life as part and parcel of the deep reality.

As we found that spiritualism in general breaks into a more intimate and a less intimate species, so the more intimate species itself breaks into two subspecies, of which the one is more monistic, the other more pluralistic in form. . . . The philosophy of the Absolute agrees with the pluralistic philosophy which I am going to contrast with it in these lectures, in that both identify human substance with the divine substance. But whereas absolutism thinks that the said substance becomes fully divine only in the form of totality, and is not its real self in any form but the *all*-form, the pluralistic view which I prefer to adopt is willing to believe that there may never be an all-form at all. . . . You see now what I mean by pantheism's two subspecies. (Pp.25-35, *passim*.)

The line of least resistance, then, as it seems to me, both in Theology and philosophy, is to accept along with the superhuman consciousness, the notion that it is not all-embracing, the notion, in other words, that there is a God, but that he is finite, either in power or in knowledge, or in both at once. (P. 311.)

Professor James, as we saw above, classes his Pluralism as a subspecies of pantheism; now, with characteristic inconsistency, he wishes to call only *one* being of his pluralistic universe, *God,* though all have the same divine nature.

Modern philosophy's treatment of God, and the relations existing between Him and the universe of His creation, is, in general, filled with inconsistencies of a like kind.

Opposed in its conclusions to all these false opinions is our reasoned study of God, which, begun in *God and Reason,* and continued in *God Infinite and Reason,* finds its completion in the present volume. As its title suggests, the questions here to be treated have to do with the relations which exist between God and the world, and which, presupposing the free production of the world by God, necessarily arise from the nature of God—self-existent, absolutely necessary, infinite—and the nature of all things in the world—produced, contingent, finite.

Our study of these relations will show us, first, that God, with a full and absolutely infallible knowledge of all that would come to pass in the world, freely called it forth from nothingness into existence, freely created it; secondly, that nothing in the world, no matter how small, after having been brought into existence, can continue to exist, unless God directly and continually gives it its existence; thirdly, that no being, thus continually receiving its existence from God, can perform any action, or bring anything, however insignificant, into existence, unless God, as the Primary Cause of all things, concurs with it in performing that action, and producing that thing. After these truths have been established, a rather thorough discussion of the nature of this concurrent action of God with actions of creatures, and especially with free actions, will immediately follow.

The last question which will engage our attention, and bring to a close our reasoned study of God, will be that of God's providence in ruling the world. It is a question of supreme importance, demanding, as it does, a solution of the so-called *Problem of Evil,* a problem which is said by our adversaries to be "the crux of theism."

"This is the terrible mystery of evil," writes F. C. S. Schiller *(Riddles of the Sphinx)*, "which for two thousand years has been a stumbling-block to all practical religion, tried the faith of all believers, and depressed and debased all thought on the ultimate questions of life, and is as 'insoluble a mystery' to the theologian now as it was at the beginning." (P. 307.)

There is, nevertheless, a solution of this mystery; and a patient estimate of the nature of evil and of the infinite perfections of God, will show us that notwithstanding the presence in the world of evil, both physical and moral, the providence of God, all-wise and all-loving, is over His creatures, directing them all, according to their different natures, to the end for which everything that is made is necessarily made—Himself, the Alpha and Omega, the Beginning and End of all things, All-wise, All-powerful, All-holy, All-loving.

Before discussing these questions, however, and as a help to their better understanding, some of the more difficult points concerning God's knowledge, which in our former treatment of that subject, in *God Infinite and Reason,* were designedly left untouched, call for an explanation. This will be given in *Thesis I,* in its various corollaries, and in the solutions of the most important difficulties commonly urged against the conclusions we shall there defend.

BIBLIOGRAPHY

Alexander, S., LL.D., F.B.A., *Space, Time and Deity*. London: Macmillan and Co., 1920.

Beckwith, Clarence Augustine, *The Idea of God*. New York: The Macmillan Co., 1924.

Boedder, Bernard, S.J., *Natural Theology.** New York: Benziger Brothers, 1891.

Calkins, Mary Whiton, *The Persistent Problems of Philosophy*. New York: The Macmillan Co., 1908.

*Catholic Encyclopedia,** Vol. XVI, Index and Reading Lists; Lists of Reading in Theodicy, Cosmology, Psychology, and the History of Philosophy. Also under titles: Baius, Bañez, Bellarmine, Congregatio de Auxiliis, Congruism, Grace, Molina, Suarez, and others. New York: The Encyclopedia Press.

Christlieb, Theodore, D.D., *Modern Doubt and Christian Belief*. (Translated with author's sanction, chiefly by Rev. H. U. Weitbrecht, Ph.D.) Edinburg: T. and T. Clark. (New York: Charles Scribner's Sons.)

Conybeare, Frederick, M.A., *Myth, Magic and Morals*. London: Watts & Co., 1910.

[Cotton, ed.], *Has Science Discovered God? A Symposium of Modern Scientific Opinion*. (Gathered and Edited by Edward H. Cotton.) New York: Thomas Y. Crowell Company, 1931.

D'Arcy, M. C., S.J., *Mirage and Truth.** New York: The Macmillan Co., 1935.

———, *Pain and the Providence of God.** Milwaukee: The Bruce Publishing Co., 1935.

———, *Thomas Aquinas.** London: Ernest Benn Limited, 1930.

Driscoll, Rev. John T., S.T.L., *God.** New York: Benziger Brothers, 1904.

Garrigou-La Grange, Rev. R., O.P., *God: His Existence and His Nature,** 2 vols., St. Louis: B. Herder Book Co., 1934.

Gilson, Étienne, *The Philosophy of St. Thomas Aquinas.** (Authorized Translation from the third revised edition of *Le Thomisme,* by Edward Bullough.) St. Louis: B. Herder Book Co., 1924.

Grabmann, Dr. Martin, *Thomas Aquinas.** (Authorized Translation, Virgil Michel, O.S.B., Ph.D.) New York: Longmans, Green and Co., 1928.

Haeckel, Ernest, *The Riddle of the Universe*. (Translated by Joseph McCabe.) London: Watts & Co., 1913.

Hammerstein, L. von, S.J., *Foundations of Faith* *; Part I, *The Existence of God*. (Translated from the German.) New York: Benziger Brothers, 1897.

Hettinger, F., *Natural Religion*.* New York: Fr. Pustet, 1890.

Hull, Ernerst R., S.J., *God, Man and Religion*.* Bombay: The Examiner Press, 1914.

James, William, *A Pluralistic Universe*. New York: Longmans, Green & Co., 1909.

——, *The Will to Believe, and other Essays*, New York: Longmans, Green and Co., 1909.

Joyce, George Hayward, S.J., M.A., *Principles of Natural Theology*.* New York: Longmans, Green and Co., 1923.

Kane, R., S.J., *God or Chaos*.* New York: P. J. Kenedy and Sons, 1912.

Knox, Ronald A., *Caliban and Grub Street*.* New York: E. P. Dutton & Co., Inc., 1930.

Matthews, Shailer, D.D., LL.D., *The Growth of the Idea of God*. New York: The Macmillan Co., 1931.

McCormick, John F., S.J., *Scholastic Metaphysics*,* Part II, *Natural Theology*. Chicago: Loyola University Press, 1931.

Noyes, Alfred, *The Unknown God*.* New York: Sheed and Ward, 1934.

Otto, M. C., *Things and Ideals*. New York: Henry Holt & Co.

Paulsen, Friedrich, *Introduction to Philosophy* (second American from third German edition, translated, with the author's sanction, by Frank Thilly.) New York: Henry Holt & Co., 1907.

Pius XI, Pope, *Encyclical*, "Quadrigesimo Anno," * May 15, 1931. The Catholic Mind, vol. XXIX, p. 257. New York: The America Press, 1931.

——, *Encyclical*, "Nova Impendet," * Oct. 2, 1931. The Catholic Mind, vol. XXIX, p. 469. New York: The America Press, 1931.

——, *Encyclical*, "Caritate Christi Compulsi," * May 3, 1932. The Catholic Mind, vol. XXX, p. 229. New York: The America Press, 1932.

Pringle-Pattison, A. Seth, *The Idea of God*. New York: Oxford University Press, 1920.

Riley, J. Woodbridge, Ph.D., *American Philosophy: The Early Schools*. New York: Dodd, Mead & Co., 1907.

Robinson, Daniel S., Ph.D., *The God of the Liberal Christian*. New York: D. Appleton & Co., 1926.

Ronayne, Maurice, S.J., *God Knowable and Known.** New York: Benziger Brothers, 1888.

Royce, Josiah, Ph.D., *The Religious Aspect of Philosophy.* New York: Houghton Mifflin Company.

———, *The Spirit of Modern Philosophy.* New York: Houghton Mifflin Company.

Sasia, Rev. Joseph C., S.J., *The Future Life.** New York: Benziger Brothers, 1918.

Sertillanges, A. D., O.P., *Saint Thomas Aquinas and his Works.** (Translated by Godfrey Anstruther, O.P.) London: Burns, Oates & Washbourne, 1932.

Schiller, F. C. S., M.A., D.Sc., *Riddles of the Sphinx.* New York: The Macmillan Co., 1910.

Shallo, Michael, S.J., *Scholastic Philosophy.** Philadelphia: Peter Reilly, 1915.

Sharpe, Rev. A. B., M.A., *The Principles of Christianity.** St. Louis: B. Herder, 1906.

Steuart, R. H. J., S.J., "The Two Voices." * *The London Tablet,* Oct. 7, 1939. London: The London Tablet, 1939.

Thomas Aquinas, Saint, *On the Power of God.** (Literally Translated by the English Dominican Fathers.) London: Burns, Oates and Washbourne, 1932.

———, *Summa Contra Gentiles.** (Literally Translated by the English Dominican Fathers from the latest Leonine Edition.) London: Burns, Oates and Washbourne, 1923.

———, *Summa Theologica.** (Literally Translated by Fathers of the English Dominican Province.) London: R. and T. Washbourne, 1912.

Turner, William, S.T.D., *The History of Philosophy.** New York: Ginn & Co., 1903.

Ward, James, Sc.D., Hon. LL.D., Hon. D.Sc., *The Realm of Ends, or Pluralism and Theism.* Cambridge, England: The University Press, 1912. (New York: G. P. Putnam's Sons.)

Woods, H., S.J., *The Creator Operating in the Creature.** San Francisco: The Gilmartin Co., 1928.

NOTE

The bibliography offered, though by no means complete, will be found sufficient; a complete one would include many other books and articles in English and other languages.

Approval is given only to those books and articles marked with an asterisk (*).

Acknowledgment is made to the publishers for permission to take excerpts from the books listed, as follows: *

THE APPLETON-CENTURY COMPANY
    Robinson, *The God of the Liberal Christians*
THOMAS Y. CROWELL COMPANY
    Cotton (ed.), *Has Science Discovered God?*
DODD, MEAD AND COMPANY
    Riley, *American Philosophy, the Early Schools*
GINN AND COMPANY
    Turner, *The History of Philosophy*
HENRY HOLT AND COMPANY
    Otto, *Things and Ideas*
    Paulsen, *Introduction to Philosophy*
HOUGHTON MIFFLIN COMPANY
    Royce, *Religious Aspects of Philosophy*
    Royce, *The Spirit of Modern Philosophy*
LONGMANS, GREEN AND COMPANY
    Grabman, *Thomas Aquinas*
    James, *A Pluralistic Universe*
    James, *The Will to Believe*
THE MACMILLAN COMPANY
    Beckwith, *The Idea of God*
    Calkins, *The Persistent Problems of Philosophy*
    Matthews, *The Growth of the Idea of God*
CHARLES SCRIBNER'S SONS
    Millikan, *Science and the New Civilization*

GOD INFINITE, THE WORLD, AND REASON

THESIS I

God, from all eternity, with an absolutely infallible knowledge, knows Himself and all the possibles and futuribles. In the light of this knowledge He decrees from all eternity and immutably the existence of the world, and, consequent on this decree, knows, also from all eternity and with absolute infallibility, all things in the world, man's free actions included, and under their varying temporal relations of future, present, and past existence.

PRENOTES TO THE THESIS

In our previous thesis on God's knowledge (cf. *God Infinite and Reason*) we were concerned solely with the infinite perfection of that knowledge, considered in itself and in its all-embracing inclusion of all things knowable. In our present thesis, God's knowledge of all these various knowable objects is again considered, now, however, rather in its relation, first, to His eternal, immutable, absolutely efficacious decree calling the world into existence in time; and secondly, to the world itself which, in consequence of that decree, will be, as God from all eternity knows it will be. In corollaries following the proofs of the thesis, God's knowledge and the objects of His knowledge will be considered from other viewpoints.

Since we wish, then, to show in this thesis, among other things, that God knows from all eternity all things knowable, it will be useful, before we develop our formal proof of these points, to repeat with slight changes, some passages from the *Prenotes* to the thesis on God's immutability (cf. *God Infinite and Reason*), in which we enumerated the different classes of objects which include all things knowable, and showed how the knowability of these objects from all eternity, i.e., their eternal objective truth, is established.

37

The different classes of objects which include all things knowable; the knowability of these objects from eternity.

1. *God.* In this class God alone is found; the only neces-, sary being possible, the source of all other beings, the most real of all real beings. It is quite evident, then, that He is knowable. That He is knowable from eternity is equally evident, since He exists with absolute necessity, hence, eternally. This point has already been proved in *God Infinite and Reason.*

2. *All the possibles.*

A possible is anything that is intrinsically capable of receiving existence.

A pure possible is anything that is intrinsically capable of receiving existence but never exists.

A non-pure possible is anything that is so capable of existence, and which, moreover, sometimes does exist.

In this class, then, are all pure possibles; and all non-pure possibles, i.e., all sometime actual, finite things, considered, however, not as sometime actual, but merely as possible. That all produced things may be so considered, follows from the fact that existence is not absolutely necessary for any of them. That pure and non-pure possibles are knowable, must be admitted if it can be shown that they are something, i.e., not nothing. And they are something, i.e., not nothing, for nothing cannot be conceived in a wholly positive concept, nor can it say a positive relation to existence; possible beings, however, can be so conceived, and can say such a relation. For example, a man, either a purely possible one, or an actual one considered merely as a possible, is conceived wholly positively as a rational animal and is intrinsically capable of existence. So of all other possible things.

The eternal knowability of the possibles is shown in this way. The intrinsic capacity that a possible has for existence is independent of any determined time, i.e., a definite time-element does not enter into the question of its capacity for existence. Hence, no possible moment of time can be assigned as the first moment when a possible is a possible. Therefore, a possible is such from eternity; hence, its objective truth, i.e., its knowability, is also eternal.

3. *All the futuribles.*

A futurible is that certain free act, from amongst those, in any possible definite set of circumstances, possible to a finite intelligent being, which *de facto* would be chosen by him, if in virtue of God's creative decree he were ever placed in those circumstances.

A pure futurible is such an act which would be, but never will be, so chosen because the condition will never be verified, i.e., the individual in question will never be placed by God in those circumstances.

A non-pure futurible is such an act which not only *would* be, but *de facto, will* be so chosen, because the condition will be verified, i.e., the individual in question will one day be placed by God in those circumstances.

Since this class includes all futuribles, it includes not only all pure futuribles, but also all non-pure futuribles, considered, however, not as non-pure futuribles, but merely as futuribles, i.e., as pure futuribles. That non-pure futuribles may be so considered must be admitted, seeing that actual future existence is not absolutely necessary for a futurible.

That all futuribles, both pure and non-pure, considered merely as futuribles, are knowable must be also admitted if it can be shown that the proposition, in which a futurible is expressed, enunciates an objective determined truth. In other words, that the following proposition, for example, is objectively true: If John were placed by God in a definite set of circumstances, and given all the aids necessary for the eliciting of a free action, though he would have the power to choose any one of the many possible courses of action open to him with regard to the matter about which he is deliberating, *de facto* he would choose this definite one.

To prove this we appeal to two undeniable principles. The first is: Whatever exists must at each moment of its existence be in one definite state. The second is the principle of contradiction: A thing cannot at the same time be and not be; be this and not be this; be in this definite state and not be in this definite state.

In the light of these two principles let us consider our example. We find that though John, at the moment of his existence we are considering, might freely be in any one of the many states presented to his choice with regard to the matter under deliberation, he would, in virtue of our first principle, and supposing that he would elicit a free act—which is the only case we are supposing—*de facto* be freely in one definite state. Again, in the hypothesis that he would be in this one definite state, it is absolutely impossible, in virtue of our second principle, for him to be, at the moment in question, in any other. The state in which John would be, we call, in our example, this definite one. Which one it is, of the many states John might have chosen, is unknown to us. It would, however, be knowable in itself, for it would be a definite state. Consequently, it would be known to God, who, since He is infinite actual knowledge, as has been proved (cf. *God Infinite and Reason*), necessarily knows all things knowable.

A futurible, therefore, as such, is knowable, for it is something. It is something, for it can be conceived in a wholly positive concept which represents the definite action which conditionally *de facto* would be chosen; moreover it says a positive relation to existence, for it is that act which *de facto* would exist if the free agent were put in the definite set of circumstances considered. Nothing, however, cannot be repsented in a wholly positive concept, nor can it say a positive relation to existence.

A futurible, in truth, is more than a possible, for it is not merely one of the possible actions which a free agent is capable of choosing if placed in a definite set of circumstances, it is more; it is that one which *de facto* he would choose.

The futuribles are eternally true, as are the possibles, and for the same reason: namely, their objective truth is independent of any definite time. This is evident from a consideration of the proposition in which the truth of the futurible is enunciated, which makes no mention of any definite time. It is evident also, if we consider that neither the objective truth of the possibles, nor the objective truth of the futuribles, tie God down to any determined moment for bringing the world into existence. Therefore, neither the possible nor the futurible demand any definite time for their existence; in other words, their objective truth is independent of any determined time.

4. *All things that will be.*

Under this heading are included all things that at some time or other actually exist. They are all called future things, and only future things, with regard to all points of possible time which preceded the beginning of the world, i.e., the beginning of actual time. With regard to all points of time after the world's beginning, i.e., with regard to all points of actual time, each one of them may be considered as future, present, and past. As future, with regard to all points of time preceding its existence; as present, with regard to the time of its actual existence; and as past, with regard to all points of time following its existence.

A future thing is a thing not now existing but which will exist.

A present thing is a thing existing at the moment called *now*.

A past thing is a thing not now existing but which has existed.

The objective truth of all things actual, considered as future, present, and past, in their different relations to different points of possible and actual time, may be shown thus.

With a full knowledge of everything that is knowable prior to, i.e., independently of, His decree of creation: in other words, with a full knowledge of Himself, of all the possibles, and of all the futuribles, God decrees the existence of every being, and of every action of every being, that will exist, including free agents, with all the different circumstances of their existence; and all this for every moment of that existence. Immediately, with regard to all objects affected by that decree, and with regard to them only, new relations arise. They are no longer merely possibles and merely futuribles, but with regard to each one of them for the points of time preceding, coinciding with, and following, the existence of each, the following propositions are respectively true; this object will be; this object is; this object was. The objective truth, therefore, of a future thing as such, a present thing as such, a past thing as such, is established.

The same proof, somewhat further developed, establishes also the eternal nature of this truth, and hence the knowability from eternity of everything actual considered under its various relations to different points of time, as future, pres-

ent, past. The further development of the proof is this. The
eternal truth of the future, present, and past, considered as
such, is established, if it can be proved that God's creative
decree, which irrevocably determines that truth, is eternal.
This has already been done in our proof for the moral immutability of God's will (cf. *God Infinite and Reason*). What
God decrees, He decrees from eternity, immutably, for all
creatures, under all circumstances, for all time.

It is to be carefully noted that when we speak of God's
knowledge of Himself, the possibles, and the futuribles, as
being prior to His decree calling the world into existence;
and of His knowledge of all things as future, present,
and past, as *following* that decree, there is no question of any
durational before or after. God's knowledge and will are
really identical: they are eternal. What is meant is this. Since,
for sake of clearness, in our treatment of God's infinite, simple perfection, we make a mental, though imperfect, distinction between His knowledge and His will; and since nothing
unknown can be willed, we conceive the decree or will of
God as conditioned by, or dependent on, and, in this sense,
as following His infinite knowledge of all things knowable
independently of that decree. In the same way, since an act
of knowledge cannot be had independently of its knowable
object, we consider God's knowledge as presupposing, i.e.,
depending on, the objective truth of the objects He knows.
It depends on that truth, however, not as on a cause but as
on a *sine qua non* condition of that knowledge. Hence, as
God's decree of creation establishes immutably the future
existence of things, and as they cannot be known as future
independently of that decree, God's knowledge of them as
future depends on His decree of creation, as on a *sine qua
non* condition of that knowledge. In that sense this knowledge is said to be consequent on that decree.

5. *All relations, and all entities (things) fashioned by the
mind.*

A *relation* is an accident the whole essence of which,
when it is looked at merely as a relation, consists in referring
one thing to another, i.e., in expressing the bearing of one
thing on another. The thing referred is called the *subject*
of the relation; the thing to which it is referred, the *term* of

the relation; and the particular perfection or aspect or formality, in virtue of which the reference is given, the *foundation* of the relation. There are *real* relations, and *logical* relations, i.e., relations fashioned by the mind. What constitutes the one and the other is fully explained in Ontology. In Ontology also will be found other divisions of relations and a full explanation of the whole question.

Entities fashioned by the mind are entities (things) which, consequent on a consideration of some aspect of reality as found in the several orders of possible, futurible, and actual beings, the mind forms, and which, consequently, so exist objectively in the intellect that they cannot exist outside of it. They are commonly called logical entities, conceptual entities. The phase, or objective aspect, of reality, the consideration of which is the basis in their formation, is called their foundation. They are to be clearly distinguished from other so-called conceptual entities, which, however, are not rightly so called, seeing that they have no foundation in reality and are nothing but impossible combinations of objective concepts; for example, a square circle.

Some examples of rightly called logical beings or entities are: (a) blindness, i.e., the privation of vision, considered as a thing; (b) darkness, i.e., the absence of light, considered as a thing; (c) the objective concept "animal" looked at in its universality, i.e., as a *genus* embracing in its predicability all animals; under which formality it can exist only in the intellect.

The knowability of relations and logical entities is clear from the description of them just given. They assuredly are not absolute nothing; moreover man can know them.

What is more, as real relations are given as soon as the objective truth of the absolute realities on which they depend is given, and as logical entities are knowable just as soon as the real foundation for them is given, it follows that relations and logical entities are also eternally knowable; and this, because, as we have already proved, all those realities on which they depend, namely, God, the possibles, the futurables, and all actual beings—future, present, and past are eternally knowable.

God's Knowledge considered in itself and in comparison with man's knowledge.

In our former thesis on God's knowledge (cf. *God Infinite and Reason, Thesis VII*), and in its corollary and scholions, a sufficient explanation of these points has already been given. A re-reading of this explanation will help much to a better understanding of the present thesis and the questions to be taken up in its corollaries, etc.

Adversaries

Either directly or indirectly, God's infinite knowledge, which is here defended, looked at in itself or as provable by unaided human reason, is denied either explicitly or implicitly almost universally by modern non-Catholic philosophers of all schools. Among these are professed *Atheists* of all types; *Pantheists;* countless overthrowers of Reason as a guide in any of the weightier interests of man's life, and, in a special way, those who reject an infinite God. (Cf. *Adversaries* mentioned *passim* in *God and Reason* and *God Infinite and Reason.*)

Proof of the Thesis

Part I—*God, from all eternity, with an absolutely infallible knowledge, knows Himself and all the possibles and futuribles.*

What is knowable from all eternity God knows from all eternity with an absolutely infallible knowledge.

But God, the possibles, and futuribles are knowable from all eternity. Therefore.

Maj.*—If God did not know from all eternity, and with an absolutely infallible knowledge, all these objects, His knowledge would not be infinitely perfect. We have proved, however, that it is infinitely perfect. (Cf. *God Infinite and Reason, Thesis VII.*)

Min.—The knowability from all eternity of all these objects has been shown in the *Prenotes to the Thesis*.

Part II—*In the light of this knowledge God decrees eternally and immutably the existence of the world.*

* See *Appendix.*

If God, the possibles, and futuribles, eternally knowable, are knowable prior to, that is, independently of, God's decree calling the world into existence, and if that decree is eternal and immutable, in the light of the knowledge of these objects God decrees eternally and immutably the existence of the world.

But God, the possibles, and the futuribles, eternally knowable, are knowable prior to God's decree calling the world into existence, and that decree is eternal and immutable. Therefore.

MAJ.—The truth of the Major follows from the fact that God's knowledge is infinite. (Cf. *God Infinite and Reason, Thesis VII.*)

MIN.—That God is knowable prior to His decree of creation is immediately evident; that the possibles and futuribles are knowable prior to it, follows from the fact that their objective truth is absolutely independent of that decree. This has been already shown.

That God's decree bringing the world into existence is eternal and immutable has already been proved. (Cf. *God Infinite and Reason, Thesis IV.*)

PART III—*Consequent on His decree calling the world into existence, God knows, from all eternity and with absolute infallibility, all things in the world, man's free actions included, and under their varying temporal relations of future, present, and past existence.*

If God's decree calling the world into existence is eternal, immutable, and infinitely efficacious, consequent on that decree, God knows, from all eternity and with absolute infallibility, all things in the world, man's free acts included, and under their varying temporal relations of future, present, and past existence.

But God's decree calling the world into existence has those qualities. Therefore.

MAJ.—The truth of the Major is shown as follows:

With a full knowledge of all things possible, and of all the acts which free agents, in all possible circumstances, would choose if called into existence, God, from all eternity, freely decreed the existence of the world. By that decree He immediately determined the existence of each individual being in it, the definite time and conditions of that existence, every event occurring during it, and the definite moments of time at which those events would occur.

Consequent on that decree, then, of each being and each event in the world, with regard to all points of time *prior* to its existence, *during* it, and *following* it, the following objective judgments were from all eternity respectively true, hence, knowable, and, therefore, known by God: That being, that event, is not now, but will be; that being, that event, is now existing; that being, that event, is not now, but was. The truth of the Major is established.

It is to be clearly understood, however, that by His decree God does not determine man's free acts. He determines merely that those acts *will* be, which, prior to His decree, He knew *would* be, if man were created. Man, and man alone, *determines* the acts, with God concurring but not determining; man, and man alone, chooses them; man, and man alone, is responsible for them.

MIN.—That God's decree is eternal and immutable has already been proved. (Cf. *God Infinite and Reason, Thesis IV.*) That it is absolutely efficacious has also been proved. (Cf. *op. cit., Thesis IX.*)

COROLLARY I—*Can the possibles be said to constitute, in any way, an actual, infinite multitude?*

The possibles, as such, are beings which do not exist in the physical order, but are intrinsically capable of so existing. In themselves they are innumerable. They are infinite, then, in a broad sense, that is, countless, not, however as actual beings but as potential ones, seeing that possibles beings without end are intrinsically capable of receiving existence. They cannot, therefore, all exist simultaneously in the physical order.

With regard to these points Scholastic philosophers in general are in agreement. They admit, furthermore, that, though all the possibles cannot exist simultaneously in the physical order, all are actually known in God's one infinite act of knowledge.

Hence arises the question: Do the possibles, as they exist objectively as actually known in God's one act of knowledge, in any way form an actual, infinite multitude? Some Scholastic philosophers answer affirmatively; others, negatively. The negative answer appears to be more probable, and for the following reason.

If the possibles, as known in God's one, infinite act of knowledge, could be said to be, as known, actually infinite, God would have to cognize them as a *completed,* or fully actuated, conceptual, i.e., known, multitude. As the possibles, however, in themselves, can never form a complete, or fully actuated, real multitude, in no sense can they be known as forming a fully actuated or completed multitude.

An example will make this clearer. God's eternity is, in itself, actually infinite. God knows His own eternity. His eternity, as known by Him, is also actually infinite. Possible time is, in a broad sense, infinite, that is, as it is impossible to assign any first moment of possible time, so it is impossible to assign any last moment. In its intrinsic possibility, therefore, time is without beginning or end. God knows, in His one infinite act of knowledge, all possible points of time. If, now, the possible points of time, as known in God's act of knowledge, could be said to be, in any sense, actually infinite, God would have to cognize possible time, as known, as equalling His eternity. This, however, is impossible, as time by its very nature may grow endlessly. It may ever increase, but never be fully actualized. It can never equal eternity, and, hence, in no way can it be cognized as equalling it.

COROLLARY II—*Some points to be noted concerning the futuribles.*

A *futurible,* as we have seen, is that certain free act, from amongst those, in any possible definite set of circumstances, possible to a finite intelligent being, which would *de facto* be chosen by him, if in virtue of God's creative decree he were ever placed in those circumstances. That the futurible, as such, is objectively true, and from all eternity, we have proved. Its truth may be expressed in the form of a conditional proposition. For example: If I (God) were to place Peter in this definite set of circumstances, and offer to concur physically with him in placing any one of the actions here and now within his power, though he would have the power to choose *this* or *that, de facto* he would choose *that.*

The following remarks will help to a clearer understanding of these propositions.

1. It should be quite evident that, though the proposition given above is conditional in form, it is not a conditional proposition in the strict logical sense. In a strictly so-called conditional proposition the truth of the antecedent is so necessarily connected with the truth of the consequent that the admission of the former is necessarily the admission of the latter. In a conditional proposition, however, which enunciates the truth of a futurible, the placing of the free agent in the definite set of circumstances does not make the act which follows, follow necessarily. It is a free act, contingent on the choice of the free agent. The placing of the free agent in the definite set of circumstances, supplies him with the occasion or the motives or with both, for doing any one of the things which are presented to his will as possible. It does not determine his action. His action is free. *He* determines it.

2. Two or more actions are possible to a free agent in those circumstances in which he is about to act freely. Since, however, at the moment of action he must be in some determined state, it is objectively true, that some one definite action from amongst the two or more possible ones would *de facto* be chosen by him. What is more, in the hypothesis that *this action* would be chosen, it cannot but be the action chosen. Hence, though the admission of the truth of the antecedent of a conditional proposition enunciating a futurible does not *necessarily* mean the admission of the truth of the consequent; that is, though *antecedently* to the choice of the free agent his action is not necessary, *consequent* on his choice of this action rather than that one, it is necessarily *this action* and not *that,* which will be freely put if the free agent is placed by God in the definite set of circumstances in question. If, then, it be asked: *If a free agent were to be placed by God in a definite set of circumstances in which he would act freely, would one determined action necessarily follow?* the answer would be: *This determined*

action would necessarily follow with a necessity consequent *on the free agent's choice, not* antecedent *to it.*

3. According to some philosophers, the objective truth both of the futurible and of the absolutely future free act depends on actual decrees of God, by which the objective truth of these free acts is determined. In these decrees, therefore, as comprehensively known by God, that objective truth is also known to Him. This opinion, which is urged under different forms, must be rejected as false, for the simple reason that the free act of man is determined, and can be determined, only in itself, that is, by man alone when he freely places the act. No decree of God can determine it.

When we say, however, that the free act of man is determined by man alone, we do not mean that his determination is made independently of God. The free act of man depends on God in many ways. In the first place, looked at as a possible act, it depends, like all the other possibles, on the essence of God—the fundamental exemplar of all the possibles. Again, as a futurible—and our present inquiry is concerned only with the futuribles—though its objective truth does not, in our opinion, depend on *an actual decree* of God which determines that truth, it *does depend* on a *conditional* decree of God, which, however, in no sense *determines* that truth. Just what that dependence is will appear in the following conditional proposition, which enunciates somewhat more fully than has already been done, the objective truth of a futurible. Here is the proposition: If I (God) were to decree the existence of Peter in this definite set of circumstances, and to offer to concur indifferently with him in performing any one of the actions which, so circumstanced, he might possibly choose, though he might, consequent on this offer, freely do anyone of these actions, he would, *de facto,* with Me *concurring in,* but *not determining,* his action, freely do this.

Corollary III—*Is there any objective medium in which God can know man's free acts?*

True and False Answers to the Question

As the free act of man is, and can be, determined only in itself, that is, by man *when* he freely places the act, there

can be no objective medium of knowledge in which, prior
to, or independently of, man's free act, that act can be known
as already determined, and in which, therefore, God could
know it, either as a futurible or as an act which *de facto
will be.*

Not a few philosophers and theologians, as already noted,
deny the above statement. They assert that such a medium is
given, and in it, as a consequence, God knows infallibly and
from all eternity all man's free acts, both the pure futuribles
and those which *de facto will be.* They differ not a little,
though, when it comes to telling just what that medium is.

All their explanations, however, are to be rejected for
the simple reason that if the free act were determined in
any other way than in itself, that is, by the free agent *when*
he acts freely, it would not be a free act, seeing that to act
freely and to determine one's choice, are one and the same
thing.

Before explaining in brief, as we shall presently do, the
principal false opinion concerning God's eternal knowledge
of man's free acts, it will help much to a better understanding of this whole matter to tell in a few words what is meant
by an *objective medium of knowledge,* to give its various
divisions, and note under which may be found an objective
medium in which God can truly be said to know man's free
acts.

An objective medium of knowledge is any object, which,
as known, is a means through which is acquired a knowledge
of another object.

An objective medium of knowledge EX QUO, i.e., *through
which* deductively, another object is known, is an object,
which, as known, leads one by a reasoning process to the
knowledge of the other object. The medium, and the object
known in it, as is quite evident, are cognized in really distinct acts. As we have already proved, God knows no object
in this way. Reasoned knowledge is knowledge acquired in a
finite way.

An objective medium of knowledge IN QUO, i.e., *in which*
not-deductively, another object is known, is an object which,
as known, is a means through which, yet in the very same act
in which it is known, the other object is known, because of a

necessary nexus between the two. When discussing the question of the objective medium of God's knowledge of various objects, authors distinguish two kinds of mediums *in which*.

1. A medium *in which*, which *ontologically*, that is, in the order of reality, *determines* the objective truth of the objects known in it. When such an medium is given, then, it is absolutely necessary, and with a necessity antecedent to them, for the objects known in it to possess that objective truth which the medium has already determined, and, determining, revealed.

It is impossible, as we have already noted, that a medium of this kind be given *in which* God eternally and infallibly knows the free future acts of man, for if such a medium were given, the acts of the will would be determined prior to the will's action. In other words, the acts would not be determined by the will; would not be free.

2. A medium *in which*, which *ontologically*, that is, in the real order, *does not determine* the objective truth of the objects known in it, but which, *presupposing* their objective truth as already determined, is necessarily connected with it, and so is a medium *in which* it can be known. God's essence may be truly said to be a medium of this kind *in which* all the futuribles and all the free acts of man that will be, are known by Him eternally and infallibly. For though God's essence, i.e., the fact that God is, does not determine what man under certain conditions, *freely would do,* or *de facto* freely will do (man himself determines that), still, supposing this determination to be given, it is necessarily represented, as a thing objectively true, in that essence, the infinite exemplar of all objective truth, and, hence, of this objective truth also.

God, then, knowing His essence as showing forth, though not determining, the futuribles and free future acts of man, knows them in His essence, as in an objective medium *which does not determine* their objective truth.

In view of these explanations no objective medium can be admitted *in which* man's, conditionally or absolutely future, free acts, prior to their determination by him, can be known by God with absolute certainty. Not a few such mediums are proposed by various groups of philosophers and

theologians. It will be sufficient for our purpose to explain
the opinion of one group, as all are to be rejected for the
same reason, namely, they destroy free will.

This opinion, the principal one of those we consider
impossible, is commonly called the opinion of the Thomists.
Not a few philosophers and theologians, however, speak of
it as the opinion of the Bannesians. Their claim is—and it
appears to be at least solidly probable—that St. Thomas never
taught this opinion. Its originator, and strenuous champion
was Domingo Bañez, a Spanish Dominican (1528-1604). From
him, its defenders get their name—Bannesians.

According to this opinion God knows all man's future free
acts, both those that would be and will be, in His actual decrees by which He physically *predetermines,* that is, prior to
the will's free act, which act would be or will be put. When
the Bannesians say that God's physical predetermination, as
it actually affects the will, is prior to the will's free act, they
do not mean that it is prior in point of time. Temporally
the physical predetermination is simultaneous with the will's
free act. It is prior, however, in this sense, that the act of the
will, which is said to be free under God's physical predetermination, cannot in any way be elicited without this determination, and hence, absolutely depends on it. What is more,
in this absolute dependence it is so determined in its action
that it must necessarily follow along the lines physically determined for it. It can only put that act which God has physically predetermined it shall put.

That the will, in acting freely, depends, according to the
Bannesian explanation, on the physical predetermination of
God in such wise that it really has the power to put only one
act, and, consequently, in our opinion, is really not free at
all, will appear immediately from the following definition,
given by the Bannesians themselves, of God's physical predetermination.

A *physical predetermination (premotion,* as it is sometimes less accurately called), which is the effect in time of
God's eternal, physically predetermining decree, is an impulse (a motion, a passing or non-permanent quality) proceeding from God alone and received in the created will
prior (in the sense noted above) to its free action, by which

the will is given the proximate power to act (or is reduced to action), and which by its very nature is so connected with the free act that without it the will is absolutely incapable of any action whatever, and with it, is moved irresistibly, inescapably, to put that action, and only that action, to which it has been predetermined by this divine impulse.

In the case of the futurible, the actual decree of God is *objectively conditioned,* and hence, the physical predetermination it decrees in the case of the pure futurible, will never be given, since the condition will never be fulfilled. In the case of the free act which actually will be, the actual decree of God is objectively absolute. The physical predetermination it decrees will be given at the time appointed.

Examples of the two decrees, the first for a futurible, the second for a free act which actually will be, will make this point clear:

(1) I (God) actually decree to give to Peter this physical predetermination to that particular free act, *if I decree* to put Peter in those definite circumstances. In the case of the pure futurible God does not fulfill this condition.

(2) I (God) actually decree to give to Peter *absolutely* this physical predetermination to that particular free act. This decree fulfills the condition of the former decree, in which the same act was known as a futurible.

This opinion of the Bannesians we reject absolutely. God most assuredly can infallibly know in these physically predetermining decrees, as in objective mediums, the acts to which He predetermines the will. The very nature of the physical predetermination, however, makes it absolutely impossible that these acts should be free. Without the physical predetermination, the will cannot determine itself, for it cannot act at all; with the physical predetermination, the will cannot determine itself, for it has the power to act in one way only, namely, in the way in which God has physically predetermined it. This system, therefore, destroys man's free will.

COROLLARY IV—*The formal object of God's knowledge, or the objective medium in which God knows all things knowable, is the Divine Essence.*

The formal object of God's knowledge is its primary object, which is known by God in itself, i.e., in no objective medium, which specifies the divine act of knowledge, and which is the objective medium in which God knows all other knowable objects. It is clear from this definition that the formal object of God's knowledge and the objective medium in which God knows all finite objects are one and the same thing.

That the *Divine Essence* is this object is shown as follows:

1. It is the primary object of God's knowledge and known in itself, i.e., in no objective medium, for in perfection it is infinite, all other objects are finite; it is the source of all reality, hence, no object can be prior to it as a medium in which it can be known.

2. It specifies God's act of knowledge, for, as the primary and sole infinite object of that knowledge, it is the only object between which and God's infinite knowledge there is formal or absolute equality.

3. It is the objective medium in which God knows all other objects; not, however, all in the same way. A consideration of the various classes of objects will make both these points clear.

(a) The *possibles* are known by God in His Essence, as in a medium which determines their ontological truth, for God's essence—the source of all reality—is the infinite fundamental exemplar, of which the possibles are necessarily possible finite copies.

(b) The *futuribles* are known by God in His Essence, *not*, however, as in a medium which determines their ontological truth, but which presupposes it. If they were not so known, God's essence would not be, as it is, the infinite fundamental exemplar representing all objective truth.

(c) *All things that will be necessarily*, i.e., independently of man's free action, God knows in His essence, supposing it to include His creative decree, as in an objective medium determining their ontological truth, for God's creative decree determines irrevocably their future existence. God also knows these future events objectively in the same way in which He knows the futuribles.

(d) *All things that will be freely*, presupposing their objective truth as futuribles and God's knowledge of that truth, God knows in His essence including His creative decree, as in an objective medium which irrevocably determines their ontological truth as acts which will be, seeing that God's decree purifies the only condition which is necessary for a futurible to become a free act which will be. God's decree, therefore, does not determine the act inasmuch as it is free— the will of man does that—but it determines that the free act, which without God's decree would remain a pure futurible, absolutely will be.

God also knows all these future events in the same way in which He knows the futuribles.

Corollary V—*How the different objects of God's knowledge co-exist, as knowable objects, with that knowledge from all eternity.*

We have shown that from all eternity God knows all things knowable—Himself, the possibles, the futuribles, and all things that some time will be, which from all eternity are knowable as future, present, and past, with regard to those points of time at which *de facto* they are respectively future, present, and past. If all these various objects, then, are knowable, as such, from all eternity, they must be, as such, objectively true from all eternity, and hence, as such, co-exist from all eternity with God's knowledge. Where do they so exist? This is the question we wish to answer.

With regard to *God,* as an object of His own eternal knowledge, the answer is quite easy. As a knowable being, He exists eternally in the order of actual beings—the physical order.

The *possibles,* whose objective truth, and, hence, knowability, from all eternity, has already been shown, co-exist with God's knowledge from all eternity as possible beings— beings existing in the metaphysical order.

The *futuribles,* the objective truth, and, hence knowability of which, from all eternity has also been shown, co-exist with God's knowledge from all eternity as futuribles —beings existing in the order of futuribles.

The objective truth from all eternity of *all future things,* as future things has already been established. They co-exist,

then, from all eternity with God's knowledge as things which
will be, future things—things existing in the order of future
things.

Things which are *actually present* and things which are
actually past are known by God *from all eternity* as actually
present and past, when they are so. It is quite evident, then,
that God does not have to await their actual existence or
actual ceasing from existence to know them as present or
past.

It is also quite evident that a thing which actually exists
at this moment, or begins to be actually a past thing at this
moment, does not co-exist *from all eternity* with God's knowledge as an actually existing thing or as an actually past thing.
How then do the actually present things and actually past
things so co-exist, *from all eternity* with God's knowledge,
that from *all eternity* they may be knowable as *actually
present* and *actually past* with regard to the moments of time
when they are so actually present and past?

Our answer is that present and past things co-exist with
God's knowledge *from all eternity,* i.e., before they are actually present or actually past, *as future things.* Because of
their existence *from all eternity* in the order of future things,
they are knowable from all eternity as things present, for the
moments of their actual existence; and as things past, with
regard to the moments succeeding their actual existence.
This will be easily understood if we remember that God's
eternal decree of creation, which establishes the eternal objective truth of all things that will be, determines their existence for definite points of future time.

For those points of time, therefore, it is objectively true
that those things will be *actually* existing. They are known,
then, by God as actually *present* for those points of time; as
future with regard to all prior points of time, i.e., prior to
the time of their actual existence; and as *past,* with regard
to all subsequent points of time, i.e., subsequent to the time
of their actual existence.

Those things which will be, then, co-exist with God's
eternity, as actual beings, only during the time of their existence; they co-exist with God's eternity as actually past things
only for the time following their actual existence. Before they

actually exist they co-exist with God's eternity as *future things*—things which will be.

Though all existing things, therefore, are continually changing—they will be, they are, they were—God's knowledge of them from all eternity as things that will be, that are, that were, is absolutely changeless, seeing that their objective truth from all eternity as things that will be, that are, that were, with regard to different points of time, was eternally and irrevocably established by God's creative decree.

Corollary VI—*Divisions of God's knowledge: Simple Intelligence, Vision; Necessary and Free Knowledge; Scientia Media.*

God's knowledge which is really one, absolutely simple, immutable act, is, for our clearer understanding, conceptually divided by us as follows:

Simple Intelligence is the knowledge by which God knows all the pure possibles, and all other finite beings looked at as if in the state of pure possibility.

Vision is the knowledge by which God knows all things ever actual. By this knowledge God knows Himself, and all other things at any time actual, as they are objectively—future, present, and past.

Necessary Knowledge is the knowledge by which God knows all those things which, in no hypothesis, could be other than they are. The primary object of this knowledge is the Divine Essence—God Himself; the secondary objects are all the possibles.

Free Knowledge is the knowledge by which God knows all those things whose objective truth depends upon His own free will. By this knowledge God knows His own free acts, inasmuch as they are free, and all other things as actual—future, present, and past; their actual existence being freely willed by Him.

Scientia Media is the knowledge by which God, independently of any actual divine decree, or of any other medium, determining their objective truth, knows all the pure futuribles, and all non-pure futuribles, precision having been made from their absolute future existence, considered as pure futuribles.

This knowledge is called *"media"* because it intermediates not only between God's knowledge of Simple Intelligence and of Vision, but also between his Necessary and Free Knowledge.

It intermediates between the first two by reason of its object—the futuribles. A futurible is *more* than the object of Simple Intelligence, the possibles, because it is *not only one* of the acts possible to a free agent in a definite set of circumstances, *but that one* which he would *de facto* choose if he were put in those circumstances. It is *less*, however, than the finite object of Vision, the absolute future, which is not merely the act *which would be put* conditionally by the free agent, but which *de facto will be put,* since the condition will be verified.

It intermediates, moreover, between *God's Necessary Knowledge and Free Knowledge,* for it has a share in the qualities of both. It is *independent* of *any actual decree* in God, and in this it is *like to God's Necessary Knowledge;* it is, however, a *knowledge which is contingent in God* (contingent on the choice of the free agent), and in this it is *like to God's Free Knowledge.*

SCHOLION—*Modern philosophy and God's infinite Knowledge.*

A God of infinite knowledge very rarely, if ever, finds a place in the attempted solutions of the world's problems offered by modern philosophers. He is ruled out in different ways. By some, because they see no reason for admitting the existence of a real God of any kind; by others, who, though they admit God to be a real being of some kind, either explicitly deny Him infinite knowledge, or implicitly do so, by insisting that He is a finite being.

It will not be necessary to establish the truth of these statements here. In *God and Reason* and *God Infinite and Reason* will be found many citations from the works of many modern philosophers which fully justify them. To these we refer the reader. They give a fair picture of the chaotic state of modern philosophy.

DIFFICULTIES

1. If God can know Himself, He must reflect on Himself. But God cannot reflect on Himself. Therefore.

D. Maj. He must reflect on Himself, i.e., He must know Himself by an act of knowledge superadded to the act by which He is, *N.*; He must know Himself by the very act by which He is, i.e., by His essence, which is infinite actual existence and knowledge, *C.—Cd. Min.*

2. If the knowledge of an object perfects the knower, God cannot know objects outside of Himself. But the knowledge of an object perfects the knower. Therefore.

D. Maj. If the knowledge of an object perfects a knower whose knowledge is partially *caused* by the object, and who, therefore, passes from a state of not-knowing to a state of knowing that object, God cannot, etc., *N.*; if it perfects a knower whose knowledge is in no sense caused by the object, but who, Himself being infinite actual knowledge, is determined by His very essence to know inimmutably and eternally all things knowable, God cannot, etc., *C.—Cd. Min.*

3. That which neither exists, nor will exist, cannot be known. But the futuribles, as such, neither exist nor will exist. Therefore.

D. Maj. What in no sense of the word is a thing, i.e., a real being or a conceptual being, cannot be known, *C.;* what is not, and never will be an actual thing, but is, nevertheless, something more than a possible thing, since it is that one of the acts possible to a free agent which *de facto* would be chosen, if such a free agent were given the power by God to put that act—such a thing cannot be known, *Subd.;* with certainty by a finite intellect, *C.;* with certainty by God, who is actual infinite knowledge, *N.—Cd. Min.*

Even a finite intellect in certain cases, can know a futurible, though not with certainty. For instance, if I have a friend of long standing, whose habits of life are fully known to me, I can tell, with a very high degree of probability what he would do if he were placed in a certain set of circumstances. This, however, is to know a futurible.

4. An action objectively uncertain, i.e., undetermined, cannot be known with certainty. But a futurible is an action objectively uncertain, i.e., undetermined. Therefore.

D. Maj. An action in no way determined, i.e., neither by a necessary cause, nor by a free cause, neither absolutely nor conditionally, cannot be known with certainty, *C.;* an action which is

not determined by a necesary cause, nor by a free cause absolutely, but is determined by a free cause conditionally, cannot be
known, *Subd.*; cannot be known with certainty in its cause, *C.*; in
itself, *Subd.*; by a finite intellect, *C.*; by God, who is infinite actual knowledge, and hence, knows whatever is knowable, *N.—Cd.
Min.—D. Cons.*

5. If a futurible is an action objectively certain, i.e., determined, there should be a necessary nexus between the
antecedent and consequent of the following proposition: If
Peter were placed in these circumstances, he would freely
do that. But there is no such nexus. Therefore.

D. Maj. The truth of the antecedent necessitates the truth of
the consequent, i.e., there should be a nexus which is necessary
antecedently to Peter's conditional choice of this definite consequent, *N.*; presupposing Peter's choice, the consequent would
necessarily be; and hence, there should be a nexus which is necessary consequent on Peter's choice, *C.—Cd. Min.*

6. If the futuribles are known by God from all eternity,
they must be present as knowable objects to God's eternity.
But the futuribles cannot be so present. Therefore.

D. Maj. They must be present as actual objects, either present,
future, or past, *N.*; they must be present as objects, i.e., free actions, which would be if certain conditions were fulfilled, *Subd.*;
and so, they are present, in the strict sense of the word, that is, as
actions actually existing in the physical order, *N.*; and so, they
are present, in a broad sense of the word, that is, as actions objectively certain in the order of futuribles, *C.—Cd. Min.*

7. If God knows from all eternity actual objects, as
present, past, and future, they must co-exist as present, past,
and future with God and from all eternity. But actual
objects cannot so co-exist with God from all eternity. Therefore.

D. Maj. Actual objects, *before they actually exist,* must co-
exist with God *from all eternity,* as *already actually existing, or
as already actually past, N.*; actual objects, *before they actually
exist,* must co-exist with God *from all eternity,* as *future objects,*
that is, as objects which will exist at a definite point of time, and
by reason of this existence in the order of future things, are therefore knowable, and hence, are known by God: (a) *as future,* with
regard to all points of time preceding their actual existence, (b)

as present with regard to the time of their actual existence, and
(c) *as past,* with regard to all points of time following the time of
their actual existence, *C.—Cd. Min.*

Eternity—*God's duration*—is, as we saw in *God Infinite and
Reason, Thesis VI,* in the words of Boethius's classical definition, *"Interminabilis vitae tota simul et perfecta possessio"*
("Limitless life perfectly possessed as a simultaneous whole").
Whatever exists in time, then, since it must co-exist with eternity,
a simultaneous whole, necessarily co-exists with *the whole* of
eternity, but not *wholly.* That is, it does not co-exist with eternity,
inasmuch as eternity eminently contains all points of time, prior
to, and succeeding the time of its existence. It will be easy, now,
to understand the full meaning of our distinction of the above
difficulty. According to that distinction, an existing thing, *before
it actually exists,* is present to God's eternity as a thing which
will be—*a future thing,* and as yet only a future thing; *when it
actually exists,* it is present to God's eternity *as an actual thing;
after it exists,* it is present to God's eternity *as a thing actually
past.* In each one of these states it co-exists *with the whole of
eternity,* but not *wholly,* i.e., not inasmuch as eternity eminently
contains all points of possible and actual time prior to and following, respectively, each one of these states. (Cf. this thesis,
Corollary IV; also *God Infinite and Reason, Thesis VI,* with its
Corollaries and *Difficulties.*)

8. If God knows all things present, past, and future, as
such, His knowledge is changeable. But God's knowledge is
not changeable. Therefore.

D. Maj. His knowledge would be changeable, if, in order to
know things as present and as past, He had to wait till they were
actually present and *actually* past, *C.;* His knowledge would be
changeable, if, in order to know things as future, present, and
past, He does not have to await the actual existence of anything,
but from all eternity and before anything existed, by reason of
his eternal, immutable decree of Creation which infallibly determines the future existence of all creatures and the determined
times of such existence, He knows that they will be existing at
those points of time, and hence, He knows them (a) as *future beings* with regard to all points of time *prior to the time when they
will actually exist,* (b) as *present beings, with regard to the points
of time when they will exist,* and (c) *as past beings, with regard to
all points of time succeeding their actual existence*—God's knowl-

edge is changeable: if, in this way, He knows the present, past, and future, as such, *N.—Cd. Min.* (Cf. this Thesis, *Corollary V.*)

9. If God could know from all eternity all future free acts, those acts would necessarily exist. But free acts cannot necessarily exist. Therefore.

D. Maj. Those acts would necessarily exist with a necessity antecedent to the act of the will, and, hence, which would really deprive the will of the power of choosing, *N.*; those acts would necessarily be with a necessity consequent on the choice of the will, known by God from all eternity, first, as a conditioned future, i.e., a futurible, and, secondly, because of his creative decree fulfilling the condition, as an absolutely future free act, *Subd.*; and the fact that God knows these acts as future is the reason why they necessarily, i.e., infallibly, will be, *N.*; from the fact that God knows them as future *we know* that they will be necessarily, i.e., infallibly, *not as necessary* but as free acts, *C.—Cd. Min.*

10. If the future acts of man which are said to be free, are not necessary with a necessity antecedent to the action of the will, man has the power of falsifying God's knowledge. But man has not that power. Therefore.

D. Maj. If man's free acts are not in that way necessary, he would be able to falsify God's knowledge, if the extrinsic determinant of God's knowledge *was not the free act,* but man just as he was about to put it, *C.*; if that determinant *is the free act itself,* which man will put, which God knows from all eternity, and before the actual existence of anything, as a futurible, and, consequent on His decree of Creation, as a free act which infallibly will be—in this hypothesis man could falsify God's knowledge, *N.—Cd. Min.*

11. If God's knowledge is prior to man's future free act, that act cannot be the extrinsic determinant of God's knowledge. But God's knowledge is prior to man's future free act. Therefore.

D. Min. If God's knowledge is in every sense prior to man's free act, that act cannot be, etc., *C.*; if God's knowledge, because eternal, is prior to the *actual* placing of man's free act, but presupposes, as a necessary condition of that knowledge, that act's objective truth, determined from all eternity, as a futurible, and, through God's eternal decree of Creation, as an act which infallibly will be—if God's knowledge is so explained, man's free future act cannot, etc., *N.—Cd. Min.*

12. If future free acts are contingent, i.e., if it is uncertain which one of the acts possible to a free agent will be chosen, certain knowledge of them is impossible. But future free acts are contingent. Therefore.

D. Maj. If future free acts are contingent or uncertain, in such wise that, before their actual choice in time, they can in no way be said to be necessary, determined, certain knowledge of them, is impossible, *C.*; if they are contingent or uncertain, but in such wise that, before their actual choice in time, they can be said to be certain, determined, necessary, with a necessity which is consequent on the choice of the free agent, as futurible in the order of futuribles, and, God's eternal decree of creation being presupposed, as future free acts in the order of future things: if they are in this way contingent, certain knowledge of them is impossible, *Subd.*; in the case of a finite mind, *C.*; in the case of an infinite mind which from all eternity, being actual infinite knowledge, must know with absolute certainty among other things, everything which is objectively true in the order of futuribles, and free future things, *N.—Cd. Min.—D. Cons.*

13. In order that God might know all things as possible in His essence there should be an absolutely necessary nexus between His essence and the possibles. But there can be no such nexus. (If there were such a nexus, the possibles would be necessary beings.) Therefore.

N. Min. The proof given of the *Minor,* however, is to be distinguished thus: The possibles would be necessary as actual beings, *N.;* as potential beings, *C.*

14. God's essence cannot be a medium in which He knows the possibles, if the possibles are not contained in it. But the possibles are not contained in it. Therefore.

D. Maj. It cannot be such a medium if His essence in no way contains the possibles, *C.*; if His essence, which is in perfection actually infinite, and which in its infinite simplicity contains all perfections, does not contain the possibles as they are in themselves, but includes all their perfections in an infinitely perfect degree, and, hence, without imperfection and limitlessly: if it contains the possibles in this way, it cannot be such a medium, *N.—Cd. Min.*

15. If God physically predetermines man's free actions, He can know those actions in His decree physically predetermining them. But God physically predetermines man's free actions. Therefore.

N. Min.

Prob. Min. If God does not physically predetermine man's free acts, man will have the power to place an action which God cannot prevent. But man cannot so act. Therefore.

D. Maj. Man will have the power to put an action which God cannot prevent by His will already freely determined to concur with the man in the putting of that action (which will of God is consequent on His knowing by His Scientia Media what the man would freely do if placed in a position to put the action): that is, man can put an action which God cannot prevent, because He has already determined not to prevent it, *C.*; which God cannot prevent by His will, considered antecedently to His determination to concur with the action, *Subd.*; which God cannot prevent absolutely, that is, either by not creating the man, or by denying His concursus to the action, or by placing the man in other circumstances in which the action would not be possible, *N.*; which God cannot prevent if He wishes the man to exercise his freedom in the matter, *Subd.*; man will have the physical freedom or power to go counter to this conditional will of God, *C.*; man, though he has the physical freedom or power to go counter to God's will so conditioned, would *de facto* go counter to it. *Tr.*

The last part of the distinction has to do with the possibility of finding a man who would be an *absolute rebel* with regard to God, that is, a man who would reject every possible effort of God to bring him, for example, to freely turn away from a temptation to sin. That the man would have the physical power to do so, is evident, since he is supposed to be physically free in the matter; for, no matter how strong the motives to reject the sin, he has always the power of choice. The question, however, is, could God present motives so strong, that the man would *de facto* freely follow them?

The most probable answer appears to be, that it would be impossible to find a man who (keeping the example given) *could* and *would freely* resist any effort that God might make to turn him from a sinful to a virtuous action.

The reason for this answer is the following: It is true that when a man acts freely he has the physical power to reject any course of action, no matter how strongly it may attract him, in favor of one whose attractive force is next to nothing. It would be a sign, however, that he was acting quite irrationally, if merely for the sake of following his own sweet will, he would choose to refuse a course of action which he saw clearly would benefit him immeasurably, to follow one which he also saw clearly would harm him in the same way—immeasurably. Now, God, who is ever seeking man's greater good, in His infinite wisdom and power, can so enlighten the intellect of man with an absolutely clear understanding of the foolishness of one course of action, and so strengthen his will with motives for rejecting it, that, though he has the physical power to choose it, *de facto* he would *freely* reject it.

In our example, then, God foresees that with the present intellectual light that man has, and with the present motives attracting him, the man would sin. God wishes the man freely to reject that sin. He achieves that result by giving him that increase in knowledge of the heinousness of sin and of the worth of acting virtuously, and that strengthening of will with more powerful motives, which, He foresees, will lead him *freely* to reject the sin and do the virtuous deed. In this wise, without any predetermining on the part of God (which predetermining, as we see it, destroys man's free will), God's supreme dominion, even in this respect, over His creatures is fully safeguarded. God's supreme dominion, as exercised by His absolute will, is of course, in the physical order, absolutely irresistible.

It is to be clearly noted, however, that, though God has given man physical liberty, including the power to choose between morally good and bad acts, it is absolutely impossible that man should ever be given moral liberty, that is, that he should ever be released from the obligations of the moral law. Hence, in the case in which, having foreseen that a man in a certain set of circumstances, would freely sin, God decrees to put man in those circumstances, though He must concur in the physical putting of the sinful act of the man, if the man is to exercise his freedom, still He not only does not concur in the moral guilt, but He absolutely forbids it, giving man always sufficient aid and strength to reject it. He promises reward, if he will do so, and eternal reward if the man will persevere in well-doing; He threatens punishment if man will perversely choose the sinful act, and eternal punishment, if he perseveres till death in grievous sin. In this way, if God permits the man to use his free will in sinning—we say, *permits,* for God never *intends* the sin, and, what is more,

His permission of it is only possible on the condition that He can draw good from it—God's supreme dominion over man, in the moral order, is also fully safeguarded.

16. If a man knowing thoroughly the character and habits of another man can foretell with great probability what he would do if he were placed in a definite set of circumstances, God with His infinite knowledge, from a consideration of the same man when fully prepared to act freely, should be able to foresee with absolute certainty the act which he will freely put. But a man knowing thoroughly the habits and character of another man can do that. Therefore.

N. Maj. Until the will makes its choice, the choice which it will make is not absolutely settled. In other words, its objective truth is not definitely established; it is not as yet objectively certain. It is impossible, then, for any intellect, considering the man merely when fully prepared to act, to know with absolute certainty the definite act which will follow, seeing that it is not as yet objectively certain which will be the definite act to be chosen.

17. If the objective truth of a futurible depends on God's decree, God can know it in that decree, as an objective medium of knowledge. But the objective truth of a futurible depends on God's decree. Therefore.

D. Maj. If its objective truth depends on an actual decree of God which predetermines absolutely that objective truth, God can know that truth in such a decree, *C.*; if it does not depend on any actual decree of God, but only on a conditional one, which in no way determines the action of the will, but in virtue of which, if God were to offer to concur in whatever act the will might choose to put, the determining of the act would be done by the will, with God concurring in it, but not determining it: if the decree is of this kind, God can know the futurible in it, *N.—Cd. Min.*

The world was brought into existence by the free creative act of God.

Prenotes to the Thesis

We have proved elsewhere that God is the unproduced, necessarily existing, personal, First Cause of all existing beings other than Himself. We have proved, furthermore, that the decree of His omnipotent will bringing all these things into existence was placed in the light of His infinite knowledge of all possible worlds that might be made, and of everything possible that could or would take place in them, either necessarily or freely, if they were made.

In the present thesis, and those which follow, we are to study the nature of this inflowing of God's omnipotence into the world He did make. As the result of this study we shall find, first, that the world, because of its utter dependence as a contingent being on God, could come into existence only from absolute nothingness and by His free creative act; secondly, and because of that same dependence, that nothing in the world, no matter how small, after having been brought into existence, can continue to exist, unless God directly and continually gives it its existence; and, thirdly, because of that same dependence, that no being thus continually receiving its existence from God, can perform any action, or bring anything, however insignificant, into existence, unless God, as the First Cause of all things, concurs with it in performing that action and producing that thing. In the closing theses of our reasoned study of God, His wise providence, in the exercise of His omnipotence in ordering and governing the world of His creation, will be considered.

The question which we are now to discuss is the way in which the world originated. For the sake of clearness in this discussion, and in the proofs which are to follow, it will be necessary to explain accurately the meaning of the terms as used by us in the twofold proposition we offer for proof, namely, *the origin of the world was due to God's creative act; God was free in the exercise of this act.*

The world as we here use the term, is the complexus of all things existing other than God, whatever their nature may be. It includes, therefore, not only this visible world of ours, but also all other beings, whatever they may be, whose existence God may have decreed. When we say, moreover, that the world, so understood—

Was brought into existence by God's creative act, we do not mean that all beings, at any time existing in the world, were, or are, created. That statement would be false. What we do mean is this; the world in its original state came into existence by God's creative act. Or, to put it more clearly, the original (being or) beings of the world, that is, those beings which were immediately produced by God, and prior to whom, no other beings were produced, were, and could only be, produced by His creative act.

Whether or not any being other than these original ones owe their existence also to creation will appear later. Later, also, will be considered three other questions, from the solution of which the present thesis prescinds, namely, the origin of our knowledge of creation; the possibility of the eternal creation of the world; and the possibility of any produced being possessing the power to create.

Creation, taken in the strict sense and as signifying action, in which way it is taken in our thesis, may be defined in different ways, from different viewpoints. These definitions, which are substantially identical, are the following:

1. Creation is the production of a thing out of nothing, i.e., the bringing of a thing into existence from actual absolute nothingness. It should be quite evident that, in this definition, *nothing* is not considered to be the *matter* out of which the thing was made, as though *nothing* could be fashioned into something. The meaning of the phrase, *out of nothing* is *not out of anything.* Hence, when a thing is created, it is made, but *not out of anything;* it is brought into existence, from a *quasi* starting point of actual absolute nothingness, hence, totally; its *existence* is conceived as *following on* its *total non-existence.* A more explicit formulation of this

definition, and one which explicitly stresses the difference between creative and non-creative production is the following one:

2. Creation is the production of a thing when neither the thing itself, *as such,* nor any subject, out of which, as a material cause, it could have been made, pre-existed. For instance, if a marble statue was not fashioned by a sculptor, but was created, using the word creation in the strict sense, then the statue, *as such,* had no previous existence, nor did the marble, i.e., the material now existing in it, have any previous existence. Had the marble previously existed, the statue would have been *fashioned* by the sculptor; it would not have been *created.* The first part of the above definition, namely, that prior to its creation, the thing, *as such,* had no existence, is true of all production, both creative and non-creative. For if the thing, *as such,* already existed, the action which was supposed to produce it would have nothing to produce. The second part of the definition, namely, that no subject, out of which, as a material cause, the thing could have been made, pre-existed, is true *only* of creation.

It follows, then, that *creation* is *not change.* To change a thing is to make an actually existing thing pass from one actual state to another. A change may be either *substantial,* as when the food we eat is changed into our flesh, or *accidental,* as when a block of marble gradually is given new form and becomes a statue. In creation, on the contrary, there is no actually existing thing which becomes something else. Prior to the existing created thing there existed only the physical efficient cause who created it, that is, brought it from actual nothing into existence.

A further explanation of what is meant by the *subject out of which,* as *material cause,* something, *substantially* or *accidentally* new, is made, will help, perhaps, to a better understanding of our definition of creation.

If the total term, or complete effect, which is the result of a non-creative action is considered, the subject, or material cause, out of which it is produced, is a constituent part of it —the determinable part; that part, namely, which is determined by the new substantial or accidental form, to be *this* substantially or accidentally new thing.

In the case of a *substantial change,* the determinable constituent part of the new substance is the prime, or fundamental, matter which existed in the substances, from which
the new substance was made, united with their respective substantial forms. This matter, in the change, has been deprived
of those forms to make way for the new substantial form
which united with it makes the new complete substance. An
example will make this clear. Hydrogen and oxygen are
changed into water. The subject, or material cause, *out of*
which the water is made, is a constituent part of the water,
namely, that part which is determined, by union with the
new form of water, to be water. This subject, or material
cause, is the prime, or fundamental matter which previously
existed in the hydrogen and oxygen. In the change, it has
given up the substantial forms of hydrogen and oxygen, in
order to take on the new form of water. The result of the
substantial union of the two is the new substance, water.

In the case of an *accidental change,* however, the subject,
or material cause, out of which the accidentally new thing is
made, is the whole substance of the thing which is changed,
and which, in the change loses one accidental form to make
way for another. An example is our block of marble which is
changed into a statue. The subject, or material cause, out of
which the complete statue is made is the marble which under
the expert hands of a sculptor gives up the accidental shape
it happens to have, namely, that of an irregular block, takes
on a new shape accidental to it, and stands revealed as a beautiful statue.

When we consider, then, the whole new thing which results from a non-creative action, we see that the subject, or
material cause, out of which it is made, is a constituent part
of it. This, however, is not true if we consider not the whole,
complete, term of the action, but that part which is newly
called into being, namely, the new substantial or new accidental form.

They are said to be produced out of the subject, or material cause, not in the sense that it is a constituent part of
them, but only in the sense that those forms have a potential
existence in the subject or material cause out of which they
are produced; that is, out of which they are drawn, or educed,

into actual existence by the efficient cause. In their production, therefore, these forms intrinsically depend on the sustaining action of the subject, or material cause, out of which they are made, i.e., drawn or educed into actual existence, and in their after-existence they also depend on it intrinsically.

It is to be clearly understood that the term, material cause, in general, signifies the determinable part of a compound, the determining part of which is its form, the formal cause. The material cause, in the case of substantial changes, is always matter—prime matter. In accidental, changes, however, the material cause, the determinable part in the change, may be a spiritual substance. For instance, when the soul, a spiritual substance, produces a thought, a spiritual accident, it is changed accidentally. It does not, however, create the thought but, as an efficient cause proximately prepared to act, produces it with itself concurring as the subject, or material cause, out of which the thought is educed, and which it determines.

Another point to be carefully noted is this. The human soul, which is an incomplete spiritual substance, though it presupposes a subject existing previous to its own production, in no sense presupposes a subject *out of which,* as a material cause, it is made, but only a subject *in which* it is produced, to which it is essentially united; which it informs, making it a living human being—a man. The matter in man is the material cause *out of which* the composite being, man, is made, but *it is not* a material cause *out of which* the soul is produced. The soul in its production and in its after-existence is intrinsically independent of matter. It is produced out of nothing. It is created by God.

A third definition of creation, which follows, will be easily understood in the light of the explanations given above.

3. Creation is the production of a thing totally. The two former definitions stressed the absolute, complete nothingness which precedes the production of the object which is created; this definition stresses the absolute completeness of being which is given that object by creation.

God freely created the world. This assertion is made in

the second part of our thesis. Its meaning is clear. God was in no way obliged to create the world. From all eternity He willed its existence. If it pleased Him, He could have willed to leave it in its original nothingness. Though its existence was willed by God from all eternity, that existence was not from all eternity. Both Revelation and reason, as will appear in a corollary to our thesis, tell us that the world had a beginning.

Adversaries

The number of Philosophers, especially modern ones, who, either directly or indirectly, reject our thesis, is all but countless. In our Introduction the views of some of them have been presented in their own words. They may be classed as follows.

1. *Kant* and countless Kantians who with him hold that reason cannot know anything outside of the phenomenal order. Reason, therefore, can tell us nothing about God, or the origin of the world from God by creation. In *God and Reason*, and *God Infinite and Reason* will be found many references to Kant and modern Kantians.

2. *All Atheists;* by far the largest number of whom will be found to be crude Materialists. Though Materialism has lost much of its following in these later days, still it is the basic philosophy of anti-God Communism and radical Socialism.

3. *All Pantheists;* who in reality are Atheists. They reject, of course, a Creator-God. Not a few of the modern Scientists are Pantheists of one kind or other. In *God Infinite and Reason* the question of Pantheism is treated at some length.

4. *Many Pluralists;* some holding God to be finite. Though they speak of creation and God as Creator, they do not admit creation to be an efficient production of real beings from a previous state of total non-existence. In fact, the explanation which some of them give of the origin of beings other than God would lead one to believe that perhaps they are Pantheists.

Proof of the Thesis

Part I.—*The world was brought into existence by the creative act of God.*

If the world in its original state was brought into existence by God from complete nothingness, it was brought into existence by the creative act of God.

But the world in its original state was so brought into existence by God. Therefore.

Maj.—The Major appears to be evident. For when we state in our thesis that the world was brought into existence by the creative act of God, we mean only this, that the world in its original state was brought into existence by God from complete nothingness. It is to be noted, however, that the world in its original state, is the world as made up of the original (being or) beings of the world, those, namely, which were immediately produced by God and before whom no other produced beings existed.

Min.—*That* the world owes its existence to God follows from the fact that God is the first and only unproduced cause of all things produced. This has already been proved.

That some (being or) beings, produced by God were immediately produced by Him, beings, namely, before whom no other produced beings existed, must also be admitted, for if no being immediately resulted from God's productive act unless a being prior to it had been produced, there would be an infinite regression with nothing produced.

That those beings which were so immediately produced by God were produced from complete nothingness remains to be proved.

It is proved as follows.

If the beings which were so immediately produced by God, prior to their production, actually existed in no way at all, they were produced from complete nothingness.

But prior to their existence they existed in no way at all. Therefore.

Maj.—The Major is immediately evident.

Min.—Prior to their production they actually existed in no way at all, for—

(a) They had no prior existence *as such* beings, that is, as they were after production, for if they had, the action which was supposed to have produced them would have produced nothing.

(b) Nor did anything out of which they could have been made exist prior to their production. For since they were beings so immediately produced by God that no produced being existed before them, the only thing existing prior to them was God Himself. God, however, a being unproduced, existing with absolute necessity, absolutely simple, absolutely immutable, infinite, could in no way be the subject out of which were made or produced, contingent, composite, changeable, finite beings.

PART II.—*The world was freely created by God.*

If the world was not freely created by God, the existence of creatures was willed by God necessarily, either as the desired end, the final cause, of the divine creative will, or as a means necessary to that end. But the existence of creatures was not so willed by God. Therefore.

MAJ.—The Major is evident. The disjunction it enunciates is complete.

MIN.—(a) The existence of creatures was not willed by God necessarily as the desired end, the final cause of the divine creative will. The end, the final cause or reason, of the divine creative will is in no way found in creatures. It is God's own infinite Goodness. It is the love of this infinite Goodness which leads God to bring creatures into existence. St. Thomas will give us the reason.

The principal thing willed is to every willer the cause of his willing. . . . Accordingly if God wills principally something other than Himself, it follows that something other than Himself is the cause of His willing. But His willing is His being, as we have shown. Therefore something else will be the cause of His being, and this is contrary to the notion of the first being. (*Contra Gentiles,* Bk. 1, c. 74.)

Whoever loves a thing in itself and for its own sake, loves in consequence all things wherein it is found. . . . Now God wills and loves His own being, in itself and for its own sake. . . . And all other being is a participation, by likeness, of His being. . . .

Therefore, from the fact that God wills and loves Himself, it follows that He wills and loves other things. (*Loc. cit.*, c. 75.)

(b) The existence of creatures was not willed by God
necessarily as a means to the attainment of the end of the
divine creative will. We turn again to St. Thomas for our
proof.

As to the things willed by God, we must observe that He wills
something of absolute necessity: but this is not true of all that
He wills. For the divine will has a necessary relation to the divine goodness, since that is its proper object. Hence God wills
His own goodness necessarily. . . . But God wills things apart
from Himself in so far as they are ordered to His own goodness
as their end. Now in willing an end we do not necessarily will
things that conduce to it, unless they are such that the end cannot be attained without them. . . . Hence, since the goodness of
God is perfect, and can exist without other things, inasmuch as
no perfection can accrue to Him from them, it follows that His
willing things apart from Himself is not absolutely necessary.
Yet it can be necessary by supposition, for supposing that He
wills a thing, then He is unable not to will it, as His will cannot
change. (*Summa Theologica*, 1, q.9, a.3.)

Scholion I.—*Unaided reason and the notion of creation.*

Can unaided reason come to a knowledge of creation, that
is, creation in the strict sense of the word; the production,
namely, of a thing *totally,* or, as it is technically expressed,
ex nihilo sui et subjecti? Some philosophers say that reason
cannot. If it could, they insist, some at least of the pagan
philosophers would have done so. However, they did not;
not even Aristotle. Others hold that Aristotle probably arrived at a concept of creation.

The view on this point taken by Bishop Turner in his
article on "Aristotle," in the *Catholic Encyclopedia,* appears
to be the correct one. He writes: "It would be hazardous to
say that he [Aristotle] taught the doctrine of creation. This
much, however, may be safely said: He lays down principles
which, if carried to their logical conclusion, would lead to
the doctrine that the world was made out of nothing."

Grabmann, *Thomas Aquinas,* says practically the same
thing: "The relation existing between God and the world is
determined by the divine act of creation. Thomas, whose

mind had been enriched by the creationist theism, is clearer and goes much farther than Aristotle, who never arrived at a notion of creation despite remarkable approaches to it." (P. 110.)

Independently, however, of what pagan philosophers taught, what answer are we to give to the question? The true answer seems to be that though unaided reason can—the proof of our thesis shows this—and, therefore, could arrive at the idea of creation, still the idea seems actually to have had its origin in divine revelation. Pohle-Preuss, *The Author of Nature and the Supernatural* (slightly modified), states the whole case quite clearly:

Though the Scriptural and Ecclesiastical concept of creation was more or less unknown to the most enlightened pagan philosophers of antiquity, as Plato and Aristotle, it is not one at which it was impossible for human reason to arrive without supernatural aid. With the possible exception of the teleological, all the arguments (we should rather say, at least some of the arguments, notably from motion, from produced being, from contingent being), by which we are able to demonstrate the existence of God, show when fully developed that He is the absolute creator of the universe, and they would not be complete without this final conclusion. *De facto,* however, human reason is indebted to divine revelation for the true concept of creation, which philosophers *might have* found, but, in matter of fact, *did not* find. (P. 8.)

SCHOLION II.—*The creative power belongs to God alone.*

In a thesis, to follow later, it will be proved, as a certain conclusion, that every action, and the effect produced by it, of which a creature is the efficient physical cause, must have God also as a physical, efficient, immediate cause, the First Cause, producing with the creature, but not under the same aspect, the same whole action, and the same whole effect. Taking this, then, as a certain conclusion, the proposition to be proved in our scholion is to be understood in this sense: the creative power so belongs to God alone that it is absolutely impossible for a creature to possess it. Hence, even though he were supposed, in his action, to be totally dependent on the concurrent immediate action of God, it would be impossible for him to be the creator of anything.

Various proofs of this statement are given. We shall develop only one; a simple one, easily understood, yet as convincing as some of the harder ones. To this will be added another from St. Thomas.

Our proof is this. The perfection of the essence or nature of a being is shown in the perfection of his actions. Hence, a being who has a nature which is essentially different from, and essentially higher than that of another being, should have a power of acting essentially different from, and essentially higher than his.

If that be true, and it is true (for the nature of a being is the source from which his active power flows), then God who, as the only infinite being possible, has a nature infinitely superior to that of any other being, and in which it is absolutely impossible for any other being in any way to participate, must have an active power also infinite, and as such infinitely superior to that of any other being, and in which no other being can in any way participate.

Now, that power is none other than the creative power. Two reasons will show this.

1. That power which is infinitely above any other power should assuredly be the highest and most perfect which can be exercised in the production of beings.

The creative power, however, is the highest and most perfect, because it is necessarily the first, the original active power to be exercised in the production of being, and as such, therefore, is independent of the previous exercise of any other active power of production, and of any subject on which it must act. The other active powers of production, those, namely, which produce substantial and accidental changes, are dependent in both ways; they presuppose the initial and original exercise of the creative power, and are dependent on the subjects which they change.

2. If the creative power is not that active power which so belongs to God alone that no other being can participate in it in any way, then such a power is impossible. For no matter in how many other ways the action of a creature would be different from God's action and inferior to it, still, if it could create, under one aspect its active power would be on a level with God's, and so would in some way participate in it,

namely, inasmuch as it would act independently of any subject. We have proved, however, that God must have an active power in which no other being can in any way participate. Therefore, no creature can in any way possess the creative power.

God, as Creator, therefore, is absolutely independent in His action; He depends on the concurrent action of no other being; He depends on the previous action of no other being; He depends on no subject. A creature, on the contrary, since in its action it can in no way participate in God's way of acting, must be dependent in these three ways. It is impossible for it, then, to possess in any way the creative power.

The proof just given shows that a creature can in no way possess that power to create; hence, neither as a principal cause, nor, if such were possible in creation, as an instrumental one. That instrumental casuality, however, can have no place in creation, St. Thomas will show us in the following passage.

Some have supposed that although creation is the proper act of the universal cause, still some inferior cause, acting by the power of the first cause, can create. . . . But such a thing cannot be, because, the secondary instrumental cause does not participate in the action of the superior cause except inasmuch as by some thing proper to itself it acts dispositively to the effect of the principal agent. . . . Now the proper effect of God creating, is what is presupposed to all other effects, and that is absolute being. Hence nothing else can act dispositively and instrumentally to this effect, since creation is not from anything presupposed which can be disposed by the action of an instrumental agent. So, therefore, it is impossible for any creature to create, either by its own power, or instrumentally. *(Summa Theologica,* I, q.45, a.5.)

Scholion III.—*It is impossible for any creature to have existed from eternity.*

We know with certainly from divine Revelation that the world has not existed from eternity. God, who freely created it, brought it into existence in time. It had a beginning. "In the beginning God created heaven and earth." The question now arises: Could God, since He was free in creating the world, have given it an existence from eternity? Or, to give as broad a scope as possible to our inquiry: Could God have given existence from eternity to any creature? Since God, however, can do whatever is intrinsically possible, our question should rather be put this way: Is it possible for any creature to have existed from eternity? To that question, which Revelation does not answer, philosophers give several answers.

Some claim that reason can give no certain arguments either for or against the possibility of a creature existing from eternity. Others insist that reason can prove with certainty the impossibility of existence from eternity of any kind of succession. According to them, therefore, it would be impossible to create a world in which there would be beings in motion from eternity, or subject to any other kind of successive change from eternity, or succeeding one another in any way from eternity. At the same time, however, the supporters of this opinion assert that reason cannot give any convincing argument showing that a produced being who would be absolutely permanent, and, hence, exclude succession of any kind could not exist from all eternity.

Finally, according to a third group of philosophers, and their opinion, which is now most commonly held, appears to be the true one, reason can give certain proof that existence from eternity is not possible for any produced being, whatever be its nature, either absolutely permanent, or in any way in succession, in itself or with regard to others.

St. Thomas, in his earlier years, appears to have favored the first opinion mentioned above. Later, however, he admitted that a world in which there would be generations of men from eternity could be shown with certainty to be impossible. His reason for holding this restricted form of the second opinion explained above, was the following. As the human soul, when once created, does not cease to exist, to admit the possibility of men generating one another successively from eternity would be to admit that an actual infinite multitude of souls could exist at any one moment, that is, simultaneously. Since, however, St. Thomas, in his later years, was convinced that an infinite multitude of beings existing simultaneously was impossible, he quite consistently admitted also the impossibility of a world in which men would generate one another successively from eternity.

Another point to be noted is this. Since the reason, given by St. Thomas to prove that successive generations of men from eternity are not possible, is used among other reasons, and rightly so, to exclude from the same possibility all produced beings, those who hold the last opinion mentioned above are justified in claiming, as they do claim, that it is but a logical extension of St. Thomas' maturer judgment, and, hence, that in principle at least he is in agreement with them.

In support of this opinion, then, which holds that existence from eternity is impossible for any creature, and which opinion appears to be the true one, we offer the following argument.

Every created being is a contingent being, that is, a being to whom existence is not absolutely necessary. Furthermore, if existence is not absolutely necessary to it, no definite state in which it exists is absolutely necessary to it. A contingent being, then, is a being who can pass from one state to another, a mutable being, a being intrinsically capable of changing. If such a being, therefore, could exist from eternity, at the present moment of its existence it would have, or at least it might have, undergone actual successive changes from eternity.

But actual succession in existence of any kind from eternity is impossible, whether it be found in successive changes in a being, or in a series of beings generating one another or merely coming into existence one after another. The following reasons will make this evident.

1. The notion of succession in existence essentially includes the notion of before and after in duration. In other words, a successively existing thing, for instance motion, is one whose parts do not exist at the same time; one necessarily comes after another. A series of successively existing beings is one in which the beings come into existence not at the same time, but one after another.

Now, nothing which includes in its concept the notion of before and after in duration can exist from eternity. Let us take the example of successive changes in a being, and what is true of them is true of all kinds of succession in existence.

As these successive changes in a being are supposed to be actual, then some one of them must be actually from eternity. That one, however, actually existing from eternity, since it would necessarily succeed another, must suppose that other to have taken place prior to eternity. It would suppose, in other words, an absolute impossibility.

2. Another absurdity, which necessarily flows from the supposition that actual successive changes from eternity are possible in any being, is the following. That being, or rather the world, to make the example a definite one, in the course of its existence should be able each day to reach some definite stage in its development. Yet it could never reach any such definite stage, let us say, its present one, if to reach it, it had to pass, as it would have, through successive stages from eternity. The reason is this. Successive changes from eternity reaching to the present time, if they could take place, would form an infinite actual multitude, seeing that they would be actually without beginning, actually limitless, actually numberless, and, so, actually infinite. Now, an infinite actual multitude of successive changes cannot be passed over. To pass over them would require the lapse of an infinite actual multitude of periods of time. But the lapse of an infinite actual multitude of periods of time is impossible. A duration of time that can be passed over is necessarily limited.

Probably a simpler way of reaching the same conclusion is this. If I start with the present state of the world, which is supposed to have been reached after successive changes from eternity, and work backwards noting each successive change, I could never pass over all the changes that had taken place from eternity. I must ever keep on my journey. In like manner, then, the world journeying from eternity through successive changes towards the present point in the world's development must be ever on its way, must pursue an endless journey. Its present state of development could never be reached. But it *has* been reached. Therefore, the world's journey was not, nor could it be, from eternity.

3. A third proof, showing that actual successive changes of any kind from eternity are impossible, is the one that led many of the supporters of the opinion we are defending to

claim that in holding it they are in principle following St. Thomas. *The proof runs as follows.*

The infinite actual multitude of successive changes which would take place, if actual successive changes from eternity were possible, would necessarily imply the possibility of an infinite actual multitude of beings existing simultaneously. Such a multitude, however—St. Thomas also concurs in this judgment—is impossible.

That an infinite actual multitude of beings existing simultaneously would be implied in the first supposition, is proved this way. It would be possible for God each time one of these changes took place to create a man. As the soul, when once created, remains in existence, an infinite actual multitude of souls would exist at the present moment, that is, simultaneously. The same would be true about a multitude of stones created in the same way by God, and preserved in existence by Him to the present moment.

The impossibility of an infinite actual multitude of beings existing simultaneously is shown in many ways.

St. Thomas gives this proof.

Every kind of multitude must belong to a species of multitude. The species of multitude are to be reckoned by the species of numbers. No species of number is infinite; for every number is multitude measured by one. Hence it is impossible for there to be an actually infinite multitude. . . . Likewise multitude in nature is created, and everything created is comprehended under some clear intention of the Creator; for He does not work aimlessly. Hence everything created must be comprehended in a certain number. Therefore it is impossible for an actually infinite multitude to exist. *(Summa Theologica,* 1, q.7, a.4.)

Francis McGarrigle, S.J., offers the following proof.

An infinite multitude of units would seem to commit us to such self-contradictory assertions as that two infinites do not form a greater multitude than one infinity, both being limitless as is their sum. We must likewise say than an infinity has in it an infinity of units, an infinity of couples and an infinity of all numbers, in fact an infinity of infinities. By coupling up each unit with its successor, we could divide infinity in halves and the result would be of necessity two infinities, since two finite multitudes will not make an infinite one. Thus infinity divided by two would equal infinity multiplied by two. The same would be true if we divided an infinite multitude into thirds, fourths, or any other fractions. Since the multitude is supposed to be infinite, such divisions of it could be infinite in number, with a result that we have an infinity of infinities, on each of which we can institute the same process. Because of these and similar reasonings, anything like real infinity referring to quantitative units has been well rejected by eminent mathematicians, such as the French MM. Cauchy and Poincaré. ("The Infinite, The Variable, An Eternal Universe," *The Irish Ecclesiastical Record,* Feb., 1933, p. 125.)

Difficulties

1. If we cannot understand how a thing is created we act irrationally in claiming that the world was created. But we cannot understand how a thing is created. Therefore.

D. Maj. If we cannot understand perfectly the nature of the creative act, but we can demonstrate the necessity of admitting the fact of the world's creation, we act irrationally, etc., *N.*; if we can do neither, we act irrationally, *C.—Cd. Min.*

Ronayne explains it this way: "The *fact* of creation reason can conclude to, but the *act* itself being intrinsically infinite, it cannot *fathom.* It cannot fathom even its own creative-like power of thought; though it is most certainly conscious of that power. It is through this mysteriousness of the operation of the soul that St. Thomas introduces us to the consideration of God's creative act. 'Since, then,' he says, 'by the act which is in us we are able to proceed not only to actions that abide in us, such as intelligence and volition, but also to actions that pass on to outward things, and through which certain things are made by us; much more can God, in that He is in act, not only understand and will, but also produce an effect. And thus He can be the cause of being to other things.' *(Contra Gentiles,* Bk. 2, c. 6.)"—*(God Knowable and Known,* p. 107.)

2. If we could demonstrate the fact of creation, we should have a concept of creation. But we have no concept of creation. Therefore.

D. Maj. We should have a concept of creation, such as we have of actions which fall within our experience and are immediately known, all of which effect changes either substantial or accidental, in things already existing, and hence produce the new thing only partially—which concepts are called proper ones, *N.*;

we should have a concept of creation, as of an action which does not fall within our experience, which is not immediately known, but whose existence is demanded by, and proved from, things we experience, and which action supposes no subject already existing, and hence, which does not change things and make them only partially new, but which produces totally what it produces —which concept is called an analogical concept, *C.—Cd. Min.*

Concepts of things which fall within our experience are called *proper,* because the notes or perfections they represent are found in the things we experience—are *proper* to them. Concepts of things not like things falling within our experience, but the existence of which is proved from things we experience, for example, the spiritual soul of man, God, creation; and which concepts represent notes or perfections derived from the things we sensibly experience (all our knowledge is so derived) but changed or modified (applied analogically, i.e., in a different way) to fit those actions or objects which are above things of sense, are called *analogical* concepts.

Our concept of creation is of this kind. It is like our proper concept of an action which produces changes, inasmuch as it represents the bringing of something into existence; it is unlike it, inasmuch as it represents something as brought into existence *from nothing.*

3. If, starting with nothing, no result can be produced, creation is impossible. (Creation is the production of something from nothing.) But starting from nothing, no result can be produced. Therefore.

D. Maj. If, starting with nothing, that is with neither efficient cause nor material cause, no result can be produced, creation is impossible, *N.;* if starting with no material cause, but supposing an efficient cause, no result could be produced, creation would be impossible, *Subd.;* creation would be impossible, if, starting with no material cause, a finite efficient cause could produce nothing, *N.;* if an infinite efficient cause could produce nothing, *C.—Cd. Min.*

4. If an infinite cause could create, something would be made out of nothing. But something cannot be made out of nothing. Therefore.

D. Maj. Something would be made out of nothing, that is, nothing would be a material cause that would be changed into something, *N.;* starting with no material cause, i.e., with nothing as a *quasi* starting point, something would be produced by an infinite efficient cause, *C.—Cd. Min.*

Hettinger refers as follows to this rather puerile difficulty, which, however, even in these later days has been advanced against our doctrine of creation.

"The axiom of the Epicureans, 'From nothing nothing is made,' which our modern philosophers quote so triumphantly, is of no real weight. As an argument against the theory [it is not a theory] of creation, its strength rests only on imagination, which substitutes phantasms for intellectual ideas, and represents creation as the act by which imaginary nothing is changed into the universe, just as the earth itself, by the organic process of assimilation, is changed into flowers and fruit. Hence if the phrase 'out of nothing' means pre-existing matter, which is transformed into and has become the world, the axiom, 'Out of nothing, nothing is made,' is true, and it does not require any great acuteness to apprehend it. But the phrase, 'God created the world out of nothing,' was employed to exclude any idea of pre-existing matter, and it is by a direct perversion of its sense that 'nothing' can be understood as the matrix, origin and matter of being." (*Natural Religion*, p. 95.)

5. If that which is said to be created, prior to its existence must have been a possible thing, creation is impossible. (In that case the production of a thing could not be "ex nihilo subjecti," that is, it would have to start with something from which it was produced.) But that which is said to be created, prior to existence must have been a possible thing. Therefore.

D. Maj. Creation is impossible, if a possible thing, as a possible thing, is in any way an actual thing, *C.*; if it is in no way an actual thing, *N.* (The added proof is also to be distinguished—In that case the production of a thing, if it were the creation of a thing, would have to start with *something actually* existing N., with something possible of existence, *C.*)—*D. Cons.*

Prior to its creation a thing is *actually*, totally nothing; it is not, however, nor can it be, in any way nothing with regard to its possibility. If it were not intrinsically possible it could not be brought into existence in any way.

6. "When anything is made, its becoming precedes its having been made. But this is impossible, unless there is a subject in which the becoming is sustained. Therefore it is

impossible that anything should be made from nothing." (St. Thomas, *Summa Theologica*, I, q.45, a.2, Obj. 3.)

D. Maj. Its becoming precedes its having been made, if in its making there is succession, *C.*; if there is no succession, that is, if the making is instantaneous, *N.—D. Cons.*

St. Thomas answers this difficulty as follows:

"In every making wherein there is succession, a thing is becoming before it has been made. . . . Now this cannot happen in creation. Because the becoming which would precede being made, would need a subject. And this could not be the creature itself whose creation is in question, since it is not before it is made. Nor would it be in the maker, because to be moved is not the act of the mover, but of the thing moved. It follows that becoming would have for its subject some pre-existing matter of the thing made. But this is incompatible with creation. Therefore there can be no succession in creation. . . . It follows therefore that creation is instantaneous." (*Summa Contra Gentiles*, Bk. 2, c. 19.)

7. If creation implies the passing over of an infinite distance, namely, from nothing to being, it is impossible. But creation implies the passing over of an infinite distance, namely, from nothing to being. Therefore.

R.1.—Tr. Maj.—N. Min. Our first answer to this difficulty, a denial of the Minor, is the answer given by St. Thomas, "This objection proceeds from a false imagination. as if there were an infinite medium between nothing and being; which is plainly false. This false imagination comes from creation being taken to signify a change existing between two terms." (*Summa Theologica*, I, q.45, a.2, in reply to Obj. 4.)

*R.2.—*That creation cannot be properly said to be a passing over an infinite distance, the following reasons, some of which St. Thomas has already given us, make abundantly clear. First, creation, objectively, is instantaneous; a passing over is successive. Again, between nothing and the effect produced in creation there is no medium passed over; if there was, nothing would have to be an actual term, and it is not; what is more the effect would be produced not instantaneously but successively, which is also false. Finally, there is nothing truly infinite in creation looked at objectively, either on the side of nothing, which is not actually infinite but simply, actually nothing; or on the side of the being created, which must always be a finite one. On the side of reality, as compared with nothingness, the only being who can be said, in the proper sense of the word, to be infinitely removed from nothing, is God, who alone is, or can be infinite.

Since, however, the only opposition to *being*, is *no being*—nothing, and since, therefore, figuratively speaking it may be said that nothing is farther removed from being than nothing itself, we may in the same sense conceive creation as though it were a passage over a so-called infinite distance from nothing to being, which passage, however, on the side of being, may not be conceived even figuratively to cover an infinite distance, seeing that the only being which can be created, or in any way produced, is, as was said above, a finite one. This answer to the objection is given by Suarez (*Metaphysics,* D.20, s.2, n.37). In form it runs as follows:

D. Maj. If creation, in any proper sense, could be said to be a passage over an infinite distance between nothing and being, either on the side of nothing or on the side of being, creation would be impossible, *C.*; if, only figurativly speaking, creation may be looked at as a passage from nothing to being, through an infinite distance on the side of nothing, seeing that nothing is farther removed from being than nothing, but not through an infinite distance on the side of being, seeing that produced being is necessarily finite, creation is impossible, *N.—Cd. Min.*

8. If God freely willed the existence of the world, His will is contingent. But God's will, the will of an absolutely necessary being, cannot be contingent. Therefore.

D. Maj. His will, looked at in its entity, which is God Himself, is contingent, *N.*; looked at as the infinite divine act by which God tends toward objects inasmuch as they are good, *Subd.*; it is contingent in its tendency toward its primary object, which is God Himself, or with regard to possible beings, inasmuch as they are, as such, necessarily connected with God as possible imitations in a finite way of His infinite goodness, *N.*; it is contingent, that is free, in willing the existence of finite things, *Subd.*; in such wise that it would be possible for God to pass from the willing of one term to the willing of another, *N.*; no such passage being possible, the will of God is free with regard to the existence of finite things, i.e., God, who willed the existence of this world could have willed the existence of no world, or of any other possible one, *Subd.*; and had He done so, He would be in any way intrinsically changed or changeable, *N.*; He would be changed, that is, different only extrinsically, that is, the same infinite will which has this world for its term, i.e., which freely willed this world, would have had, without any change in itself, another term, i.e., would have freely willed the existence of no world, or of any other possible world, *C.—Cd. Min.*

The above solution differs from the solution of the same difficulty which we formerly gave in *God Infinite and Reason.* It is a better solution than the former one, as it leaves the intrinsic immutability of God absolutely untouched. It is to be noted that this difficulty, namely, the reconciliation of God's free will with His intrinsic, absolute immutability, is a crucial one, and all authors admit, that no matter what solution is given, the matter will still contain a mystery. The mystery is this: how God's will, remaining intrinsically, immutably the same, could have had as its term, in place of the present world, another world or no world. The solution we formerly gave is given by not a few authors of note. As it grants that God, though *actually,* intrinsically immutable, may be considered to be *virtually, intrinsically mutable,* we now reject it for our present solution which denies that God can in any way be intrinsically mutable. A few words in explanation of this solution will not be out of place.

God freely willed the existence of the world. He could have willed instead, the existence of another, or the non-existence of any world, understanding, however, as we proved in *God Infinite and Reason,* that whatever He wills is immutably willed, and, hence, that in God there is no passing from one willing to another. Now, had God willed the existence of another world, or the non-existence of any world or any being, His will, assuredly, in some way would not be the same as His present will. Would that difference connote any change or changeableness in God? Or, to put the question in another way—Could God, remaining in Himself in every way immutably the same, have willed this world, or, in its stead, another or no world? Seeing that we have already proved that God is in every way intrinsically immutable, our answer to the first question is, that the difference would in no way connote any change or changeableness in God; and to the second question, that God, remaining in Himself in every way immutably the same, could have willed instead of this world, another or no world.

The reason for our answer is to be found in the infinite perfection of God and God's will. To make this answer clear, it will be helpful to compare man's free will and God's free will.

When man freely wills, his will suffers two intrinsic changes and an extrinsic one. The first intrinsic change takes place when his will passes from the remote to the proximate power to elicit the free act, and the second, when it passes from the proximate power to the free act itself, which is intrinsic to the will. The extrinsic change is in the relation which arises with regard to the term of the act, which from being not-willed, is now willed. Furthermore, man's will, when it is fully and proximately prepared to elicit a free act, is actively indifferent to all the possible choices given it in any definite case. This means that the *very same proximate power* which the will exercises in choosing one act and its term, was capable of choosing, in its stead, any one of the other possible ones. In other words, man's will, when proximately prepared to elicit a free act, has the simultaneous power to choose any one of the acts possible to it, to the exclusion of the others.

With God, however, the case is different. He is not, nor can He be, in potency to any act. He is act, *Infinite Act.* His will, too, is infinite, not only in its entity, under which aspect it is identified with Himself, but also when considered as the faculty by which He tends in love towards objects, inasmuch as they are good.

This infinite act of will, therefore, by which God necessarily loves Himself and all possible creatures, as such, and freely wills the existence of creatures, *because it is an infinite act,* excludes all passage, from remote potency to act, to proximate potency, and from proximate potency to act, to act, itself; that is, it excludes as absolutely impossible those intrinsic changes which are found in man's will. What is more, and *again because it is an infinite act,* it is with regard to the terms or objects of its free act or choice, *actually actively indifferent,* and, hence, in freely willing the existence of this world, it was fully and actually capable, *remaining absolutely unchanged,* of willing, in its stead, another world, or no world, or no creature whatever.

We saw that the human will, in proximate potency to act freely, was actively indifferent with regard to the various free *acts* and their terms, possible to its choice in any definite set of circumstances. We see now that God's infinite will, is *in act actively* indifferent, not to possible *acts,* but to all the *terms* possible to His free choice. God, therefore, is, in freely willing, absolutely immutable intrinsically. He would be changed extrinsically with regard to the term of His free act, in the sense that, intrinsically remaining the same, He might have had another term to His act, but not in the sense that He might pass in willing from one term to another.

Thesis III

All existing things other than God, in order that they may continue in existence, require by their very nature God's positive and direct conservation.

Prenotes to the Thesis

In order that contingent beings, that is, beings which have not the reason for their existence in themselves, may begin to exist, it is absolutely necessary that God, as an immediate, physical, efficient cause, give them such beginning of existence, in other words, bring them into existence, cause them to begin to exist.

This assertion, which is immediately evident with regard to beings produced by God alone, will be proved in *Thesis IV* to be true also with regard all beings of which other contingent beings also are the cause. In that thesis we shall show that it is absolutely impossible for any creature to perform any action, unless God so concurs in its performance that, whilst the whole action of the creature and its effect proceed from the creature, the same whole action and effect proceed also from God; from each as from an immediate, physical, efficient cause; from God, as the First Cause, under one formality; from the creature, as a secondary cause, under a different formality. Of this, however, more, later.

In order, then, that a contingent being—and all beings other than God are contingent beings—may *begin* to exist, it must necessarily have God as an immediate cause of that beginning of existence. Must it, however, in like manner also have God as an immediate cause continually giving it its existence as long as it remains in existence? Our thesis answers this question affirmatively when it asserts that all existing things other than God, in order that they may continue in existence, require by their very nature God's positive and direct conservation.

90

The word *conservation,* then, refers to the permanency in existence of a contingent being and may be used in an active sense, as when we speak of God's conservation of creatures, or, in a passive sense, when we say that the conservation of all creatures is due to God's action.

Conservation may be of different kinds. A general notion of it, and its various divisions and their definitions will make for a clearer understanding of our thesis.

To *conserve* a thing, in general, is to bring about, in some way or other, the continuation or permanency in existence of that thing.

Negative conservation of a thing is attributed to one who, though he has the power and the right to terminate its existence, permits it to continue in existence.

Positive conservation of a thing is had when a physical, efficient cause by its action brings about the continuation in existence of the thing.

Indirect positive conservation (per accidens) is had when the conserving cause by its action brings about the continuation of a thing in existence, by protecting it from the action of anything that might destroy it, or by supplying to it whatever is necessary for its continuing in existence. In this wise, a living being positively and indirectly conserves himself in existence, when he rejects foods that would destroy, and selects those which will prolong his life.

Because this kind of conservation is not required in the case of every contingent being, but happens *(accidit)* to be required only in the case of some, it is sometimes styled, as was noted above, conservation which is required *per accidens.* The beings who require it are those only which can perish through natural causes. What is more, it is required by them not uninterruptedly but only when occasion demands it, that is, when something must be supplied to keep those beings in existence, or when they are to be protected from something which could destroy them.

Direct positive conservation (per se) is had when the conserving cause physically, immediately, and continually without interruption, inflows into the very being of the thing conserved, causing it to continue to exist.

All contingent beings, whatever be their nature, in order

that they may continue in existence require with absolute necessity this kind of conservation. On that account it is sometimes called conservation which is required by the very nature *(per se)* of things. This kind of conservation, inasmuch as it is God's action, is the immediate, uninterruptedly continuous, physical inflowing of the omnipotence (efficacious will) of God, into the very being of all contingent things, existing for a time or perpetually, the effect of which is their continuance in existence.

A thing is said to preserve another directly and in itself, namely, when what is preserved depends on the preserver in such a way that it cannot exist without it. In this manner all creatures need to be preserved by God. For the being of every creature depends on God, so that not for a moment could it subsist, but would fall into nothingness, were it not kept in being by the operation of the Divine power. (St. Thomas, *Summa Theologica,* 1, q.104, a.1, *in corpore.*)

It is to be noted, and emphatically, that when we assert that God must necessarily preserve positively and directly all contingent beings, we do not say that God in all cases is the sole preserving cause. Creatures, in certain cases may also be causes directly and positively conserving other contingent things, but never, however, unless they themselves be directly and positively preserved in existence by God, as is proved in the present thesis, and never, as the *Thesis IV* will prove, without the concurrent action of God producing with them the whole action by which they so preserve other contingent things.

The truth of our thesis is admitted universally by Scholastic Philosophers as absolutely certain.

Adversaries

Our thesis presupposes, as already established by reason, God's existence as the one, necessarily existing, infinite, first cause by creation, of the universe, together with all His other perfections shown, in our previous theses, here, and in *God and Reason,* and *God Infinite and Reason,* to belong to God. All the adversaries, therefore, to these reason-proved conclusions may be said to be indirectly adversaries to our present thesis.

Directly opposed to it are those Deists, of an extreme type, who held, as Christlieb puts it, that God

... exists only *above* the world as a personal spirit, who, after creating the world of His will, now acts toward it like an artificer with a finished machine, which mechanically pursues its natural course according to the laws laid down for it, and no longer requires the immediate assistance or interference of its maker. ...

The being, personality, and supramundane nature of the Deity, and the creation of the world by Him, are thus acknowledged; while, on the other hand, *any continuous* active presence of God in the world, and any living interposition in its affairs are denied. (*Modern Doubt and Christian Belief*, p. 101.)

It must not, however, be supposed that all Deists held that after creating the world, God left it to exist and act independently of Himself. As Ward, rightly remarks:

... [With regard to] mere deism [which] leaves the world once started to go of itself, it is sufficient to reply that this supposed tenet of Deism is really inconceivable. ... If there is a Creator at all, he can never stand aside and wholly apart from his world.

But the ascription of such a tenet to Deists generally, to the English Deists of the 18th century, for example, is a grievous misconception. What they denied was not the divine immanencé *in toto,* but only such occasionalistic interferences as miracles, special revelation, and special providence imply. They were in fact what we should now call naturalistic theists. (*Pluralism and Theism*, pp. 260f.)

What Ward says of the English Deists may be said in general also of the Deism commonly advanced elsewhere, and, in particular by not a few American philosophers of the 18th century. They denied God's supernatural intervention with nature's laws. Woodbridge Riley, in his rather lengthy account of Deism in America, makes this clear. He writes:

The movement affected the lives of eminent men; it was perhaps best defined by one of its minor prophets, a disciple of the notorious free-thinker, Thomas Paine. Said Elihu Palmer: "Deism declares to intelligent man the existence of one, Perfect God, Creator and Preserver of the Universe; that the laws by which he governs the world are like Himself immutable; and that violations of these laws, or miraculous interference in the movements of Nature must necessarily be excluded from the grand system of universal existence." (*American Philosophy, the Early Schools,* pp. 191ff.)

Proof of the Thesis

If all existing things other than God, in order that they may continue in existence, require, by their very nature, the positive and direct conservation of some efficient cause, they require by their very nature God's positive and direct conservation.

But all existing things other than God, in order that they may continue in existence, require, by their very nature, the positive and direct conservation of some efficient cause. Therefore.

Maj. If all such existing things require, that they may continue existing, such conservation from some efficient cause, and if God is not such cause where only one is given, and one of such causes where more than one are given, no adequately sufficient reason can be given why such things continue to exist—for, in that case a creature, who, by the very fact that he is a contingent being, has, in no way, in himself the reason for his beginning or his continuing to exist, would be sole and adequate sufficient reason why another contingent being remains in existence. This, however, is absolutely impossible.

God alone is Being by virtue of His own essence, since His essence is His existence; whereas every creature has being by participation, so that its essence is not its existence. Therefore, as Augustine says: "If the ruling power of God were withdrawn from His creatures, their nature would at once cease, and all nature would collapse." (St. Thomas, *Summa Theologica,* 1 q.104, a.1, *in corpore.*)

Min. All existing things other than God, in order that they may begin to exist, necessarily depend on the action of a physical, efficient cause giving them that beginning of existence, for they are all contingent beings, and, as such, have, in no way, in themselves the sufficient reason for their existence. That existence, then, they must receive from another, their physical efficient cause, who gives them their very being, causes them to begin to exist.

Now, as a contingent being, while he remains in

existence, must ever remain a contingent being, and, hence, in no way can have the reason for his existence in himself, it necessarily follows, that as he, because of his contingency, required a physical efficient cause to bring him into existence, by giving him his very being, so also he requires continually while he exists, and because of that same contingency, the continual action of a physical, efficient cause who, continually giving him his very being, causes him to remain in existence. All existing beings other than God, therefore, in order that they may continue in existence, require the positive and direct conservation of some efficient cause.

Suarez puts it this way, rather pithily: "The same want which is in the very being of a creature in the first instant of its existence, and which makes it depend on the action of another for its coming into existence, remains in the creature as long as it continues in existence." *(Metaphysics,* Disputation 21, s.1, n.16.)

Confirmatory Proof

As no being, outside of God, has in any way the reason for its existence in itself, and as it depends on the omnipotent efficacious free will of God for it, it follows that God, the supreme and omnipotent source and Lord and Master of all existing things should be able, if He so wills, to annihilate such a being, that is, to deprive it utterly of existence.

Unless, however, God positively and directly conserved creatures in existence, He could not utterly deprive a being of existence. For annihilation, the outcome of which is *simply nothing,* since it cannot be a positive act, whose effect would be something, must necessarily be the withdrawal, or the cessation of the positive and direct conserving action of God, which withdrawal means that the creature simply *is not.*

What is more, if God did not have the power to annihilate creatures—which as we have just shown supposes necessarily that He positively and directly conserves them in being—some creatures, namely finite spiritual substances, once they had come into existence, could never be deprived of that existence even by God. As a consequence, supposing their existence, they would be by their nature absolutely necessary beings, which necessity, however, their essential contingence must necessarily deny. Therefore all existing beings other than God require His positive and direct conservation in order that they may continue in existence.

The reason why a finite spiritual substance, once it had received existence, could not, in the supposition that God did not conserve it in being, be deprived of its existence, and would so be constituted a being in existence independent of God, is the following. If God did not conserve such a being, He could not as we have shown, annihilate it. And yet only by annihilation could it be deprived of existence, for no positive action could destroy it, seeing that it has no component parts into which it could be dissolved by a positive action. Nor does it, in case it happens to be a finite spiritual substance united with a body, which is true of man's soul, intrinsically depend for its existence on its remaining united with the body. Hence, if by a positive action a man is killed, his soul still remains in existence apart from the body. A finite spiritual substance, therefore, if God did not positively and directly conserve it in existence, could never, even by God, be deprived of its existence. It would be independent of God in its existence, which independence its nature as a contingent being denies.

Suarez states the argument clearly:

God's omnipotence demands that He should be able to reduce to nothingness, if He so wills, the creatures He has brought into existence. . . , There are many things which cannot be deprived of their existence by any action which could go counter to it, for example, an angel. . . . Hence it follows that if God were in every instance obliged to use a positive action in destroying things, He could not annihilate such things. Therefore, in order that He may be able to do so, it is necessary that annihilation should be brought about by the withdrawal of an efficient action. The withdrawal of such action, however, can be had only on the supposition that creatures, both in their production and conservation, depend necessarily on such efficient action. (*Metaphysics*, Disp. 21, s.1, n.14.)

COROLLARY I—*God's action and its effects, in the production and conservation of various classes of beings.*

1. The permanency of a produced being in existence, inasmuch as it depends on God, is the immediate effect of the exercise of God's omnipotence, that is, of His efficacious will. Hence, as those creatures which come into existence through creation, begin to exist because God wills that beginning, so they continue to exist because, and as long as, and only as long as, God wills that continuance. The effect, therefore, of conservation, as such, in things which are created, namely, spiritual substances, prime matter, and complete substances produced from nothing, does not differ *really* from the effect of creation, as such. In both cases it is the total existing thing. Between the two effects, however, there is a perfect, objective, *conceptual* distinction. The effect of the creative act is the total existing thing, connoting its previous total non-existence; the effect of the act of conservation, is the same total existing thing, connoting, however, its previous total existence. This same truth is expressed otherwise in the statement, that the act of creation, by which a being is brought into existence from nothingness by God, and the act of conservation by which it is continued in existence by Him, in their effects, differ not *materially* but *formally* only. It is clear from this, what is meant when it is said that God's conservation of a created thing is a continued creation of it.

2. Besides things which are created, and of which, consequently, God is the sole cause, there are many others which are produced by creatures, or secondary causes, God always concurring, but owe their permanence in existence in no way to the conserving action of these causes but to that of God alone. This happens when the producing secondary causes, cease to act as soon as they have produced the things in question. Examples of things so produced, are material substantial forms, and accidents which continue in existence after the action of the secondary causes producing them has ceased.

In these cases, therefore, the permanent effect, which had God and creatures as concurring *producing* causes, has God alone continuing His action as their *conserving* cause.

3. Creatures, that is, secondary causes, at times by their actions, not only produce effects, but also by a more or less

lengthy continuation of these actions positively and directly preserve such effects in existence. As we will prove in the *Thesis IV*, no creature can begin or continue any action unless God, as the First Cause, concurs in its production and continuation as an immediate, physical, efficient cause of the whole action and its effect. God, therefore, by His concurring action not only produces with the creature, the latter's action and its effect, but also with him preserves both in existence.

The combined actions of God and the creatures, looked at as productive, have *really* the same result as these actions looked at as preservative; the difference is only conceptual. In both cases it is the result produced; in the former, its previous non-existence is connoted, in the latter, its previous existence.

COROLLARY II—*God has the absolute power to annihilate creatures. This power He will not exercise.*

St. Thomas *(Summa Theologica,* 1, q.104, aa.3, 4, *in corpore)* gives the following reasons for these assertions.

1. *God has the absolute power to annihilate creatures.*

Some have held that God, in giving existence to creatures, acted from natural necessity. Were this true, God could not annihilate anything since His nature cannot change. But . . . such an opinion is entirely false and absolutely contrary to the Catholic faith, which confesses that God created things of His own free will. . . . Therefore, that God gives existence to a creature depends on His will; nor does He preserve things in existence otherwise than by continually pouring out existence into them, as we have said. Therefore, just as before things existed, God was free not to give them existence, and so not to make them; so after they have been made, He is free not to continue their existence; and thus they would cease to exist; and this would be to annihilate them. (Q.104, a.3.)

2. *God will annihilate no creature.*

Some of those things which God does in creatures occur in accordance with the natural course of things; others happen miraculously, and not in accordance with the natural order. . . . Now, whatever God wills to do according to the natural order of things may be observed from their nature; but those things which occur miraculously, are ordered for the manifestation of grace, according to the apostle, "To each one is given the manifestation of the Spirit, unto profit" (I Cor. 12:7); and subsequently he mentions among others, the working of miracles.

Now, the nature of creatures, shows that none of them is annihilated. For, either they are immaterial, and, therefore, have no potentiality to non-existence; or they are material, and then they continue to exist, at least in matter, which is incorruptible, since it is the subject of generations and corruption. Moreover, the annihilation of things does not pertain to the manifestation of grace; since rather the power and goodness of God are manifested by the preservation of things in existence. Wherefore, we must conclude by denying absolutely that anything at all will be annihilated. (Q.104, a.4.)

Difficulties

1. A being which cannot lose its existence, does not require God's positive and direct conservation in order that it may remain in existence. But some beings other than God, for example, finite spiritual substances, cannot lose their existence. Therefore.

D. Maj. A being which exists with absolute necessity—and there is only one such being, God—and hence, absolutely excludes the possibility of losing its existence, does not require, etc., *C.*; a being which does not exist with absolute necessity, and which nevertheless, cannot lose its existence, does not require, etc., *Subd.*; if it cannot lose its existence, only in the sense that no creature, or secondary cause, can deprive it of existence, it does not require, etc., *N.*; if it cannot lose its existence, in the sense that God cannot deprive it of existence, it does not require, etc., *Subd.*; if God by His absolute power cannot deprive it of its existence, it does not require, etc., *C.*; if God cannot deprive it of its existence only because He has already decreed not to do so, it does not require, *N.—Cd. Min.*

2. If a creature can produce an effect which continues to exist after the creature has ceased acting, God should be able to produce an effect which could continue to exist without His preserving action. But a creature can produce such an effect. Therefore.

D. Maj. If a creature can produce an effect which continues to exist without the preserving action either of the creature or of God, God should be able, etc., *C.*; if a creature can produce an effect which continues to exist without the preserving action of the creature, God should be able to produce an effect which would continue to exist without His preserving action, *Subd.*; if the creature can so act precisely because he is a finite being, and, hence, a being whose effect may continue to exist independently of him, God should be able, etc., *N.*; if such a mode of action would not imply any imperfection, God should be able, etc., *C.—Cd. Min.*

God cannot grant to a creature to be preserved in being after the cessation of the Divine influence; as neither can He make it not to have received its being from Himself. For the creature needs to be preserved by God in so far as the *being* of an effect depends on the cause of its being. So that there is no comparison with an agent that is not the cause of *being* but only of *becoming*. (St. Thomas, *loc. cit.*, a.1, reply to Obj. 2.)

3. If God positively and directly preserves creatures in being, His preserving act should produce an effect distinct from His producing act. But there is no distinction with regard to the effect of both acts. Therefore.

D. Maj. Really distinct, *N.*; conceptually distinct, with a perfect objective distinction, *C.—Cd. Min.*

As was stated above, the effect of the productive act is the existing thing produced, connoting its previous non-existence, the effect of the preserving act is the same, connoting its previous existence.

4. If God necessarily preserves all things in being, it would seem that creatures exercise no preserving or sustaining power with regard to other creatures. This, however, appears to be false. Therefore.

N. Maj. Indirect preserving power is within the competence of some creatures. Direct preserving power is also within their competence with regard to those accidents which, with God concurring, they efficiently produce, and sustain in being, for example, enduring mental actions. With regard to other accidents, as material causes they sustain God's action in directly preserving them, and so this action is in no sense continued creation. With regard to complete substances, and the human soul, an incomplete spiritual substance, creatures exercise no positive and direct preserving power at all.

5. If all creatures have an innate tendency to continue in existence, and if, in addition some are able to preserve themselves in existence, it would seem that creatures do not

require God's positive and direct conservation. But all creatures have such a tendency, etc. Therefore.

D. Maj. If all creatures, presupposing that God positively and directly preserves them in existence, have an innate tendency to continue in existence in conformity with the laws of nature, and if some creatures are able to preserve themselves indirectly, creatures do not require, etc., *N.*; if creatures had that tendency independently of God's direct preserving action creatures would not require, etc., *C.—Cd. Min.*

Thesis IV

No action of a creature is possible unless God physically and immediately concurs in its production.

Prenotes to the Thesis

We have seen that no creature can continue to exist unless God continually, positively and directly preserves it in existence; that is, unless God continually gives it its very being.

In this thesis, going a step farther, we assert that no creature can perform any action, whether it be one which merely produces an effect, or one which also preserves it in existence, unless God also concurs physically and immediately in the performance of that action, and in such wise that the whole action and its effect are produced by both God and the creature, but under different formalities. They proceed *from God*, as the *sole primary, necessary cause* in the production of actions of all kinds and their effects, inasmuch as they are something; *from the creature*, as *secondary*, and *contingent cause* in the production of all actions and their effects within the sphere of the creature's activity, inasmuch as they are *this* or *that* something.

With regard to the *fact*, that it is absolutely necessary for God to concur, in the way just described, with every action of every creature Scholastic philosophers are in unanimous agreement. They differ widely, however, in their explanations of the precise nature of that concursus, and especially in the vitally important question of God's concurrence with the free acts of the human will. The point is this: to determine whether or not God's decree to concur with His creatures has the effect not only of concurring simultaneously with them in their actions, but also of determining them when on the point of, and prior to, acting, in such wise that only one definite action, with which He will concur, can be put by them.

It is quite evident that if God's decree to concur did so predetermine man's will, God, knowing with infinite knowledge His decree, would know what definite act the man would put in any definite set of circumstances, and prior to the will's determination of the act. In which case the act, in our view, could not be free.

In our previous thesis on God's knowledge (*Thesis I, Corollary III*) we ruled out any such decrees as mediums in which the free acts of man, either the futuribles or those which will be, can be known by God. Our reason for their rejection was that given above. They destroy free will.

Again, it is also quite evident that, if God's decree to concur with His creatures, so predetermined them that they could put only one act in a given set of circumstances, God's supreme dominion over His creatures would be absolutely safeguarded. It is impossible to see, however, as we have already noted, how under these conditions man would remain free. Some other way of safeguarding God's absolute dominion must be found.

In *Thesis V* this whole matter of the *precise nature* of God's physical concursus will be considered, and at some length. Our present thesis has nothing to do with it. Here we are concerned only with establishing the *fact* that God must physically and immediately concur, and in the way described above, in the production of every action and its effect, of every creature.

That our present thesis aims at establishing only the *fact* just mentioned, which all Scholastic philosophers admit, *is to be carefully noted*, for in the definitions and explanations of the various kinds of God's concursus, to be given presently, some references may be made here and there to the opinion we shall hold with regard to the precise *nature* of that fact, especially on the disputed points mentioned above. Our thesis is true no matter what opinion may be held on those matters.

If, now, it be asked why it is that all Scholastic philosophers are in complete accord in admitting that God must necessarily concur physically and immediately with all creatures in all their actions, the answer is, that the absolute necessity of that concursus, just as the absolute and universal necessity of God's positive and direct conservation of all creatures, is demanded by the contingent nature of all produced beings. And the contingent nature of all produced beings, in themselves, and in all their actions with their effects, must be admitted by all philosophers.

As a consequence, not only the absolute necessity of God's positive and direct conservation of all creatures must be admitted by all philosophers, as we showed in *Thesis III*, but also the absolute necessity of the physical and immediate concursus of God with all the actions of all His creatures must be admitted by them, no matter what opinion they may favor in their explanations of the precise nature of that concursus.

This utter and essential incompetence of the creature to explain itself; its essential dependence in everything—in its becoming, in its continuing in being, in its every action, with its effect—a dependence which calls with absolute necessity, and universally and continually, for the immediate causal influx of a sustaining power, not contingent but absolutely necessary, is the mystery of the next-to-nothingness of creatures. God acting alone, or God acting with His creatures—but always God—must be ever giving what being they have by His conserving power and His concursus. So that, in the strictest sense, it is absolutely true that a creature without God's continual, causal, sustaining influence, conserving and concurring, is nothing and can do nothing. With God it is something and can do something, but only if *God* preserves it in being, and produces with it, under the *univer-sal* formality of *something* the whole action and whole effect, which *it* produces under the *particular* formality of *this* or *that* something.

We hasten now to give the various divisions of God's *concursus,* with their various definitions, noting again, and emphatically, that though the opinion, which we shall hold on the disputed points concerning the precise *nature* of God's concursus, will, almost of necessity, be included in some of them, still both the truth of our thesis, and the validity of its proofs, are altogether independent of that opinion, or of any other opinion, on the same matter. They are true no matter how these disputed points may be explained.

Divine Concursus, in general, is the co-operation of God, as the sole primary cause, with His creatures, as secondary causes, in the production of their actions and the effects produced by their actions.

Moral Divine Concursus is the co-operation which God gives to intelligent beings for the performance of *morally good* actions, by presenting prior to those actions, to their wills through their intellects, motives drawing them on, or urging them, to the performance of such actions. This co-operation of God in no way interferes with man's physical liberty. Man, therefore, has always the physical power to go counter to any of these promptings, even when by so doing he would commit sin. This concursus is a *mediate* concursus with regard to the putting of the good act which it invitingly or urgingly proposes to the will's free determination, or choice, seeing that it is given prior to that choice. God's Moral Concursus is of two kinds, *natural* and *supernatural.* Both the natural and the supernatural, looked at as they are found in the free agent, consist of an act of the intellect cognizing, and presenting to the will, some truth which inclines the will towards the putting of the good action; and an act of the will by which the will is so inclined.

Through these acts, God is said to, and does, concur towards the putting of the free good act. For since God really and sincerely wishes the salvation of all men, He efficaciously wishes also that man should have all the means by which, his freedom remaining intact, he is led, either directly (positively), or indirectly (negatively), towards the gaining of that end.

It is to be noted that the end for which man is created is a supernatural one, the seeing of God face to face, the Beatific Vision. Only good actions, in their essence supernatural, lead directly (positively) to the attaining of that end; naturally good actions, however, indirectly (negatively), that is, by removing obstacles, lead to it. Those who have not been drawn by God to the light of supernatural faith can perform only naturally good actions. By performing these, they prepare themselves indirectly (negatively) to receive the gift of supernatural faith. God, therefore, who wishes them to be saved, draws them on to the putting of actions naturally good, by a natural, moral concursus. This concursus is given through the natural influence of creatures, for instance, of parents, of teachers, of good friends, of the commands and prohibitions of the Natural Law written in the hearts of all men, and of other laws imposed by lawfully constituted authority, all of which incline and urge us naturally to choose what is right, and reject what is wrong.

There are two kinds of God's natural, moral concursus. One, which is in every sense of the word natural, is had when in the ordinary course of events the natural influence of creatures, noted above, invites and urges the putting of the good act; the other, which is in itself, or in essence, natural, but in the way in which it is given is supernatural, is had when God, by a special interference—not necessarily a miracle —with the ordinary course of events, put us in the way of receiving the natural influence of creatures which inclines us to well-doing. Through both of these concursuses, therefore, man is invited or urged only to good actions which in their essence are natural, and which, consequently, lead only indirectly (negatively) to man's last end, which is supernatural— the Beatific Vision.

In another order, essentially higher than the natural order, is the moral concursus of God which, in its very essence, is supernatural, and which draws man on and gives him power to put good actions intrinsically supernatural, and leading directly (positively) to man's last end. In the case of this supernatural concursus, it is the Holy Spirit Himself who illumines the intellect of man, presenting motives which incline his will to the putting of the supernaturally good act, and it is the Holy Spirit Himself who inspires the act by which the will is so inclined. If man answers this call of the Holy Spirit—and he has the power to reject it—the good act he puts is one leading positively and directly to man's supernatural end.

The above-mentioned acts of the intellect and will, by which God through His moral concursus, either natural or supernatural, draws man on to the putting of good actions, are all *indeliberate* acts, that is, acts not freely, not deliberately, but necessarily elicited. For if the initial acts of intellect and will, which precede and invite to the putting of a free act were not, and of necessity, indeliberate acts, or, in other words, if a free act necessarily postulated a prior free act, an actually infinite multitude of free acts would have to precede the putting of any one of them. Which is absurd.

Another point to be noted about God's moral concursus is this. The indeliberate acts of intellect and will which, through their intentional value, respectively as knowledge and volitional tendency, invite and urge to the putting of good actions, are also physical entities, spiritual accidents. In their production, therefore, as in the case of all other actions of creatures, God concurs physically and immediately, as our thesis states, and as the proofs of our thesis will establish. This physical concursus, which is *immediate* with regard to these acts, is *mediate* with regard to the free act to which they incline the will, and is an integral part of the mediate physical concursus of God required for that act. On this point, more, when we explain, as we shall presently do, in what the physical and mediate concursus which God gives to His creatures consists.

Physical Divine Concursus is the co-operation, in the production of all the actions of all creatures, which God gives, by actually supplying, either alone or with other creatures, all those things which He should supply, in order that His creatures may have the full power to produce, and may actually produce, those actions.

Physical Divine Mediate Concursus consists in the supplying by God, as stated above, of all those things, which, on His part it is necessary for Him to supply, in order that His creatures may have fully the power to pass from non-action to action. This concursus is given by God:

1. *In general:* (a) inasmuch as God gives to His creatures the remote and proximate principles *by which* they have the power to act, namely, their natures and faculties; (b) inasmuch as He positively and directly preserves in existence both natures and faculties, and all the habits which creatures have acquired (and, in the supernatural order, all infused habits); and (c) inasmuch as, acting alone or concurring immediately with other creatures, He sees to it that His crea-

tures are supplied with everything else necessary to prepare them proximately for action.

2. *In particular,* that is, in the case of man and his power to act freely: inasmuch as God has given to the human will a natural inclination to good in general, or happiness, as such, in virtue of which inclination the will naturally tends towards that which is good (sometimes it is only apparently so), in particular objects. And so, when such objects, without previous deliberation—and in indeliberate acts of the intellect and will a free act must always find its origin—are presented to the will by the intellect, the will spontaneously, that is, indeliberately, goes out towards, is attracted by, such objects. This spontaneous, necessary, indeliberate tendency towards objects which, without previous deliberation, have been presented by the intellect to the will as in some way good or attractive, in some cases may be exceedingly slight, in some exceedingly violent. In fact, at times it may be so violent, that even after the will has deliberately turned towards something else, the rejected object may still attract it most forcibly. This going-out, or attraction, of the will to an object deliberately rejected, is, of course, a spontaneous or indeliberate act, and as long as it remains an indeliberate act, the will is in no way responsible for it. Almost instantaneously, now, following on these indeliberate acts of the intellect and will, the intellect, again *spontaneously or indeliberately,** begins, and frequently, even if it continues to do so for some time, *indeliberately continues,* to deliberate. It sees that the object proposed to the will as good or attractive, is not attractive under every aspect. Under one aspect its acquisition appears to be desirable, under another, its rejection and the substitution of another good towards which, perhaps, at the same moment the will is supernaturally, indeliberately drawn. While this deliberation is going on—and it may last, and frequently does last, for the briefest interval—the intellect is quite conscious (we are considering only a fully deliberate free act) of its conviction that the act of will which may follow is under the will's dominion, both with regard to *whether* it will be, and *which* it will be, the natural or the supernatural

---

*. . . for, as we have shown, a free act elicited apart from others, or the first free act in a series, cannot presuppose a deliberate or free act . . .

one. For God, on His part, since He gave the will a nature by which it tends towards good, as such, leaving to it the power to determine after deliberation by the intellect, which particular good it will select, from among those offered it in any given set of circumstances, in order that the will may be fully prepared to make its choice, offers to it *His physical* immediate concursus *indifferently* to all the actions under these circumstances possible of choice.

The man is now fully prepared to act freely, to make his choice, with God ready to give His determined physical, immediate concursus, either natural or strictly supernatural, to that action, already foreseen by Him in the order of futuribles, which the will, and the will only, will determine or formally choose, God, however, concurring immediately, with a natural or strictly supernatural concursus, in the action which is the choice.

Physical Divine Immediate Concursus is the co-action or co-operation of God with the action of the creatures in such wise that whilst the creature, in the order of contingent or secondary causes, is the cause of the whole action and whole effect, God, also, as the sole necessary or first cause, is the cause of the whole action of the creature and its whole effect. Whence it follows that God and the creature are *partial* causes of the creature's action, and its effects, in the sense only that neither of them is whole cause, and not in the sense that neither of them put the whole action and whole effect. The whole action and its effect is put by both, though under different aspects. On this point more will be said in the next thesis.

God physically concurs by His efficacious will, by which He immediately produces, with the creature, the creature's action and the effect produced by its action.

Adversaries

Those mentioned in the previous thesis are, in the same way, directly and indirectly, opposed to this thesis also. Like the previous thesis, too, this thesis, in the sense in which we defend it, is upheld unanimously by Catholic philosophers and theologians. Indeed, according to some, a denial of it would be, objectively at least, close to heresy; according to

others, simply heresy. Among the earlier Scholastics, however, there was one somewhat notable exception to this
unanimous teaching, Durandus, a Dominican, famous, not so
much for erudition or depth of knowledge, as for the strange-
ness of his opinions. Turner says of him:

> By his independence of thought and his advocacy of certain
> principles which his contemporaries considered dangerous, Du-
> randus earned the title of *Doctor Resolutissimus*. Still he never
> exceeded the limits of orthodoxy. Indeed, the independence
> which he advocated, and which he formulated in the principle
> "Naturalis philosophiae non est scire quid Aristoteles aut alii
> philosophi senserint, sed quid habeat veritas rerum" [Philoso-
> phy's aim is to discover not what Aristotle or any other philos-
> opher thought about things, but what is objectively true], had
> been professed before his time and formulated almost in the same
> words by St. Thomas and the other great schoolmen. . . .
> His rejection of Divine co-operation with secondary causes
> . . . is the doctrine by which Durandus places himself in most
> pronounced opposition to the current thinking of his time. The
> Scholastics of the thirteenth century unanimously taught that
> God is not only creator and preserver of all finite things, but
> also co-operator in all the actions of secondary causes. Durandus
> maintains that all the actions of the creatures proceed from God
> inasmuch as it is God who gave creatures the power to act, but
> he denies that there is an immediate influxus of the creator in
> the actions of the creature. (*History of Philosophy*, Pp. 400ff.)

That St. Thomas taught and defended the doctrine enunciated in our thesis has been, and is, the common opinion
of Catholic philosophers and theologians. It is an opinion
which may be safely said to be founded in fact. (Cf. *infra,
Scholion,* for passages in confirmation.) Our conclusion, then,
is that St. Thomas did not (though an attempt has been
lately made to show that he did), hold the opinion, later
and surely held by Durandus, namely, that God does not
co-operate immediately with His creatures in their actions.

PROOF OF THE THESIS

If it is absolutely impossible for a contingent being to
act unless its action also proceeds efficiently and immediately
from a necessary cause, no action of a creature is possible

unless God physically and immediately concurs in its production.

But it is absolutely impossible for a contingent being so to act. Therefore.

Maj.—The Major is evident, for we have already proved that the only possible necessary cause is God. (*God and Reason, Thesis V.*)

Min.—*It is absolutely impossible for a contingent being to act unless its action also proceeds efficiently and immediately from a necessary cause.*

The truth of the Minor is to be admitted for the following reasons.

1. We proved in *Thesis III* that in order that a creature may continue existing God must, as an immediate, physical, efficient cause continually give it that existence. This immediate, physical, efficient action of God giving a creature its very existence, is absolutely necessary because, and simply because, a creature is a contingent being, namely, in no way having the reason for its existence in itself, and, hence, in no way giving an *adequate, sufficient* reason for the existence of another being.

Now, an action of a creature is *a contingent thing.* The adequate, sufficient reason, therefore, for its existence cannot be a contingent being. Therefore, a necessary being, God, must also give it its existence, and this He does, as an immediate, physical, efficient cause of it.

2. As the active power or potency of a being has its source in the being's essence or nature, it follows that the actions of a being cannot be of a higher perfection than its essence or nature.

Now, since every creature, in order that it may continue in existence, requires as we proved in *Thesis III,* that God, as an immediate, physical, efficient cause continually give it that existence, it follows that God, as an immediate, physical, efficient cause must also give existence to its action. Otherwise the actions of a creature, in that case independent of God's immediate action, would be of a higher perfection than its essence or nature, which of necessity depends on such action.

3. A third proof of our Minor is derived from God's supreme dominion over all creatures—contingent beings, in themselves having no adequate reason for their existence. The proof runs as follows:

Just as God's supreme dominion demands that a creature, who, as a contingent being, has in itself no right or title to existence, should be capable of being reduced to *absolute nothing*, so also His supreme dominion demands that the action of a creature, which, as a contingent being, has no reason in itself, and no adequate reason in any other contingent being, for its existence, should be capable of being directly and immediately impeded by God.

But as the annihilation, or reduction to absolute nothingness, of a creature is possible only if God withdraws His immediate, physical, efficient action preserving the creature in existence, so the direct and immediate impeding of the action of a creature is possible only if God withholds His immediate, physical concursus with the action.

God, therefore, must physically and immediately concur in the production of all the actions of His creatures.

COROLLARY—*A few words on the opinion concerning the nature of God's physical concursus, which appears to be the true one.* It will be explained more fully in *Thesis V*.

Our present thesis, as has been stated more than once, is concerned only with the *fact* that God of necessity concurs physically and immediately in producing with creatures their actions and the effects of these actions. It prescinds altogether, therefore, from the truth or falsity of any of the opinions advanced in explanation of the nature of that concursus. In our former thesis (*Thesis I, Corollary III*) on God's infinite knowledge, we showed that God's knowledge of man's free future acts, both those conditionally, and those absolutely future, must exclude, as absolutely impossible, an objective *medium in which* they could be known, one which determined those free acts prior to their determination by the will.

We admitted, therefore, in God a knowledge called *Scientia Media*, by which God knows all man's free future acts, as futuribles—that is, all the free acts which man *would* put in any definite set of circumstances in which he might be found, independently of any medium of knowledge predetermining them. The admission of the *Scientia Media* is essential to the explanation of the nature of God's physical concursus with man's free actions, which appears to us to be the only true one. We note this, because our inquiry into the nature of God's physical concursus is concerned therewith mainly as affecting man's free actions. The reason for this narrowing of our inquiry will appear in *Thesis V*.

God's physical and immediate concursus, then, as we explain it, is placed simultaneously with the action of the creatures. It is conferred by God on creatures acting *necessarily* under the guidance of His knowledge of all things possible, and on creatures acting *freely* under the guidance also of His *Scientia Media*. It is the *actual, determined* concursus which God *confers on,* or *gives to,* the acting creature. To this concursus there is another corresponding one, which it *not* an actual concursus *given* to the acting creature, but a concursus *offered* to the creature prior to its action, in order that it may have the full power to act. This concursus, in our opinion, as offered to free agents is *not* a *determined concursus* but an *indifferent* one, that is, in virtue of it, God stands ready to give His actual physical concursus *indifferently* to any one of the actions, possible of choice to the free agent, which the will may choose. This *offered* concursus, therefore, leaves the will when fully prepared to act, in no way determined with regard to any choice it may wish to make. In no way does it interfere with the will's freedom.

Essentially different, therefore, is our simultaneous concursus from the previo-simultaneous concursus of the Bannesians, of which mention has already been made in our previous thesis *(Thesis I, Corollary III)* on God's knowledge. The element in it which warrants the prefix "previo" in its name, is none other than the physical predetermination which, according to the Bannesians, God gives to all creatures *previously* to their action.

Its nature has already been explained, and will again be explained in *Thesis V*. It is uselessly given, in our opinion, to necessarily acting agents, and harmfully to free agents, seeing that it predetermines the will and so destroys freedom. It makes little difference to us, then, how the Bannesians explain the concursus, inasmuch as it is simultaneous, since all of the viciousness of their explanation of the nature of God's concursus with man's free acts is found in their physical predetermination. *Thesis V* will investigate more fully all the points mentioned in this corollary.

SCHOLION—*Saint Thomas and the necessity of God's immediate, physical, concursus.*

As we noted above, only very recently has St. Thomas been classed with Durandus and some few others, who deny the necessity of God's immediate, physical concursus with creatures in their actions. Two of the writers who so class him are Father Thomas Papagni, O.P., in his booklet, *La Mente di S. Tommaso intorno alla mozione divina* (Benevento, 1902); and Father John Stufler, S.J., in his book, *Divi Thomae Aquinatis doctrina de Deo operante, etc.* (Innsbruck, 1923). A refutation of Father Stufler's argument in support of his conclusion that St. Thomas taught the necessity only of God's *mediate* concursus, will be found in *Gregorianum* (The Pontificial Gregorian University, Rome,) March, 1925. It is entitled, "Divi Thomae Aquinatis doctrina de Deo operante," and was written by Father Gabriel Huarte, S.J., a professor of the Gregorian. It shows quite clearly, we think, that St. Thomas taught, not the opinion later advanced by Durandus, but that commonly held by Catholic philosophers and theologians, namely, that God of necessity immediately concurs with creatures in all their actions. What is more—and attention is called to this point by Father Huarte—one who would care to make the comparison, would find, first, that Durandus, in explaining the opinion he wishes to refute, comes so close to using the words of St. Thomas in explaining and defending that opinion, that one would be led to believe that Durandus had St. Thomas in mind as his main adversary; and, secondly, that St. Thomas's arguments are presented as difficulties by Durandus, and *vice versa*.

A few passages from St. Thomas, selected from others of like tenor, will show quite convincingly that he may be classed with certainty as a supporter of the doctrine advanced in our thesis. The expressions in them, which, either in urging a difficulty or explaining the doctrine defended, can refer only to one thing, namely, God's immediate concursus in the actions of creatures, are in *italics*.

On the Power of God (p.3, art.7). *Does God work in operations of nature?*

Obj. 3. If God operates in every operation of nature, *God's operation and nature's are either one and the same operation or they are distinct. They are not one and the same;* since unity of operation proves unity of nature. . . . *Nor can they be two distinct operations;* because distinct operations cannot seemingly be terminated in one and the same product. . . . *Therefore it is altogether impossible that God operate in nature.*

Obj. 4. It will be replied that two operations can have the same term if one is subordinate to the other. On the contrary, when several things are *immediately* related to something, *one is not subordinate to the other.* Now both God and nature produce *the natural effect immediately.* Therefore of God's operation and nature's one is not subordinate to the other.

Obj. 6. To operate *on* a thing is not the same as to operate *in* it. Now, the operation whereby God either produces or preserves the forces of nature, has its effect *on* those forces by producing or preserving them. Therefore, this does not prove that God works *in* the operations of nature.

Reply, Obj. 3. In that operation whereby God operates by moving nature, nature itself does not operate: and even *the operation of nature is also the operation of the divine power,* just as the operation of an instrument is effected by the power of the principal agent. *Nor does this prevent nature and God operating to the same effect,* on account of the order between God [First Cause] and nature [secondary cause].

Reply, Obj. 4. Both God and nature operate immediately, although as already stated there is order between them of priority [First Cause] and posteriority [secondary cause].

[What St. Thomas had already stated is this:] If we consider the subsistent agent, every particular agent is immediate in its effect; but if we consider the power by which the action is done, *then the power of the higher cause is more immediate to the effect than the power of the lower cause;* since the power of the lower cause is not coupled with its effect save by the power of the higher cause; wherefore it is said in *De Causis (prop. 1) that the*

power of the first cause [God] *takes the first place in the production of the effect and enters more deeply therein.* Accordingly, the divine power must needs be present to every acting thing.
. . . Therefore, *God is the cause of everything's action* inasmuch as He gives everything the power to act, and preserves it in being *and applies it to action,* and inasmuch as *by His power every other power acts.* And if we add to this that God is His own power, and that He is in all things not as a part of their essence but as upholding them in their being, *we shall conclude* that He *acts in every agent immediately.*

Reply, Obj. 6. God is the cause of nature's operation *not only as upholding the forces of nature in their being,* but in other ways, as stated above. [The passage added above to the reply to *Obj. 4* states those different ways.]

Summa Contra Gentiles (Bk.3, c.70). *How the same effect is from God and from the natural agent.*

Some find it difficult to understand how natural effects are ascribed to God and to the activity of nature. For it would seem impossible *that one action should proceed from two agents; hence, if the action productive of a natural* effect proceeds from a natural body, it does not proceed from God.

Again, *if a thing can be done sufficiently by means of one, it is superfluous to do it by means of several.* . . . *Since, then the divine power sufficed to produce natural effects, it is superfluous to employ for the production of the same effects, the powers of nature also.*

Besides, *if God produces the whole natural effect, nothing of the effect is left for the natural agent to produce.* Therefore, seemingly, *it is impossible that God produce the same effects as natural things.*

However, these arguments offer no difficulty if we mind what has been said already. For two things may be considered in every agent: namely, the thing itself that acts, and the power whereby it acts. . . . Accordingly, just as it is not unreasonable that one action be produced by an agent and by the virtue of that agent, *so it is not absurd that the same effect be produced by the inferior agent and by God,* and *by both immediately, though in a different way.*

It is also evident that *there is nothing superfluous if nature produce its proper effect and God produce it also,* since nature does not produce it except by God's power.

*It is, also, clear that the same effect is ascribed to a natural
cause and to God, not as though part were effected by God and
part by the agent; but the whole effect proceeds from each, yet in
different ways; just as the whole of the same effect is ascribed to
the instrument, and again the whole is ascribed to the principal
agent.*

Difficulties

1. If God immediately concurs in producing the actions
of creatures, God's action is identified with the creature's
action. But God's action cannot be identified with the creature's action. Therefore.

D. Maj. God's action considered as it is in itself, or as it is in
God, is identified with the creature's action, *N.*; God's action
considered as it is in its effect, is identified with the creature's
action, *Subd.*; it is really identified with it. *C.*; it is conceptually
identified with it, in which case God and the creature would
produce the same act and under the same aspect or formality,
N.—Cd. Min.

God's act, considered as it is in itself, is identified with God
Himself. God's act, considered in its effect, or in what it produces, is really identified with the action, or physical influxus of
the creature producing the effect. God produces the whole action; the creature produces the whole action, God, as First and
Universal Cause, produces it under the formality of *simply
being,* inasmuch as it is *something existing;* the creature, as secondary and particular cause, produces it under the formality of
this specific and individual existing something. God and the
creature are partial causes, *in the sense* that neither of them
solely produces the action and its effect, but *not* in the sense that
neither of them produces the *whole* action and its effect. *Both*
produce the *whole* action and its effect, but under different formalities.

Examples of two causes producing by one action the same
effect under different formalities are of daily occurrence when
one of them is the principal, and the other is the instrumental
cause. Let us take the case of a man using a pen in writing.
There is one action, that of writing. It, and its effect, which also
is one—that which is written—are produced by the man, under
the formality of a motion producing a sign, representing a
thought; they are produced by the pen, inasmuch as the motion
is that of the pen producing a black ink-mark. The sign produced, then, is from the man giving the motion, under the for-

mality of *a sign representing a thought;* it is from the pen
moved under the formality *of a sign consisting of a black ink-
mark.*

2. If God, the infinitely wise Creator of the world, of
necessity gives to the creatures He produces full power to
perform all the actions natural to them, His immediate,
physical concursus is not required in the performing of
them. But God, the infinitely wise Creator of the world, of
necessity does this. Therefore.

D. Maj. If He gives them full power, in the order in which
they exist, that is, as creatures, or secondary causes, to perform
all actions natural to them, but if it is intrinsically impossible
that they should ever be independent of God, preserving them
in existence and concurring in the production of all their actions,
God's immediate physical concursus is not required by them, *N.*;
if God gives them full power and if it were possible for them
to remain in existence without God preserving them in existence, and act without His immediate physical concursus, that
concursus would not be necessary, *C.—Cd. Min.*

A creature receives from God all the power in the order in
which it exists, the order of secondary causes, to perform all
actions natural to it. It requires no other cause, therefore, in the
same order, as a complementary cause supplying some power
wanting to its nature. If it did so, its nature would be imperfect.
Since a creature, however, is essentially a contingent being, and
since all its actions are contingent things, it is intrinsically impossible that it should begin to exist, continue to exist, or act,
independently of the one Necessary Being, God, respectively,
as a producing cause; as a positive and direct preserving cause;
as an immediate, physical concurring cause.

3. If God and creatures perform the same action, the
same effect is produced by different causes. But different
causes cannot produce the same effect. Therefore.

D. Maj. The same effect is produced by two co-ordinate
causes, *N.*; by two causes, one subordinate to the other, *Subd.*; the
same total effect is produced by both under the same formality,
N.; under different formalities, *C.—Cd. Min.*

The explanations already given should make this solution
clear.

4. If God, acting alone, can produce the effects which
proceed from the actions of creatures, it appears to be super-

fluous for God to use creatures in producing those effects. But God, acting alone, can do this. Therefore.

D. Maj. It would be superfluous for God to use creatures in producing actions and their effects, if He wished by His sole power to produce them, *C.*; it would be superfluous, if God moved by His own infinite Goodness, wished to communicate that goodness in finite measure to creatures, and so not only call them into existence, preserve them in existence, but also give them power to act, with dependence, however, on His immediate concursus: supposing all this, God's concursus would be superfluous, *N.–Tr. Min.–D. Cons.*

We have transmitted the Minor, because it is not true that all actions and their effects, considered in their specific nature, can be performed by God alone. If God desires to make a being who can think, who can see and feel things, it is absolutely impossible that these perfections, which are immanent actions, be produced by God alone. God alone can produce a creature who can see and feel things, and He can concur with a creature in the action of seeing and feeling, but it is impossible for God formally to see or feel.

5. If it is right to say that God sometimes uses creatures as means, or mediums, in producing effects, it is not true that God concurs immediately with all the actions of creatures. But it is right to say this. Therefore.

D. Maj. If such an expression is rightly used, and its sense is that God sometimes uses creatures as means or mediums in producing effects, and in such wise that He in no way, or only mediately, concurs in the production of those effects, it is not true that God concurs immediately with all creatures in their actions, *C.*; if such an expression is rightly used and its sense is that, though God at times produces effects alone, at other times He uses creatures as means or mediums in their production but never without immediately concurring in the production of those effects, it is not true that God concurs immediately with all creatures in their actions, *N.–Cd. Min.*

6. If a cause using an instrument in producing an effect is not an immediate cause of its production, God, who uses creatures as instruments in producing effects, is not an immediate cause of the production of those effects. But, a cause, using an instrument in producing an effect, is not an immediate cause of its production. Therefore.

Tr. Maj. We transmit the Major, noting that though creatures are said to be instruments of God in producing natural effects (St. Thomas uses the term), still they are not instruments in the strict sense of the word. An instrument, strictly so called, is not a principal cause in the order in which it acts. Creatures, however, with God concurring, still remain principal causes in the order in which they produce their effects, that is, in the order of secondary causes. Secondly, the effect produced when an instrument, strictly so called, is used, bears primarily a resemblance not to the instrument but to the principal cause. When creatures using the powers which nature has given them, act, the effect bears a resemblance to the creature. The same is true even when man uses instruments in the production of artificial effects, for all these effects reveal the intellect of the principal cause.

N. Min. We deny the Minor, for, though a distinction might be given noting that God in using creatures to produce effects, may be said to be an immediate cause in two senses, whilst a creature using an instrument, strictly so called, is an immediate cause of the effect in one sense only, still, as to be an immediate cause in this sense, is to be an immediate cause in the sense of our thesis, we omit the distinction and simply deny the Minor.

God is an immediate cause in the sense that no other being intermediates between God and the effect produced by the creature. In His Being, or Person, He is as close to the effect as the creature is. A created cause, using an instrument, properly so called, is not an immediate cause in this sense. The instrument is between the principal cause and the effect. *Example:* A man using a pen in writing.

The principal cause of an effect, however, whether it be God or creature, is always an immediate cause in the sense that its action, its actual operative virtue, flows into or produces the effect immediately.

7. If a finite cause can produce an effect, either natural or artificial, which can act and continue to act without the immediate concursus of its maker, God should be able to produce effects, that is, creatures, capable of acting without His concursus. But a finite cause can do that. Therefore.

D. Maj. If a finite cause can produce such an effect; an effect, namely, which after its production is independent of its producer in its very being, and in its actions, and if the fact that it can so act is precisely because it is *finite,* God should be able to produce an effect which could exist without God's direct and immediate conservation, and act without His physical and immediate concursus, *N.*; if the power which a cause has so to act would not necessarily imply that it was a finite cause, God should be able, etc. *C.—Cd. Min.*

A being other than God and existing and acting independently of God is a contradiction in terms, an impossible thing. As a being other than God it is contingent and finite; as a being independent of God in its existence and operation, it would be a necessary being, an infinite being. Hence, any being, apart from whom, and utterly independent of whom, other beings exist and act, is necessarily a finite being.

8. If creatures can do nothing unless God immediately concurs with them, no effect can be produced unless infinite power is exercised. But no effect, since all of them are finite, requires the exercise of infinite power in its production. Therefore.

D. Maj. Unless a power is exercised *which is infinite in itself*—God's power—and also infinite in the effect produced, *N.*; unless a power, *infinite in itself,* but *not* infinite in its effect, is exercised, *C.—Cd. Min.*

God's power in itself is infinite. It can bring into existence anything which is intrinsically possible. An infinite effect is an impossible thing, as there can be only one necessary, one infinite being. Therefore the effect of God's action is necessarily finite. Again, it is to be noted that God's infinite power in its influx into the effect differs in kind and intensity with the different kinds of creatures, the different kinds of their actions, and the different degrees of intensity of those actions at different times. In other words, the nature and intensity of God's influx into the effect produced is determined by the creature; in causes acting necessarily, by *the nature* in the *individual causes,* in causes acting freely, by the *individual* using his free nature in determining his free action.

9. If it were possible for God to concur immediately with man's free actions, man would exercise dominion over God's concursus. But man cannot exercise dominion over God's concursus. Therefore.

D. Maj. Man would exercise absolute physical dominion over God's concursus, *N.*; a much conditioned, dominion, *Subd.*; which means that, supposing God wished to create man, preserve

him in existence and supply him with everything necessary for
the exercise of his freedom, man, exercising that freedom and
so determining his action, could do so independently of a further
condition, namely, that God wills to concur with him in so doing,
N.; could do so with an absolute dependence on God's immediate
concursus, and hence, while God leaves to man the determination
of his act, God must necessarily put *the whole act which is the
determination, Subd.*; and in so granting man physical freedom
it is possible for God to grant man freedom from the observance
of the moral law, *N.*; it is necessary for man ever to obey the
moral law, and, hence, to give an account to God for the use
of his physical freedom, receiving, according to his deserts, reward or punishment, which in the next life will be eternal, *C.*—
Cd. Min.

Man, a contingent being, has absolute dominion over nothing. His very coming into existence is conditioned on God's
willing; likewise his continuing in existence and his being placed
in circumstances in which he may act freely. On God's will also,
offering him His physical concursus indifferently to all actions
possible to man's free choice, depends man's proximate power to
elicit a free act; with a further dependence in exercising that
power, on God concurring in putting *the act which is the choice
or determination,* but in no way determining it.

He only determines, i.e., chooses the action he puts, who,
when putting it has full power to act otherwise. To *choose,* therefore, is not *merely* to put an action, but to *put one action
rather* than another. As God in granting man freedom, *leaves to
man* the choice of his action, God wills not to do the choosing
when man acts freely; therefore, though God must put with man
the whole action, He does not choose or determine it, seeing
that the choice has been left to man.

Furthermore, though God grants man physical liberty, it is
impossible for God to grant him moral liberty, freedom, namely,
from the obligation of tending towards God in the exercise of
his physical liberty. Man, therefore, though free, must render
an account of the use he makes of this great gift. If he has used
it well, and has preserved in his well-doing until death, he will
be rewarded eternally; if not, he will be punished eternally.

10. If God concurs immediately in producing all the
actions of creatures, it would be necessary for Him to concur
in the production of man's sinful actions. But it is not pos-

sible that God should concur in the production of man's sinful actions. Therefore.

D. Maj. It would be necessary for Him to concur with man's sinful actions, inasmuch as they are sinful, *N.*; it would be necessary for Him to concur with man's sinful actions, *which are* sinful, but *not as sinful,* that is, it would be necessary for Him to produce with man the act *which is sinful,* in no wise, however, choosing it, and hence, in no wise being responsible for its direction away from Himself, *C.—Cd. Min.*

The one who is free in putting an action, who has the power of choice, and, hence, who has control over the action, is the one who is responsible for its moral goodness or badness. As we saw, however, in the solution of the previous difficulty, when man acts freely, God leaves the choice of the action wholly to man. God, therefore, in concurring with a morally bad action of man, is in no way responsible for its direction away from Himself. He concurs with the action *which is* sinful, but not *as sinful.*

The gift of freedom, inasmuch as it includes the power to choose between what is morally good and morally bad, was given to us by God in order that by a right use of that gift we might win Him as our eternal reward. If, however, we are to win God as our reward, we must have the power to lose Him, that is, to separate ourselves from Him by sin. If, then, God wishes us freely to come to Him, and if, therefore, it is ours to make the choice, and if we choose to sin rather than not, God must necessarily by His concursus be a co-operator in that act, for otherwise we could not choose it. And He is a co-operator in it, not, however, a *formal* co-operator but a *material* one, producing with us our action *which is sinful,* but not *inasmuch as it is sinful.*

Thesis V

God's concursus with man's free actions does not, and cannot, physically predetermine them.

Prenotes to the Thesis

Our thesis rejects in part the opinion quite generally held by Thomists concerning the nature of God's immediate, physical concursus. It is commonly called the Thomistic opinion. Whether or not it is also the opinion of St. Thomas is a hotly disputed question. The Thomists insist that it is; others say that the matter is at least doubtful; and still others, among whom even Thomists are found, are quite convinced that St. Thomas never held the opinion. Its originator, according to these last, was Domingo Bañez, a Spanish Dominican (1528–1604). Consequently they speak of it as the Bannesian opinion. Since the settlement of this dispute, if indeed it can be settled, has no bearing on our thesis, we may well leave what little we have to say concerning it to a Scholion.

It is a fundamental tenet of Thomistic (or Bannesian) philosophy that no creature can put any action, free or necessary, unless God physically predetermines it to put that action. Admitting with us and all Scholastic philosophers the necessity of God's simultaneous concursus, which was established in *Thesis IV,* and claiming in addition, as their own peculiar doctrine, the necessity of this physical predetermination, they label the concursus which they demand as necessary, not merely simultaneous, but *previo*-simultaneous; the prefix, *previo,* referring to the physical predetermination.

This physical predetermination, which is an impulse (or push or motion) produced by God alone, is called a *pre-*motion because it is given to the creature prior to its action. This priority is not a priority in point of time, but only in the sense that the putting of the action for which it is given,

124

necessarily depends on its reception. Without it the creature cannot act.

What is more, this *pre-motion,* is, by its very nature, a *pre-determination,* for it not only moves the creature to act, but also irresistibly determines the act. Only the one determined action for which it is given can be put; and *it must* be put.

Our view on the matter is this. All creatures, the handiwork of an all-wise, omnipotent God, are complete in their natures. That is, they are fully prepared to perform those actions natural to them, when the conditions to be supplied by other creatures, and necessary for such performance, are fulfilled. *Necessarily-acting creatures,* therefore, when the conditions just mentioned are given, without any impulse or motion other than the tendency imbedded in their natures to act, and hence without the reception of any physical predetermination, are determined by those very natures irresistibly to put, and actually do put, the definite actions natural to them. They have no need, therefore, of any physical predetermination. In their case it would be simply useless.

In the case of *free agents,* however, if God were to physically predetermine them to act, He would be giving them not a merely useless impulse or determination to act, but one utterly destructive of their liberty.

It should be quite clear, now, why our thesis is concerned with the rejection of physical predetermination, only inasmuch as it affects free agents. Objectively, it makes no difference whether or not necessary agents are physically predetermined. In either case their actions would be the same. With free agents, however, the case is altogether different. Physical predetermination destroys free will. The former question, then, is relatively of minor importance; the latter, the destruction of man's freedom, of utmost importance. Hence, the restriction of our thesis.

What is more, the further exposition, to be given presently, of the Thomists' opinion, and of our own, concerning the nature of God's physical concursus, shall, following the scope of our thesis, be confined to a consideration of them only in their reference to man's free actions; and this, be-

cause the chief difficulties in this matter demanding solution
are concerned in one way or another with the safeguarding
of man's freedom.

The Thomists claim that without physical predetermination these difficulties cannot be solved; with it, a solution,
fully safeguarding man's liberty, is possible. This, our thesis
denies. Some other solution, therefore, must be found which
will leave man's liberty intact.

That our opinion offers such a solution of at least one
of the difficulties referred to, has already been shown in that
part of our first thesis (*Thesis I*) which treats of God's foreknowledge of man's free acts. The difficulty there solved was
to find how, *without prejudice to man's liberty,* God could
know with absolute certainty and from all eternity, the definite action which each free being in a definite set of circumstances would put, if he were to be created. And so also, to
find how in His eternal decree of creation, man's liberty remaining intact, God could decree the definite concursus
He would give him in time, for the performance of that
action.

The Thomists, as was shown in *Thesis I, Corollary III,*
explained that knowledge by postulating in God two different kinds of decrees physically predetermining man's will,
and so, as we think, destroyed his freedom. For a fuller knowledge of the nature of those decrees, and also for an understanding of our solution of the difficulty through the medium
of the *Scientia Media,* a re-reading of particular parts of
Thesis I, and the Corollaries, Scholions, and Difficulties connected with them, will be sufficient. That re-reading, with
the further explanation of both opinions which follows immediately, will help us also in solving other difficulties which
await us; difficulties, namely, in explaining how God, without detriment to any of His infinite perfections, and without
in any way prejudicing man's freedom, can concur with man
in his free actions.

The Previo-Simultaneous Concursus of the Thomists

The specifying and principal element in this concursus
is that which physically predetermines all the actions of all
creatures. As our thesis, however, is concerned with this ele-

ment only as it affects the will in the exercise of its freedom, the following definition of it, so restricted, given previously in *Thesis I*, leaves us in no doubt as to its all-compelling nature.

A *physical predetermination* (or *pre-motion* as it is sometimes less definitely called), which is the effect in time of God's eternal physically predetermining decree, is an impulse (a motion, a passing or non-permanent quality) proceeding from God alone and received in the created will prior (in the sense noted at the beginning of these prenotes, and in *Thesis I, Corollary III*) to its free action, by which the will is given the proximate power to act (or is reduced to action), and which by its very nature is so connected with the free act that without it the will is incapable of any action whatever, and with it, is moved irresistibly, inescapably, to put that action, and only that action, to which it has been predetermined by the divine impulse.

Taken in connection with what was said in *Thesis I, Corollary III*, when rejecting the Thomistic pre-determining decrees as an objective medium of God's fore-knowledge of man's free acts, the above definition with some few further remarks concerning it, to be noted immediately, will give us a knowledge of the Thomistic physical predetermination theory sufficient for our purpose. The remarks are the following:

1. Though it is not absolutely certain *by whom*—whether St. Thomas or Bañez—and, consequently, *when* the theory of physical predetermination with its two kinds of physically predetermining decrees was incorporated into the Thomistic system of philosophy and theology, it is certain that it was not until the latter half of the sixteenth century, that that theory and the theory of the Society of Jesus, with its *Scientia Media* and non-determining decrees, began to be more fully developed and explained, and strenuously defended by their respective champions.

· This activity, in more precisely refining, defining, and explaining the various points of their theories, was brought about in great measure, if not solely, by the many disputes, both private and public, which cropped up at that time between the two rival schools, concerning the nature of actual grace.

These disputes, at times more or less heated, went on for some twenty years, till finally Clement VIII established a tribunal—*Congregatio de Auxiliis*—to hear both sides of the controversy, and, if possible, put an end to it. Its first session was held in 1602. Before it finished its hearings, however, Clement VIII died. Leo XI, who followed him, was Pope for but a few weeks. Under his successor, Paul V, the Congregation continued its work. Altogether, from 1602 to 1607, it held 85 sessions, 17 of them during the reign of Paul V, who was present during them. The outcome of it all was a decree, issued by him September 5, 1607, condemning neither theory, and permitting both to be taught freely in the Schools. And there the matter rests.

2. What the primary aim of the Thomists was in advancing the theory of physical predetermination is not quite clear. Some say it was to explain God's foreknowledge of all things, especially all free actions that will be, or would be, if God so willed. According to others, it was to safeguard God's absolute dominion over His creatures, and above all over His free creatures.

Though this point still remains in doubt, there is no doubt concerning the primary aim of the Jesuits in steadfastly *opposing* the theory of physical predetermination, as they have always done, and as they did in a special way during the sixteenth and seventeenth centuries. That aim was, and is the defense of man's free will, which, according to their firm conviction, physical predetermination destroys. The reason for the Jesuits' insistent opposition to physical predetermination during the centuries just named, was this. At that time the doctrine of free will was being bitterly attacked by the followers of Luther, and Calvin, and by the Jansenists. The Fathers of the Society of Jesus were anxious to make use of every means available to repel these attacks. As they were fully persuaded, however, that the theory of physical predetermination, which was then beginning to be taught in the Schools, was destructive of free will, they felt that unless they attacked it vigorously their battle against the enemies from without was all but lost.

3. The definition we have given above, of physical pre-determination considered only as affecting the will in its free actions, is vouched for by the Thomists themselves. They admit that the will physically predetermined is driven irre-sistibly to put the one determined act for which the physical predetermination is given, yet they claim that that act is freely put. An insoluble mystery, say the Thomists. Our answer is that since a free act is a self-determined act of the will, a predetermined free act of the will is a metaphysical impossibility. The proof of our thesis will show this clearly. Farther on we shall show how the Thomists, in their effort to prove that it is possible to have a physically predetermined free act, give a definition of a free action which must be flatly rejected.

4. The Thomists whilst insisting that God premoves the will to act freely by means of the physically predetermining quality which irresistibly drives the will on to the eliciting of the one determined act for which it was given, insist also, as the name given to their concursus, i. e., *previo-simultane-ous,* suggests, that God simultaneously concurs with the will in producing the free act. What explanation they give of this simultaneous concursus of God, does not concern us, since we claim that the previous physically predetermining action of God, which their theory demands, makes a free act impossible.

5. The predetermining motion, i.e., the physical prede-termination, which God, according to the Thomists, gives to the will for its free act, satisfies, so they say, an absolute want on the part of the will. Without it the will cannot act. All Thomists are in agreement on this point. They differ, however, in assigning what precisely is the want which is satisfied. Some say that without the physical predetermina-tion the will is not proximately prepared to elicit the free act, hence it comes to the will, in remote potency (*in actu primo remoto*) to act, as a complement which estab-ishes it in proximate potency (*in actu primo proximo*). In other words, the will without the physical predetermination has not the full power to act; with it, it has. Others, however, say that without the physical predetermination, the will *has* the *full power* to act, but is still incapable of passing from

full potency to the actual putting of the act without the physical predetermination. The physical predetermination, therefore, is required, not to give the will the full power to act, but to apply it, so fully prepared, to the actual putting of the act.

It seems to us that here we have a distinction without a difference. Without the physical predetermination the will simply cannot actually put the free act. It has not, therefore, the full power to do so. The physical predetermination gives it that power. The settling of this dispute, however, we leave to the Thomists, for no matter how it is settled, the truth of our thesis stands. We reject physical predetermination because, under its influence, the act which is supposed to be the will's free act, and which consequently should be supposed to be determined by the will, has already (and this the Thomists admit), been determined, and irrevocably determined, by God. The will, therefore, does not, and cannot, determine it. It is not the will's free act.

6. The Thomists are consistent with themselves in holding that man is physically predetermined by God, not only when his act is morally good, but also when it is morally bad. When man sins, therefore, God moves him with a motion which is irresistible, i.e., drives him irresistibly, to the commission of the sinful act. They claim, nevertheless, that the man so irresistibly driven, sins freely, since God predetermines him to the commission of the act *which is* sinful, but not *as* sinful. Here we have another mystery, according to the Thomists; a metaphysical impossibility, as we view it. The only conclusion we can reach, then, is that the theory of physical predetermination makes God to be the author of the sinful act, inasmuch as it is sinful. More will be said on this point later.

The Simultaneous Concursus as commonly explained by the Jesuits

The Thomists who defend the doctrine of physical predetermination—and almost all of them do so—are called by some, as we have seen, Bannesians; a name derived from one of their very learned theologians, Domingo Bañez, (1528—1604) a Spaniard. If not the originator, Bañez was certainly one of the foremost proponents of the doctrine. In fact, it was his bitter attack on a work published by Luis de Molina (1535–1600), of the Society of Jesus, also a Spaniard, which added fuel to the heated controversy, and so led to the convoking of the *Congregatio de Auxiliis* referred to above. Molina's work attacked, *Concordia liberi arbitrii cum gratiae donis, divina praescientia, etc.,* was an attempt to solve the difficult problems of grace and free will, divine foreknowledge, etc. The solution offered, based on the *Scientia Media* (cf. *Thesis I*), was later more fully developed by Bellarmine, now Saint Robert Bellarmine, a Doctor of the Church; by Suarez, Vasquez, and Lessius, all noted theologians of the Society of Jesus. It is this perfected solution which is now commonly taught in that Society. It is sometimes called Molinism, and its defenders Molinists. In strict accord with its principles is the following necessarily brief explanation of the simultaneous concursus of God with the will's free acts in the natural order, with which order we are solely concerned. Though some of the points we shall touch on have already been noted in other connections, and especially in the solution of difficulties, it will be helpful to repeat them here, with others not yet explained, in a formal summary.

1. *The physical and immediate concursus of God* is the act of God's efficacious will, or omnipotence, by which, whatever there is of actual reality in the action of a creature and its effect, proceeds actually from God as an immediate, efficient cause. It can be looked at in two ways: in itself (*principiative*), and as it affects the creature's will and its free actions (*terminative*).

2. *The concursus of God in itself (principiative)* is God's action as it is in Himself, namely, the efficacious will of God; that is, the will of God actually and eternally decreeing to inflow into, or produce in time the actions and effects of creatures. It is really identified with God Himself. It is eternal, and hence, is prior to the action of the creature both in duration and in the sense that the action and effect of the creature necessarily depend on it.

This actual decree of God to concur with the free actions (we are considering only such) of creatures is concerned with the will both in its preparation (*in actu primo*) for the putting of the free act, and in the actual putting of it (*in actu secundo*).

In the Molinistic system, by this decree God *offers* to the will, in order that it may be fully prepared (*in actu primo proximo*) to act freely, that is, to make its choice, His physical concursus *indifferently* for all the acts which are possible of choice to the will in any definite set of circumstances. By it He also *confers* His *determined* concursus for that particular act which the will, God concurring but in no way determining, freely puts.

3. *The concursus of God as it affects the will, and its actions (terminative).*

Looked at in this way it is both an *offered* (*oblatus*) concursus and a *conferred* (*collatus*) one.

4. *The offered* (*oblatus*) *concursus.* The concursus of God as it affects the will remotely prepared (*in actu primo remoto*), in order that it may be fully prepared (*in actu primo proximo*), for the putting of its free act, is called the *offered* (*oblatus*) concursus; the concursus required by the will prior to (*concursus in actu primo*) its free act, and in order that it may be fully prepared to put it. In its effective power it is *many-sided, multiple* (*virtute multiplex*), for it is God's actual offer to concur physically in putting any one of the actions which are possible of choice to the will in any definite set of circumstances. It is consequently *indifferent* (*indifferens*), for the *physical concursus* is offered *indifferently* with regard to any one of the possible free actions just mentioned. *It does not* consist in any kind of reality produced by God in the will, as does the physical determination of the Bannesians, but through it the will, in order that it may be fully prepared (*in actu primo proximo*) to select any one of the actions of possible choice to it in any definite set of circumstances, has God ready to concur indifferently in the production of any one of those actions.

This offered concursus of God is *not*, therefore, an *immediate* concursus with a free action, but a *mediate* concursus in preparation for it. *It is require*d in order that the will may be fully prepared (*in actu primo proximo*) to act, and it must be *indifferent,* in order that the will may be fully prepared to *freely* act.

5. *The conferred (collatus) concursus.* God knows from all eternity through His *Scientia Media* (cf. *Thesis I*) the determined act which the will would freely put, and, hence, the determined concursus which He himself would give, if He were to place a man in a definite set of circumstances and offer to concur indifferently in the placing of any of the actions possible of choice by the will in those circumstances. In the light of this knowledge, then, He decrees to create man, to place him in those circumstances, to *offer* His concursus indifferently for any one the actions which, by His knowledge of simple intelligence, He knows to be possible of choice in those circumstances, and to *confer* that determined concursus which by His *Scientia Media,* He foresaw man by his choice would freely determine on.

The concursus so given by God is called the *conferred (collatus),* the *given (datus), the actual (in actu secundo)* concursus. It is given for one and only one determined action, that one, namely, which the will and the will only, God concurring but not determining, will determine. It cannot be used, therefore, like the *offered* concursus, for any one of many actions indifferently. It is not received in the will prior to its free action, as is the Bannesian physical predetermination, but is really identified with that action.

If, however, God's action, looked at not in itself but in its result *(terminative),* is identified with the action of the creature, both God and the creature put the same action. They are partial causes, in the sense that neither one of them alone puts the action and its effect, but they are *not partial causes* in the sense that neither one of them puts the whole action and its effect. They both put it.

It is of the greatest importance to note, however, that though God and the creature both put the whole action, still, owing to the totally different nature of the causes and of the causality which they exercise in putting it, the action, which is really one, is put by God and the creature under altogether different aspects or formalities. The following explanation will show this difference clearly.

God and the creature do not, and it is impossible that they should, inflow into the free action of the creature as co-ordinate causes. God inflows as the First, universal, and essentially independent cause; the creature as a secondary, particular, and essentially dependent cause. God as First and universal cause, produces not only the free actions of the will, but all the actions and their effects of all creatures, under that fundamental formality which is found in everything produced, the formality, namely, of being something. Without God's action there would be nothing. To God's action, then, is due that the action of the creature with its effect is *something existing,* and *not nothing.*

The creature as a secondary and particular cause, that is, as a cause existing and acting in a definite and particular species of being, produces the action with its effect under the formality of this or that *specific* and *individual* existing thing. To the action of the creature, consequently, is due that the existing thing is this or that specific individual action and effect.

St. Thomas (*On the Power of God,* q.1, a.4, Reply to Obj. 3): ". . . although the first cause has the greatest influence on the effect, its influence, nevertheless, is determined and specified by the proximate cause, whose likeness, therefore, the effect bears."

In the case of necessary actions of creatures, this specification of the act is due to the nature of the concurring individual creature, acting through the individual. In the case of free acts, it is due to the individual creature acting through his human nature; for the human individual, having been granted by God the gift of free will, has, as a consequence, individual control of his free actions. Not, however, in the sense that he is absolute master of them, for though physically free, he is never free from the obligations of the moral law. He may refuse God service, but at his risk. It is absolutely impossible that any creature should break the law of God with impunity.

As the action, then, produced by God concurring with a creature, is determined in its specific and individual nature by the creature, it is quite evident that the efficient inflow of God, into the action and effect produced by the creature, is conditioned by the creature's inflow. Hence, though both causes produce the whole action and effect, neither of them exercises an efficiency capable of producing alone the whole effect under all its formalities. The creature does not do so, because it is absolutely impossible for him to do so. Without God's concurrence there would be no action, no effect. God does not do so, because, having given the creature a nature capable of acting and producing effects within definite specific bounds, He so concurs that the creature may exercise that power, that is, He leaves to the creature the specification of the action and its effect.

The reason, therefore, why God does not alone produce wholly an action and effect which might be so produced by Him, is because He does not wish to do so. The reason why a creature does not alone produce an action and its effect, is because it is absolutely impossible for him to do so. For as it is of the very essence of a creature to depend ever on the immediate efficient inflow of God's action for his very being, so it is of the very essence of the action of a creature with its effect to depend for its being in the same way on God's action.

God's dependence, then, in action on the concurrent action of His creatures is due not to indigence but to the munificent liberality of the Infinite.

It is to be noted that the conferred (*collatus*) concursus of God, of which we have just been speaking, is really the same as the immediate concursus, mentioned and defined in *Thesis IV.* It is also called a simultaneous concursus, since its objective conferring by God is simultaneous with the action of the creature.

6. *This immediate, conferred concursus,* then, which is given by God, the First, universal, and essentially independent cause, to the freely acting creature, under the directing light of His *Scientia Media,* is said to be, and is, simultaneous with the free action of the creature, which action it does not determine. As a consequence, in the case of a sinful act, it does not make God the author of the sin, as such.

Now, it is mainly in these very points that our explanation of God's immediate concursus with man's free acts differs altogether from the explanation of the Bannesians, according to whom the principal element of God's concursus is His physical predetermination of man's free act. This predetermination, as our study of its nature forces us to conclude, prevents the creature from determining his supposedly free act, and so, in the case of a sinful act, makes God, the sole determining cause, the author of the formal sin. Since it is, then, in these points that the two systems vitally differ, it will be necessary for us to examine them more closely, and show as clearly as is possible, exactly in what sense God's concursus, as explained by us, is simultaneous, and how it leaves to the creature alone the determination of his free act, and, hence, in the case of a sinful act, though God concurs in the putting of it, the *sole* responsibility for the formal sin. These points now demand our attention.

7. *In what sense God's conferred (collatus) concursus is simultaneous with the action of the creature.*

God's conferred concursus, if it be looked at as proceeding from God, considered merely as its efficient cause, and hence no consideration being given to the nature or perfection of His efficient causality, is simultaneous with the action of the creature, looked at in the same way. It is so in point of time: neither cause acts before the other; also as regards dependence: neither acts independently of the other, and in this sense, prior to the other. They act with a mutual dependence on each other.

In point of time they are simultaneous, for the action of the creature is really identified with God's conferred concursus, i.e., with God's action looked at in its result (*terminative*). Moreover, if God's conferred concursus, which is a determined one, were prior in point of time to the action of the free creature, it would predetermine that action and so destroy its freedom. On the other side, to suppose the action of the creature to be prior in point of time to the conferred concursus of God, is to suppose that the creature for a time acts without the divine concursus. This, however, we have proved to be impossible.

They are simultaneous in the matter of dependence; that is, they are mutually dependent one on the other, for God concurs in such wise that His concursus depends on the action of the creature for its specification, and the creature necessarily depends on God's concursus for the putting of his action.

God's conferred concursus, therefore, and the action of

the creature, looked at merely as efficiently proceeding from them, are perfectly simultaneous in point of time and dependence. They take place at the same time, and they are mutually dependent one upon the other.

8. *In what sense the conferred concursus of God must be given precedence over the action of the creature.*

If, however, we consider, as we now do, the nature or perfection of God's efficient causality in conferring His concursus, and compare it with the action, or efficient causality, of the creature, looked at in the same way, it will be quite evident that God's efficient causality must be given that precedence which is demanded by His absolute Lordship over all creation.

If, then, in the system we are defending, God's absolute dominion is so safeguarded, we shall be able to answer without difficulty the many objections urged against us on the score that we defend man's liberty to the detriment of God's supreme Lordship over him.

In the first place, then, we assert explicitly, and none of our other explanations contradicts it, that God by His conferred concursus inflows into the actions of His free creatures, as the First Cause, and absolute Lord, of all things. In giving freedom to His creatures He must give them some dominion over their free acts, but never, in our system, a dominion which in any way lessens His own supreme dominion. The action of the free creature, therefore, is the action of a secondary cause; master in a limited way of his free acts but ever a subject of God's absolutely supreme dominion.

Secondly, and as was noted before, God, as the One Universal Cause, by His efficient causality produces the actions and effects of all creatures under the universal and fundamental formality of *being something*. To His causality, then, is due that the action of every creature with its effect is something, not nothing. To the causality of the creature, as a particular cause, acting within the limits natural to it, is due that its action with its effect, which owes to God that *it is something* and not nothing, is *this* or *that* something. What is more, in the case of free actions of creatures, this determination of the action is under the control of the individual. It is *his* choice. He is responsible for it. This is not true in the case of the non-free, or necessary actions of creatures.

It will be evident, then, that here God's causality is superior to, takes precedence over the causality of the creature, seeing that it produces everything under the absolutely fundamental and universal formality of *being*. To His causality is due that things *are something, not nothing*.

Thirdly, and again as we noted before, the efficient causality of God in concurring with His creatures is that of an essentially independent cause; the causality of the creature, that of an essentially dependent one. God, then, when He acts, may act alone. If He so wills, He may act in concurrence with His creatures. His dependence in this case is not one of necessity, but is due to the munificence of God in freely giving creatures not only being but also manifold activities. In all these activities, however, the dependence of the creature on the concurrent action of God is absolutely necessary. It is of the very essence of creaturehood.

9. *In what sense the free action of the creature may be said to take precedence over the conferred concursus of God.*

The free action of the creature, then, if it be looked at in its entity, is produced by God, the First and Universal, essentially independent Cause, under the formality of being *something;* and produced by the creature, a secondary, particular, essentially dependent cause, under the formality of *this* or *that* something, *this* or *that* action which is free. If, however, we consider the free action of the will not merely in its entity, but precisely *as a free* action, that is, inasmuch as it is a choice of this action rather than others it might have chosen, it proceeds from the creature's will *alone,* in no way from God's will. God puts the action which *is* the choice; the *will chooses,* that is, it puts the action *inasmuch as it is the choice, inasmuch as it is free.* Under this formality, then, the action of the will must be given precedence over the conferred concursus of God. For it is the will alone which, with God concurring but not determining, determines, that God shall concur with this free action rather than that.

To understand this we must call to mind the fact that

the will is said to determine or choose or freely put its action when, on the point of putting it, it is fully prepared to refuse to put it, or put another one. The choice, as such, then, is not the putting of the action, but the putting *rather* of *this* action *than that* one. A will, then, which would put an action having no power to do anything else, would not choose it, would not determine it.

Now, God, who has given the will the gift of freedom, if He wishes the will to exercise it, must necessarily leave to the will the determination of its own free acts. Hence, when He concurs with the will in putting its free act, He has taken from Himself the power of choice, and consequently, though He produces the whole act which *is* a determination, a choice, on the part of the creature's will, He *does not determine* or *choose* the act. The creature alone, because God so wills it, does that. Hence, when God puts with the creature's will its free act, God inflows into it as a necessary cause, a cause having no power to do anything else, and this because He wills to do so. The creature inflows into the act as a free cause, a cause having at the time the full power of doing something else. The act, then, says a relation to God as to a necessary cause, to the creature's will as to a free cause. God puts the whole act which *is* the determining or free act of the creature, but *He* does not determine it, *He* does not choose. The creature puts the whole act which *is* its determining act *and at the same* time, God concurring, *determines* or *chooses* it. The creature is responsible for it, not God.

10. *God, then, so concurs with the free act of the creature that He does not determine it.*

Essential to our explanation of the way in which God concurs with the free act of a creature, is our appeal to the *Scientia Media* (fully explained in *Thesis I*), by which God knows that if He were to offer to a free creature, in order to prepare him fully to act freely, His physical concursus indifferently for all the actions of possible choice at the time, the creature would choose one determined action, and so would *determine* His divine simultaneous concursus necessary for the putting of that action. God, then, decrees to create that free creature, to place him in a set of conditions

in which he is to act freely, to offer him His physical concursus indifferently for all the actions of possible choice under those conditions, and to confer on him His divine
determined concursus, the determining cause of which, with
God simultaneously concurring, is the creature alone, and
not God. In such wise we claim that we save man's freedom.
That, in our system, God's supreme dominion is also safeguarded will appear more explicitly in our answers to difficulties on this point. In all these answers we will appeal to
the way, insisted on above, in which God inflows by His
concursus into the actions of His creatures, not on the creatures' level, but as the First, Universal, absolutely Supreme
and essentially independent Cause of all things.

In the system of Bañez, however, whatever may be said of
the way in which God, by means of physically predetermining decrees, exercises His supreme dominion over all His
creatures, since that way destroys man's freedom, it must be
rejected. It destroys man's freedom, because the physical
predetermination, which is the immediate effect of those
decrees and which is implanted in the will by God as its sole
author, prior to the putting of the act which is supposed
to be free, takes from the creature the power to determine
his own act. This means the destruction of his liberty. The
nature of the physical predetermination, which we have defined more than once in terms supplied by the Bannesians
themselves, shows this. Without it the will can do absolutely
nothing, and its intrinsic driving power is such that, with it,
the will has the power to put only one action, namely, that
determined action for which the physical predetermination
was given by God.

11. *God's concursus with man's morally bad acts.*

This question has been touched on briefly in the solution
of some difficulties previously given. The fuller explanation
which follows will be found helpful.

Both Bannesians and Molinists must, and do, admit that
God concurs with man's sinful acts. What is more, both
must, and do, claim that God concurs with the act *which is*
sinful, but not with the act *inasmuch as it is sinful.*

The question now is: Can both systems in the light of
their absolutely opposed explanation of the nature of God's

concursus, justify this claim? Our answer is, that the Molinists can, the Bannesians cannot. Our reasons for this answer
are simple.

The cause of a sinful act, inasmuch as it is sinful, is the
one who deliberately intends and chooses it.

In the Molinistic system, the one and the only one who
deliberately intends and chooses the free act (in this case, a
sinful act), is the creature. It is true that to do this he must
have God simultaneously putting with him the whole act
which is sinful. God does not, however, on this account become the chooser of the sinful act, the cause of it, inasmuch
as it is sinful. He reprobates it. He forbids it under threat
of the severest sanctions. If a grievously sinful act remains
unforgiven until death, He will requite it with eternal punishment. Using innumerable positive means, He endeavors,
without prejudice to man's physical freedom, to draw man
away from it. Consequently, then, in the hypothesis that He
wishes man to act freely, God, who by right Divine, has
absolute physical control over the actions of all creatures,
deprives Himself of the physical control of man's free actions. Man is their master in the physical order. Man is responsible for them. If the actions are sinful, man, and man
only, intends them; man, and man only, is their cause inasmuch as they are sinful.

All this is sometimes expressed technically by saying that
God is a material and not a formal co-operator in man's
sinful acts. He does not intend them. He reprobates them.
He could impede them. This, however, neither His wisdom,
nor His mercy, nor His justice, nor His absolute dominion,
over His creatures, obliges Him to do. He simply permits
them. (More on this point will be said in *Thesis VII,* on the
Problem of Evil.)

In the Bannesian system, the case is altogether different.
In their explanation of God's concursus, it is impossible, as
far as we can see, for a man ever to act freely. Hence, if the
action he puts with God concurring, is said to be sinful, not
he, but God who alone deliberately chooses the action, is
responsible for the sin. The nature and function of the Divine physical predetermination demand, it seems to us, no
other conclusion.

Let us take the case of a man who is physically predetermined by God to commit a sin. Previous to the reception
of this physical predetermination, his will, being without
any physical predetermination, is absolutely incapable of
action. Hence, when God offers the physical predetermination to the sinful act, the will is absolutely incapable of refusing it. When it has received it, as it must, the will has
absolutely no power to elicit any action other than the sinful
action for which the physical predetermination was given.
The will, therefore, does not act freely, but acts under a
physical compulsion which is absolutely irresistible. The
will, then, deprived of all power of choice cannot be the
cause of the sinful act as such.

The Bannesians, however, insist that the will acting under the compulsion of a physical predetermination still has
the power to choose, and so is responsible for its action. In
their endeavor to explain how this is possible, they make
use of a famous distinction which appears to us to explain
nothing.

The will, they say, physically predetermined, e.g., to commit a sin, has the power to choose a virtuous act, not, however, *in conjunction (in sensu composito) with* the physical
predetermination to the sinful act, but *as separated (in sensu
diviso)* from it. Thus, they say, the freedom of the will is
clearly established and vindicated.

Our answer is, that the will, in their system, in no sense
has the power to choose, in no sense is responsible for the
act, in no sense is free, whether *in conjunction with (in sensu
composito)*, nor *as separated from (in sensu diviso)* the physical predetermination to the sinful act. For, in the first place,
it has absolutely no power to separate itself from the physical
predetermination it already has to commit the sin. That
predetermination is inexorably connected with the act for
which it was given by God. It is true that if the sinful act
is still enduring, God, if He chooses, may remove the present
physical predetermination to sin, and give another, to a virtuous act. But in all this, the will has absolutely no control
or choice. And when the physical predetermination to the
virtuous act has been received, the will has no control over
the act which follows its reception. It is driven by a com-

pelling force, which it is absolutely incapable of resisting, to put the act which is said to be virtuous.

The will is never free. Without a physical predetermination it cannot act. With it, it is forced absolutely to put the one act for which God gives it. If it is taken away, the will has nothing to do with its removal. If another, in place of it, is given by God, the will has no choice in the matter, it must receive it. And when the will has received the other, it has no control over the act for which it was given.

The will, in a word, in the Bannesian system, in every one of its actions must be physically predetermined by God. That means that the will never determines its own actions, never has the power to choose, never is free.

In the case of a sinful action, then, the will does not choose the sin, is not responsible for the sin as such. The only one who does any choosing is God, and God alone. If there be a sin, therefore, God is the cause not only of the action which is sinful but also of the action inasmuch as it is sinful.

12. *In what sense God may be said rightly to physically premove the will to its free act.*

Though the Molinistic system denies the possibility of the physical predetermination, even by God, of man's free actions, Molinists are equally insistent in denying that those free acts can be put by man unless God physically premoves the will, and in more ways than one, to their putting.

This He does, in the first place, by supplying, either alone or concurring with creatures, all that is necessary in order that the will may be fully prepared for, and so physically premoved to, the putting of whatever action it may choose.

From among these necessary prerequisites, one of which is God's offered indifferent physical concursus, special mention must be made of another, namely, the natural tendency towards good in general with which God has endowed the human will, and in which is rooted its remarkable gift of freedom. For, it is in virtue of this tendency that the will, when the good in particular objects is presented to it, after tending spontaneously or indeliberately towards such good, and then after deliberation on the part of the intellect, which in its inception, and frequently while it goes on, is also spontaneous or indeliberate, finds itself fully endowed with the remarkable power of determining its own acts, the remarkable power of acting freely.

In another way, too, God may be rightly said physically to premove the will to its free action. This premotion has to do with the free act itself. It consists in the predominantly superior, and in that same sense *pre,* or *prior,* motion or action of God, over that of the creature in the production of the creature's free act. For though the creature alone inflows into it as its determining cause, he does so with an utter dependence on the inflow into it of God, as the absolute, essentially independent Lord and Master of all creatures and all their actions. God's supreme dominion over His creatures is in no sense lessened because He has freely granted, to some of them, physical freedom, physical dominion, over some of their actions.

Adversaries

The Bannesians.

Proof of the Thesis

If a physically predetermining concursus destroys man's liberty, and, in the case of sinful acts, makes God the cause of the sinful act, inasmuch as it is sinful, God's concursus with man's free acts cannot physically predetermine them.

But a physically predetermining concursus does this. Therefore.

Maj.—The Major appears to be evident. Nothing that interferes with man's liberty can be admitted. Moreover, as a sin, as such, is the deliberate turning away of an action from God, and in the case of a grievous sin of the sinner also, it is absolutely impossible that God should be the cause of sin as such.

Min.—Part I—*A physically predetermining concursus destroys man's liberty.*

It does so because it makes it absolutely impossible for a man to determine or choose his action, for,

(a) *Without the physical predetermination* it is absolutely impossible for him to do so, for without it he can do nothing.

(b) *With the physical predetermination* it is absolutely impossible for him to do so; for, the physical predetermination by its nature is so connected antecedently with the one determined action for which it was given by God, that it is metaphysically impossible for that action not to follow.

Min.—Part II—*In the case of a sinful action, a physical predetermination makes God the cause of the sinful act, inasmuch as it is a sinful act.*

The one who is culpable in the putting of a sinful act is the one who is the cause of that act inasmuch as it is sinful. Now, he alone is culpable who had the power when he deliberately put the sinful act, not to put it. But the man who is physically predetermined to put an act which is sinful has not that power. It is metaphysically impossible, as we have shown, for him not to put the act. He has no power to choose. The one, therefore, who deliberately and freely gave him the physical predetermination to sin, that is, God, is the one who chose the sinful act, and, hence, is the cause of the sinful act inasmuch as it is sinful.

Scholion—*St. Thomas and physical predetermination.*

Whether or not St. Thomas taught the doctrine of physical predetermination is, as we noted before, a question which has been for years, and still is, hotly disputed. Much has been written in support of both views. In his work, lately published, *Divi Thomae Aquinatis Doctrina de Deo Operante,* Father Stufler, S.J., appears to show quite conclusively that St. Thomas neither taught nor held that opinion. Many passages from St. Thomas' works in support of this view might be cited. The following, very brief ones, from his *Commentary on Peter Lombard's Four Books of Sentences,* will suffice here.

. . . that the will embraces this or that definite act is due to *no other determining cause* than the will itself. (*Op. cit.,* 2, d.39, q.1, a.1.)

Culpability in the commission of a sinful act falls on him who has control over that act. Man, however, has such control owing to the fact that he has a faculty which is capable of doing

many things, *and is determined* to do some one of them *by itself
and only itself.* That faculty is the will. (*Ibid.,* a.2.)

The will in man has the power to determine with what matters other faculties in man shall busy themselves, while *it is
determined by itself alone.* (*Op. cit.,* 3, d.27, q.1, a.4.)

. . . the rational faculty [the will] has the power to opposite
things in matters over which it has control, namely, in those
matters with regard to which *it determines itself.* It has no such
power, however, with regard to those matters which *are determined for it by another.* (*Op. cit.,* 4, d.49, q.1, a.3.)

To these passages, we add, again from countless others
which might be cited, one extrinsic testimony.

Giovanni Cornoldi, S.J., a rather famous Italian philosopher of the nineteenth century, and an ardent disciple of St.
Thomas, writes: "Saint Thomas, in all his works, never, even
once, says expressly that God physically determines the will
to particulars; while a hundred times he expressly and formally teaches that the will determines itself to particulars.
Nay more, he teaches that it is determined by itself precisely
because God does not determine it, as He determines natural things, which, therefore, do not determine themselves."
(*Quale sia la concordia della mozione divina colla libertà
humana,* p. 25).

DIFFICULTIES

1. If God is Lord and Master of man, as man, that is, of
man as a free agent, man's free actions must be physically
predetermined by God. But God is Lord and Master of Man,
as man. Therefore.

N. Maj. The Major is to be denied for the simple reason
that a cause acting freely, yet physically predetermined by another, is an absolute impossibility.

Without any appeal to any kind of predetermination, the
Molinists' explanation of God's concursus fully safeguards God's
supreme dominion, and also man's freedom. The following
statements, to which they subscribe, clearly show this.

(a) Man for his coming into existence, for his continuing in
existence, for the reception of everything necessary for his full
preparation to act freely, among which is the offered and indifferent physical concursus of God, depends utterly and absolutely

on the free will of God, the Supreme Lord and Master of all things.

(b) God, through His *Scientia Media,* and prior to His decree of creation, knowing what every free creature, in whatever circumstances he would be placed, would freely do when so fully prepared, with full knowledge of what the event will be, decrees whatever He pleases concerning the existence of such creatures and all their actions, and all this without in any way interfering with the physical liberty He gives them.

(c) God's efficient inflow into man's free actions, although it is simultaneous with man's, is the inflow of the essentially independent First Cause of all actions and their effects, producing with the free agent the whole entity of the action, inasmuch as it is something and not nothing, and freely granting to the creature the determination or choice of the action, since without this, his action would not be free.

(d) Though God has granted man physical freedom, He has not granted, and it is impossible that He should grant, man moral freedom. Man is ever bound by the moral law. Hence, he is bound to render to God a strict accounting of his use of his great gift of physical freedom. If he has used it well, he will be rewarded. If badly, he will be punished. The final rewards and punishments are eternal.

2. If a creature cannot act freely unless moved thereto by God, and if God not only co-operates with the creature's free action, but is the cause giving the creature the power so to act, God physically predetermines that action. But all this is so. Therefore.

D. Maj. If these conditions are true, and if, moreover, they are fully satisfied without any appeal to physical predetermination, as will be shown immediately, God physically predetermines, etc., *N.*; if these conditions are true, and they can be satisfied only by appealing to physical predetermination, God physically predetermines, *C.—Cd. Min.*

According to the Molinists, who reject the physical predetermination of man's free acts as an absolute impossibility, the conditions mentioned above are fully satisfied by the fact that acting in the light of His knowledge of all things possible, and also in the light of His *Scientia Media—*

(a) God gives to man, and preserves in existence after they are once given, his rational nature, with all the faculties and other active potencies flowing from that nature—one of them being a free will.

(b) By Himself alone or concurring with creatures God gives to man all things necessary to prepare him fully to act freely. Among these things are His offered, indifferent, physical concursus, and especially as fundamentally necessary, the natural impulse which He imprints in man's will towards good in general. For, it is in virtue of this impulse that the will, when the limited good in particular objects is presented to it by the intellect, after tending indeliberately towards such good, and after deliberation on the part of the intellect, initially at least, and frequently while it endures, also indeliberate, finds itself fully prepared to act freely.

(c) He concurs with man in putting the free act, inflowing into it in a pre-eminent way as the First and essentially independent cause of all things, producing the whole entity of the act, in order that it may be rather than not be, and leaving to man the choice or determination of the act.

In all these different ways, then, God moves the creature towards the exercise of his free will, gives him the power to act freely, and co-operates with his free action, but does not physically determine it.

3. If God's concursus is determined by the free action of the creature, the act of the creature, which determines, must be prior to the concursus of God, which is determined. But that is impossible. Therefore.

D. Maj. The act of the creature, looked at merely in its entity or as a thing produced, since it is produced by God and the creature, with mutual dependence on each other, and at the very same time, is prior to the act of God from the viewpoint either of time or dependence, *N.*; the act of the creature, looked at not merely in its entity, or as a thing produced, but as a free act, an act of choice, as this thing produced rather than that, since in this respect the act proceeds from the creature alone, and so the creature determines the concursus of God: in this respect the act of the creature is prior to the concursus of God, *C.—Cd. Min.*

The creature determines the act, for God wishes the act to be the creature's free act. God concurs with the creature in simultaneously putting the whole act which is the determination. Hence, the creature determines God's concursus by putting simultaneously with God *the condition* necessary for that determination, that is, the act which *is* the determination. *As* the determination it is from the creature alone. He alone makes the choice.

4. A faculty which is in a state of indifference with regard to action, cannot act unless it be previously determined by another. But the will when it is about to act freely is in such a state. Therefore.

D. Maj. A faculty which is in a state of passive indifference cannot act unless it be previously determined by another, *C.*; a faculty which is in a state of active indifference, i.e., the will fully prepared to act freely, cannot act unless it be previously determined by another, *Subd.*; unless it be previously determined by another to put the definite act which is its free act, *N.*; unless it be determined by another with regard to whatever is necessary to prepare it fully to act freely, that is, to render it actively in-different and so capable of determining its own free act, *C.—Cd. Min.—D. Cons.*

Some of the Bannesians claim that a physical predetermina-tion is necessary fully to prepare the will to act freely, some others deny this, and say that the physical predetermination is required to move the will, fully prepared to act freely, to the free act. In both cases the act which is supposed to be free, is predetermined absolutely by God, and, consequently cannot be a free act of the will.

The Molinists deny absolutely that the will can be deter-mined by another to put the definite act which is its free act. They admit, however, that the will may be determined by God, either acting alone or concurring with creatures, with regard to all things necessary fully to prepare it to act freely, that is, to render it actively indifferent and so capable of determining its own free action. What those prerequisies are we have shown before, and more than once.

5. If creatures, even free creatures, in the performance of their various actions are but instruments used by God as He pleases, all their actions even free actions, must be abso-lutely determined by God. But creatures, even free creatures, in the performance of their various actions are such instru-ments. Therefore.

D. Maj. If they are instruments in the strict sense of the word, all their actions, etc., *Tr.*; if they are instruments in a broad sense of the word, all their actions, etc., *Subd.*; all necessary actions must be absolutely determined by God, *Tr.*; all free actions must be absolutely determined by God, *N.—C. Min.—D. Con.*

In a broad sense, all creatures using their natural powers may be said to be instruments with regard to God. First, because as secondary causes they all are subordinate to God, the Universal, First Cause; secondly, because all their actions and the effects produced by them are also wholly produced by God; and, thirdly, because God uses them in furthering the designs of His wise providence.

Strictly speaking, however, creatures in the order of secondary causes are both principal and instrumental causes. They are instrumental causes when they are used as subordinate causes by other creatures, the principal causes, in the production under different formalities of actions common to both, but on a plane with the higher perfections of the principal causes. Creatures acting according to their natural powers, and not subordinated as above, are in their own order, principal causes.

With regard to the actions of creatures, either as principal causes, or as instrumental causes, strictly or broadly so called, the following statements are true.

A creature which *is not free,* may be said to have its actions determined by God, inasmuch as God has brought it into existence with a nature which, when conditions necessary for its action are fulfilled, can act in one determined way only. A special physical predetermination by God every time it acts, such as the Bannesians require seems to be altogether useless.

A creature who *is free,* determines his own free action. Determination of them by another, even by God, is absolutely impossible. Our thesis is concerned with free actions only.

6. If physical predetermination is not admitted, God cannot with absolute certainty exercise a wise providence in ordering His creatures and directing them infallibly to the attainment of the end intended by Him in bringing them into existence. But God should be able to do this. Therefore.

D. Maj. He cannot wisely order and direct creatures who are not free, *N.*; creatures who are free, *Subd.*; if the *Scientia Media* is not admitted, that knowledge, namely, by which God prior to His decree of creation knows what each free creature, in no way previously determined, would do in whatever set of circumstances he might be placed by God; if such knowledge is not admitted, God could not wisely order, etc., *C.*; if such knowledge is admitted in God, He cannot wisely, etc., *N.—Cd. Min.*

7. Whatever is moved is moved by another. Therefore the physical predetermination by God even of the free actions of creatures is to be admitted.

D. Ant.—In the sense that nothing so moved has also the power to move itself, *N.*; admitting that a thing so moved, for example, a living thing, may also have the power to move itself, *Subd.*; it is moved by another when its action is necessary, excluding, however, the physical predetermination of the Bannesians, *C.*; it is moved by another in the case of free actions, *Subd.*; it, that is, the will, is moved to pass from the state of remote preparation to the state of full preparation for its free act, by another or others, and especially and necessarily by God, through the natural inclination He has given it towards good in general, as we have already explained, *C.*; it is moved by God in the putting of its free act, *Subd.*; it is in any sense of the word determined by God, *N.*; it is moved by God in the sense that God, putting, but not determining, the free act with the will, inflows into it as the First and essentially independent cause of all things, *C.*

8. If the will alone determines its free actions, and if God, though concurring with them, does not, there is something in the free action which is not caused by God. But that is impossible. Therefore.

D. Maj. If God causes the whole entity by which the will determines itself, there would be something, that is, there would be some absolute entity which would not be caused by God, *N.*; the action, which with regard to its whole entity is produced by both God and the will, would say a different relation towards God from what it says towards the creature, *C.—Cd. Min.*

The determination or choice in a free action is not *in the putting* of the action, but *in the rather putting* of *this* action *than another*. Now, *he only* has the power to choose who, when he puts the action, has the full power to refrain from putting it, or to put another action.

When God, however, concurs with a creature and wishes the creature to act freely, i.e., to choose his action, He concurs as one who has deprived Himself of the power of choosing. Therefore, though He puts the whole action with the creature, He has no part in the *rather putting* of this action than another; no power of choice. Hence, the whole action is put by the creature as a free cause, and the whole action is put by God as a necessary cause. This necessity arises from His prior will to leave to the creature the choice.

9. If physical predetermination is not admitted, God's decree regulating His concursus with man's free actions will necessarily be indeterminate, vague. But God's decree regulating His concursus with man's free actions cannot be indeterminate, vague. Therefore.

N. Maj. God's decree is not indeterminate, either with regard to the concursus it *offers*, which is indifferent, or with regard to the concursus it confers, which is determined.

With regard to His offered (oblatus) concursus, which is indifferent, God's decree is not vague. In this regard, it is formed in the light of His knowledge of all the actions which are of possible choice to the free agents in any definite set of circumstances, and offers to them, in order that their choice of any of them may be possible, His physical concursus indifferently with regard to all of them.

With regard to the concursus it confers, which is determined, God's decree is not vague. In this regard, it is formed in the light of His *Scientia Media,* by which knowledge God knows which action the free creature, when offered God's indifferent physical concursus, would *de facto* choose. It confers God's determined concursus for that act.

10. If God by His decree regulating His concursus with man's free actions, offers to man His physical concursus indifferently with regard to any of the actions man might possibly choose in any definite set of circumstances and leaves to man the actual choice, man has the power to go counter to the will of God. But man has not that power. Therefore.

D. Maj. If God offers by that decree His physical concursus indifferently and by the same decree, inasmuch as it is guided by His *Scientia Media,* God determines absolutely to confer that concursus with the action which He sees the man, placed in those circumstances would freely choose, man has the power to frustrate this consequent and absolute will of God, *N.;* man has the power to frustrate God's antecedent and conditioned will, that is, God's will wishing the man to act in a determined way, if the man also freely wills so to act, *Subd.;* man has the physical power to frustrate this conditioned will of God, *C.*; a man could be found who, though he has the physical power to frustrate this will of God, would *de facto* be morally able to resist every effort of God to bring him freely to choose the action, so conditionally wished by God, *Tr.—Cd. Min.*

The last part of this solution is fully explained in *Thesis I*, at the end of the answer to *Difficulty 15*.

11. If God's decree regulating His concursus with man's free acts confers only one determined concursus, that, namely, which man determines, there appears to be no reason why it should offer indifferently God's physical concursus with the other acts of possible choice to this man at that time. But God's decree regulating His concursus with man's free acts confers only one determined concursus, that, namely, which man determines. Therefore.

D. Maj. There would be no reason if without such offer man would fully be prepared to choose any one of the acts said to be of possible choice to him at that time, *C.*; if without such offer he would not be fully prepared, etc., *N.—D. Cons.*

Thesis VI

God governs all creatures, both collectively and individually, and in a special way, all rational creatures, with a wise providence.

Prenotes to the Thesis

The absolute necessity of the continual, immediate, physical inflowing of God's omnipotent power into every creature, giving it being, preserving it in being, and producing with it its every action, shows clearly the utter nothingness of contingent being left to itself. It shows, too, with equal clearness, the supreme and absolute dominion of God over creatures.

Having proved all these points, we wish, by going a step farther, to show in our present thesis that, whilst God rules the world with absolute right, He rules it also, in consonance with other divine perfections, with an all-embracing, wise providence.

Now, though it is true that this bare conclusion might be easily derived, as a corollary, from other theses of our Natural Theology, the importance of the matter demands the fuller treatment leading up to formal and explicit proof, which a thesis development permits. For, without such treatment, neither the nature nor the many divisions of God's providence in governing this concrete world could be understood as they should be, nor could the principles required for the solution of the many practical difficulties urged against it be properly explained. Indeed, some of these difficulties, namely, those arising from the presence of evil in the word, physical and especially moral, appear to so many, both learned and unlearned, to be insoluble, or so all but insoluble, that we shall devote the thesis which follows (*Thesis VII*) to their consideration and refutation.

The term, *Divine Providence,* like that of providence in general, may be used in a strict or in broad sense. Strictly

154

taken, it excludes divine government; broadly taken, it includes it.

Divine Providence, in the strict sense, is defined by St. Thomas, as "the plan of the order of things foreordained [by God] towards an end." (*Summa Theologica,* I, q.22, a.3.) In other words, it is the act of the divine intellect which plans from all eternity the ordering of all creatures, to be brought into existence, for the attaining of the subordinate ends proper to each one of them, and the absolutely final end common to all, determined on by God as the goal towards which, in accordance with this, His eternal plan, they are to be variously directed by Him.

It is to be noted in general, that the planning or ordering of means to an end may be of two kinds, speculative or practical. A speculative planning is the intellectual ordering of means to an end, which might be, but is not intended. A practical planning is the ordering of means to an end which is intended.

The practical intellect differs in its end from the speculative, as the Philosopher says. The practical intellect is ordered to the end of the operation, whereas the end of the speculative intellect is the consideration of truth. Hence, if any builder should consider how a house can be made, not ordering this to the end of his operation, but only to know how to do it, this would only be a speculative consideration as regards the end, although it concerns an operable thing. (St. Thomas, *Summa Theologica,* I, q.14, a.16.)

Providence, therefore, as a practical planning, a planning for an end intended, includes not only the act of the intellect planning, but also the act of the will intending both the end for which the planning is done and the following of the plan in reaching it. Consequently:

Divine Providence, in the strict sense, may be defined more explicitly as the plan of the divine intellect by which God from all eternity wisely orders all things for the attainment of their end, and especially their absolutely last end; and the act of the divine will intending the existence of creatures, the ends to be attained by them, and the carrying out of the plan in accordance with which they are to attain those ends.

It is evident from this definition that God's providence is that of a Ruler planning for the attainment of their end by his subjects, and not that of an individual ordering his own acts for the proper attainment of an end desired. For, says St. Thomas:

It belongs to Prudence [i.e., Providence] according to the Philosopher, to order things towards an end, whether in regard to oneself—as, for instance, a man is said to be prudent, who orders well his acts towards the end of life—or in regard to others, subject to him, in a family, city, or kingdom. . . . In this way Prudence or Providence may suitably be attributed to God. For in God Himself there can be nothing ordered to an end, since He is the last end of all. This reason of order in things towards an end is, therefore, in God called Providence. Whence Boethius says that 'Providence is the Divine reason itself, sealed in the Supreme Ruler; which disposeth all things.' Disposition may be said to be the reason of things towards an end, and the reason of the order of parts in the whole. (*Summa Theologica*, I, q.22, a.1.)

Divine government is the actual direction in time by God of creatures, towards their end and especially towards their last end, in accordance with the pre-ordained eternal plan of His practical intellect. Therefore: *Divine Providence, strictly so called*, is eternal; *Divine government* is temporal. *Divine providence, broadly so called*, as we noted above, includes divine providence, strictly so called, and divine government.

Two things pertain to the care of providence—namely, the reason [plan] of order, which is called Providence; and the execution of the order, which is termed government. Of these, the first is eternal; and the second is temporal. (St. Thomas, *Summa Theologica*, I, q.22, a.1.)

Divine Providence, strictly so called, or the practical planning of the order of the world is, then, eternal, and is due to God alone. It regards all creatures immediately, not only in general but also in particular, even to the lowest.

In the following passages St. Thomas touches on these points.

God has immediate knowledge of individuals, as knowing them not merely in their causes, but also in themselves. . . . Now, it would seem unreasonable, if, knowing individuals, He did not desire their order wherein the chief good of things consists, since His will is the source of all goodness. Consequently, even as He knows individuals immediately, so does He establish order among them immediately. (*Summa Contra Gentiles,* Book 3, c.76.)

It is evident that the individual [not man as a person] is for the sake of the universal nature. . . . Now, since providence has the ordering of things to their end, it follows that to providence belong both the ends and things directed to the end. Therefore, not only universals but also individuals are subject to divine providence. . . . Providence belongs to practical knowledge, since it directs things to their end. Therefore, God's providence would be imperfect if it extended no further than universals and reached not the individual. (*Op. cit.* Book 3, c.75.)

Divine Providence, in the strict sense, or God's eternal plan of the ordered universe, provides for the exercise in time, on the part of rational creatures, of both providence and government, both with regard to themselves and to others.

The rational creature is subject to divine providence in such a way, that not only is it governed thereby, but is able to know something of the nature of providence; so that it is capable of providence and government in respect to others. . . . Now, through being capable of providence, a man can direct and govern his own actions also. Therefore the rational creature participates in divine providence not only in being governed but also in governing: for it governs itself in its own actions, and other things, too. Now, every lower providence is subject to divine providence as supreme. Therefore the government of a rational creature's acts, as personal acts, belongs to divine providence. (St. Thomas, *op. cit.,* Book 3, c.113.)

Divine government, or the actual carrying out by God of His eternal plan of the ordered world, which, as noted above, is not eternal but in time, directs all creatures to their various ends, in general and also in particular. In this direction it also is immediate.

Divine government, differs, however, from the divine planning in this, that God is not alone in executing His plan. He uses creatures, as for instance, as we saw above, man, in exercising providence and government towards himself and others. God uses all other creatures, with whom He

concurs physically and immediately, directing them towards
their various ends. Though God's government, then, is immediate in the sense that He immediately directs even the
smallest individual thing to its end in its every action, it
may be said to be mediate in the sense that God makes use
of creatures, man and creatures inferior to man, in many
and countless ways as *means* in directing others to the end
for which all were made by Him.

As regards . . . the plan of the order of things foreordained
to an end . . . God has immediate provision over everything, even
the smallest; . . . as to the extension of this order . . . there are
certain intermediaries of Divine Providence; for He governs
things inferior by superior, not on account of any defect in His
power, but by reason of the abundance of His goodness; so that
the dignity of causality is imparted even to creatures. . . . God's
immediate providence over everything does not exclude the
action of secondary causes, which are the executors of His order.
(St. Thomas, *Summa Theologica*, I, q.22, a.3.)

*The kind of intention, to achieve an end planned, which
providence demands.*

The intention, which one who is truly provident has, to
achieve an end planned, must be a serious one. It is not,
however, in general, necessary that it be an absolute one.
It may be conditioned; conditioned, for example, as it is
in many instances, on the free co-operation of another, or
others, in bringing about the end desired. In which case,
however, the one primarily desiring the end must have an
absolute intention of supplying all the means within his
disposal, which are necessary for the attaining of the end,
on the part of the one, or the many, co-operating.

In this way a father acts with a wise providence, who is
desirous that his son should be a Religious. He plans, and
has a serious intention, which is absolute, of supplying all
the means within his power which are necessary for the
achievement by the son of the end desired. The achievement
itself he desires seriously, but only conditionally; on the condition, namely, that it be the untrammeled choice also of
his son's free will.

The various ends which God, in His wise providence over
the world, intends, are willed by Him, some absolutely, and

some conditioned on man's free concurrence with Him in bringing them about. More will be said on these points presently. What we have to say, however, will be better understood after we have noted briefly some of the more important divisions of God's providence in the present order of things. These divisions, it should be understood, are made by our limited intellects for the sake of clearness, and in no way go counter to God's absolute simplicity.

Some divisions of God's providence in the present order of things.

God's providence may be looked at under the following aspects:

God's Universal Providence—Under this aspect God's providence consists in the practical ordering in the mind of God, of all the creatures who will ever exist in the world, for the attaining of the common end for which He made them. All are considered as parts of the world taken as a whole—the Universe. This universal ordering, therefore, has to do with the stupendous subordination and co-ordination of the innumerable individuals, species, genera, and kingdoms of the world, for the attainment of the absolutely last end of all things created.

God's Particular Providence. To God's particular providence belongs the practical ordering in the mind of God, of all things for the attainment of the different particular ends proper to them. It is concerned with each individual thing in the world, and with the well-being of all the particular groups of beings which go to make up the world, looked at as a whole.

All things are subject to Divine Providence; not only in general, but even in their own individual selves. This is clear; for since every agent acts for an end, the arrangement of effects towards that end extends as far as the causality of the first agent extends. . . . But the causality of God, who is the first agent, extends to all being, not only as to the constituent principles of species, but also as to the individualizing principles. . . . Hence, all things that exist in whatsoever manner are necessarily directed by God to some end. . . . Since, therefore, as the Providence of God is nothing less than the reason of the order of things towards an end, as we have said, it necessarily follows that all things inasmuch as they participate existence, must likewise be subject to Divine Providence. It has also been shown that God knows all things, both universal and particular. Since His knowledge may be compared to the things themselves as the knowledge of art to the objects of art, all things must of necessity come under His plan; as all things wrought by art are subject to the rules of art. (St. Thomas, *Summa Theologica*, I, q.22, a.2.)

Looked at under another aspect, God's providence may be divided into *Physical* and *Moral*. This division is based on the difference in the means, which God from eternity plans to use, in providing respectively for the existence and physical well-being of His whole marvelously ordered creation, and for the moral well-being of a part of it, namely, man, its crowning glory. Hence:

God's Physical Providence is concerned with the means God will use to bring all creatures, including man, to the various ends natural to them; not, however, man as an intelligent being, but only inasmuch as he shares the nature and activities of the creatures inferior to him.

These means in general are: God's initial, creative selection of the various elements constituting the world, and determination of their quantity, various proportions, and collocation; His establishment of the physical laws governing the action and interaction of the various forces and powers natural to those elements; His continual preservation of them and all their forces and powers in being, and His continual, immediate, physical concurrence with them in all their actions even the smallest.

The result, then, of God's physical providence, which *de facto* is none other than the general providence we speak of in the enunciation of our thesis, is this ordered world of countless creatures and countless combinations of creatures, tending unceasingly, in virtue of His preserving and concurring action, towards the ends planned for them, individually and collectively, from all eternity.

A consideration of this result, explainable only on the hypothesis that it was brought about by a supremely wise, by a designing mind, constitutes *de facto* the *a posteriori* proof for the first part of our thesis. It is to be noted, however, that this argument taken alone does not prove the intelligence of the cause of the world-order to be infinite.

The following fuller description of that order will show clearly that only a designing mind of vast intelligence could have produced it. That it could have happened by chance, the only other alternative, is unthinkable.

The natural sciences without exception, and one's own contemplation of nature give indubitable testimony to the presence in the world of an—

Order. In the world there are innumerable beings; great and small, simple and composed of many elements and many parts; of varying degrees of perfection, non-living and living, plants, animals, man. All of these beings are so marvelously arranged, both with regard to their parts and amongst themselves, that, mutually supplying to one another all those things which are necessary for the proper performance of each one's special work, the lower continually serve the higher, and the higher, those still higher; and so are perpetuated the numberless species and genera in the various kingdoms that give us our *mundus,* our *cosmos,* our *universe.*

Most widespread. In the various kingdoms which constitute our world are innumerable individuals of innumerable species and innumerable genera; all are subject to Nature's laws; order reigns supreme.

Most complicated. The world order is produced—

1. By many elements in innumerable and complicated combinations.

2. By countless individual, efficient agents of numberless species and genera.

3. Under conditions innumerable, ever-varying and most complicated; the individual substances being subject to constant changes both accidental and substantial.

The result of all this is an order of the *greatest stability* founded on *the maximum of instability.* For, whilst kingdoms, genera, species, and the apt combination of elements endure, the elements themselves are in constant flux resulting from the action of mechanical, physical, and chemical forces operating either in their own spheres or as vitally elevated. Everywhere is found local motion, and, what is of deeper import, everywhere the destruction of inferior beings, that superior beings may exist, and, in turn, the return everywhere of superior beings, in part at least, to the earth from which that part was taken, lest, the inorganic kingdom being depleted, life vanish from the earth and death reign supreme.

Furthermore, if we consider the organic world only, and restrict our inquiry to creatures endowed with the higher forms of plant or animal life, we shall find in each of them (in some, however, more than in others), an adaptation of part to part, and function to function, most complicated. How many and varied the organs, and how marvelously united; how many and varied the functions and how perfectly co-ordinated and subordinated; in order that a living being of one of the higher species nourish itself; grow, and perfect itself; give birth to others like unto itself; defend itself against hostile forces of nature; expel whatever could be harmful to it; repair injuries, and through its mysterious sensitive faculties put itself in touch with the visible world about it.

Most constant. Not merely for days, nor weeks, nor months, nor years, but for centuries, with unfailing regularity, the countless changes and combinations which give us our world-order have been produced by Nature's forces. (*God and Reason,* pp. 116ff.)

Truly God's physical providence over the world is marvelous.

God's Moral Providence is the practical, eternal ordering in the mind of God of the means by which man, as an intelligent and free agent, in time, and under the wise government of God, will be able to live conformably to his nature, and so, if he freely wills to use the means God places at his disposal, reach the end for which God made him. And this—perfect happiness, commensurate with his merits, in the secure possession of God in knowledge and love for all eternity. This possession, as we know from Divine Revelation, is to be a supernatural one. One, namely, which human nature left to itself could never merit, never enjoy—the Beatific Vision; the immediate, or face-to-face, seeing, and consequent loving of God for all eternity by the supernaturally illumined soul.

As the means, however, eternally ordained by God for the attainment of this supernatural end, are both natural and supernatural, God's moral providence which orders them is both natural and supernatural. Now, though as philosophers we are concerned only with God's natural providence, its intimate connection with His supernatural providence justifies, we think, the few remarks we shall make about the latter, farther on. This intimate connection between the natural and the supernatural is twofold. *In the first place,* unaided reason, through means which God in His natural providence has given man for that purpose, can discover (it does so scientifically in Fundamental Theology, which follows reason as a guide) the fact of a Divine Revelation and the other supernatural truths connected with it. *Secondly,* the proper use by man of the natural means which God has given him to live conformably to his nature will surely be rewarded by the gift from God of the supernatural means necessary for the attainment of his supernatural end. Before enumerating, however, some of these means, both natural and supernatural, it will be helpful to consider not only the end for which God created man, but also the end which God wishes to attain in creating the whole visible universe, man included. (Our concern as philosophers is only with this visible creation; reason tells us nothing of an angelic one.)

God moved by His own infinite Goodness, not for the sake of increasing it—it is infinite—but for the sake of communicating it to His creatures, in order that possessing it they, and in a special way, man, might make it manifest, brought the world freely into existence. This communication of His Goodness to His creatures does not mean—it could not mean—that creatures participate in the very Goodness of God. It does mean, however, that, as concrete and actual, though finite, imitations of that Goodness, their creative cause, creatures in imitation possess, and possessing manifest, as God intended them to do, in their being and actions, in varying degrees, something of the endlessly imitable Perfection of God, the Source of all their perfections.

God, then, made creatures in order that His own, His internal glory, might be made manifest through them, and so a definite amount of external glory be given Him. This is the primary end intended by God in creating the world.

A brief explanation of the nature of glory, its various divisions, and their application to God and His creation will help to a better understanding of these points.

Formal glory: that is, glory properly so called, is the due appreciation of the excellence of anyone.

Objective glory: is the goodness or excellence of anyone, inasmuch as it is an object worthy of such appreciation.

Both may be internal and external.

Internal formal glory is the due appreciation by one of one's own goodness or excellence. If the appreciation is by another, it is *external formal glory.*

Internal objective glory is the goodness or excellence of a being manifested in himself, inasmuch as it is worthy of due appreciation by himself or others. If the goodness be manifested *in* another, *it is external objective glory.*

We may now apply these divisions to God and His creatures.

God's internal formal glory is God's infinite appreciation, in infinite knowledge and love, of His own infinite Goodness.

God's internal objective glory is the infinite Goodness of God, inasmuch as it is an object worthy of infinite appreciation on the part of God, and the highest kind of appreciation on the part of man. (It is to be noted again, that we are concerned only with this visible universe, of which man is the crowning glory.)

God's external formal glory is the due appreciation on the part of man of the infinite goodness of God his Creator. This due appreciation is based on the knowledge of God's infinite perfection, an appreciation which man gathers from a study of the stupendously ordered world he sees round about him. He finds himself master of it all. All other creatures are there to serve him. His mastership, however, he soon discovers to be a stewardship, for he himself, and the world he controls—all, all owe everything they are, and have, and can do, to the all-wise, all-powerful, all-loving God, who made them; whose law is to be obeyed; and to whom an account of his stewardship is to be rendered when demanded.

Man, therefore, rising from creatures to a knowledge of the Creator of them, and acknowledging His infinite perfection and absolute Lordship over them, realizes that the true purpose of his life, the end for which God made him, is to praise and reverence and serve God, in thought and word and deed, in humble adoration—the supremest act of service, reserved for the All-mighty alone—and by so doing to receive the reward promised him for that faithful service. And that reward, his very nature, which seeks for perfect happiness, tells him he will find in the secure possession of God, in knowledge and love, for all eternity. This possession, as we noted before, Divine Revelation tells us will be a supernatural one—seeing God endlessly, face-to-face, in the Beatific Vision. That all men may enjoy this everlasting reward, is the secondary end God had in creating this world of ours.

God's external objective glory is found in the goodness and excellence of the wonderfully-ordered visible world, all the creatures of which, wholly dependent on God their Creator and showing forth in innumerable ways His infinite perfections, give to man, as God intended them to do, abundant reason for acknowledging His transcendent glory.

God's primary end, then, in creating the world, moved thereto by His own infinite Goodness, was to manifest through creatures, in a definite degree, His own intrinsic objective glory. This end God intends absolutely. He will attain it no matter how man makes use of his liberty. Though each individual man is free to sin when occasion offers, and even to die in sin, by so acting he in no way diminishes the definite degree of external glory absolutely willed by God. When he sins, his sinning, during life, is taken by God as an occasion for obtaining in various ways, through the sinner himself or through others, compensating formal glory. The same is true if he dies in God's enmity. He will suffer for all eternity, and so will glorify God for all eternity, not formally but objectively, giving to others a reason for formally glorifying God in His Justice forever.

The secondary end God had in creating the world was man's eternal happiness. This end God wills not absolutely but conditionally; on condition, namely, that man himself freely wishes to use the means God gives him for the attainment of that happiness. If he makes use of them, and perseveres in well-doing, he will glorify God formally, seeing Him face-to-face in the Beatific Vision forever. If he rejects those means, and perseveres in his sin, he will, as we said above, in punishment glorify God's justice for all eternity, not formally, but objectively, as an object namely, for its formal glorification eternally by others.

Some of the helps which God, in His moral providence, has arranged to direct man to the attainment of the end for which he was created.

Among the *natural* helps, first in importance is the natural law, which is none other than the eternal, necessary (supposing the decree of creation) Divine Law, imprinted in the very nature of man, and manifested to him by the natural light of reason, commanding him to do good and avoid evil, that is, to live conformably to his human nature looked at in its essential relations to God, to himself, and to his fellow men and all other creatures. Other helps are the laws governing domestic and civil societies; the sanctions of reward and punishment which the natural and other laws demand; the voice of conscience warning in individual cases that this must be done and that left undone; the peace of soul and the joy which follow from heeding that voice, and the remorse and sorrow from not doing so; the desire of being esteemed by the good and the fear of losing that esteem; all nature inasmuch as it leads man to acknowledge the existence of God, and the duty of praising, reverencing, and serving Him; the trials and troubles of life as opportunities of practising the moral virtues, especially fortitude, patience, charity, and resignation to the will of God; and all the innumerable illuminations of intellect and strengthenings of will in individual cases to help those in need of them to meet successfully their various personal trials.

An explanation of the nature of the various kinds of means prepared by God in His providence for man's attainment of the supernatural end for which he was created, and of the way in which they, and the natural means fulfill God's purpose, belongs to Dogmatic Theology. Saying nothing of these points, therefore, we note merely a few of those supernatural means; miracles, Divine Revelation, the Incarnation, the Birth and Redeeming Sufferings and Death of Jesus Christ Our Savior; the sending of the Holy Ghost; the Church; the Sacraments; Sanctifying Grace; the Super-

natural Virtues; all the innumerable actual graces, both internal and external, supernatural in their essence or only in
the manner of their giving, all calling on man, even until
the last moment of his conscious life, to serve God, and, if
he has perhaps lost God's friendship, to return to Him.

Another division of God's province into *antecedent* and
consequent, will help us not a little to a better understanding of the nature of God's providence and in solving many
difficulties urged against it.

God's Antecedent Providence is His providence inasmuch
as it proceeds from His antecedent will; His will, namely,
to act this or that way with regard to His creatures, which
is formed *prior* to, and hence, prescinding from, or independently of His foreknowledge of the way in which man
will use his freedom. This will of God may be *absolute* or
conditioned.

God's Consequent Providence is His providence inasmuch as it proceeds from His consequent will; His will,
namely, to act this or that way with regard to His creatures,
which is formed posterior to, and hence, dependently on
His foreknowledge, through His *Scientia Media,* of the way
in which man will use his freedom. This will of God's is
always absolute.

*How God's own external glory in general, and man's final
state of salvation or non-salvation fall under the providential
will of God.*

In man, knowing precedes willing. This priority is real.
In God, who is absolutely simple (proven in *God Infinite and
Reason*), there is only one act; the act by which God *Is,*
which is God. By this same act, however, God not only is,
but also knows and wills. Though there is no real priority,
then, between God's knowing and willing, still the infinite
perfection of His one act, in an infinitely more perfect way,
supplies for God's knowing and willing, what a real priority,
between similar actions in man supplies. As a consequence,
for the sake of clearness in our limited knowledge, we look
on God's act of knowing as though it preceded His act of
willing.

With this distinction in mind, the following answers

to the two questions proposed above will be more easily understood.

1. *How God's external glory in general falls under His providential will.*

Prior to His creative will, God's infinite knowledge had for its object, besides Himself, every being of possible existence, every possible moment and circumstance of such existence, including every possible necessary and free action of every being, and every free action, from among the possible ones, which every free being would put, in any world He might wish to create. His infinite knowledge, then, at this stage, embraced every possible combination of all possible beings—all possible worlds, and the definite degree of extrinsic glory which each, if created, would give Him.

In the light of this infinite knowledge, with an absolute will, God freely decreed the existence of one of those possible worlds, the present world, as ordered to give Him the definite amount of external glory He desired in creating it. This will of God, however, though absolute with regard to the definite amount of external glory He would obtain, with regard to the means and manner of its obtaining, was not in every case absolute. What it was with regard to man's salvation or non-salvation in the present order, in which man was created for a supernatural end, which is the second question we wish to answer, and what it was with regard to some other particulars of deep concern to man, will now be briefly told.

2. *How man's final state of salvation or non-salvation in the present order falls under God's providential will.*

For the sake of greater clearness we divide our answer as follows:

(a) *With an antecedent and conditioned will God sincerely desires the final, eternal happiness of all rational creatures who are able to use their reason.*

This will of God is formed antecedently to His foreknowledge of the final state in which man, by the good or bad use of his free will, will die. It is not an absolute will on the part of God, but conditioned; conditioned, namely, on the free co-operation on the part of the creature with

the aids God gives him to save his own soul. Whilst this will
of God is conditioned, therefore, with regard to the actual
obtaining of salvation by man, it is in no sense conditioned
with regard to the giving by God to all men the means by
which they may, if they will, obtain salvation. Up to the very
last moment of his life, then, no matter what that life has
been, God wills absolutely to give, and does give him grace
sufficient for the saving of his soul. And up to the same very
last moment He wills conditionally the eternal salvation of
that soul, the condition being that the man has used, or, if
necessary, will use the grace sufficient for the saving of his
own soul—a grace which God gives everyone who has the
use of his reason.

(b) *God wills with an antecedent and conditioned will
the eternal salvation of all infants, and all adults who have
never had the use of their reason.*

This will of God is formed antecedently to His foreknowledge of the state, either of sanctifying grace or original
sin, in which such infant or adult will die, as the result respectively of the care or want of care of those on whom
normally (the charity of others might supply for such negligence), proximately or remotely, it depended to provide for
the actual reception by such infants or adults of the means
necessary (according to the Christian Law—Baptism) for their
salvation.

This will of God, then, though conditioned on the co-
operation of man for the actual reception of the means
necessary for the salvation of such infants or adults, is absolute with regard to the giving to all concerned everything
necessary for the supplying of those means. As a consequence,
if such infants or adults are not saved, it is due in some way
or other to man's negligence. It is hard to say, at times, and
the matter strictly speaking is outside the province of philosophy, just who was negligent, or what that negligence was.

(c) *God's providential will and the distribution in general of His actual aids towards man's salvation.*

With an absolute will, which is some cases is antecedent
to, and in other cases, consequent on His foreknowledge of
the way in which man will make use of his liberty, God
grants different actual means for the attainment of salvation

to different men. It belongs, however, to his antecedent and absolute providence, to provide all men at all times with actual means sufficient for the obeying of His law, and so, for the saving of their souls:

(d) *God's providential will and man's morally evil actions.*

Consequent on His foreknowledge of the sins men will commit in the world He wishes to create, God wills absolutely to permit those sins. It is to be clearly noted, that God does not will the sin, but only its permission. It is to be further noted, that this permission is what is technically called a *simple* permission, *merely* a permission and nothing more. What conditions must be fulfilled in order that a permission be a *simple* one, will be noted in *Thesis VII,* which will formally consider God's providence in its relation to the physical and moral evil in the world. Another point to be noted, and an important one, which also will be more carefully considered in *Thesis VII,* is that God's infinite perfection makes it impossible for Him to permit, even simply, moral evil, unless He foresaw that such permission could and would be made the occasion for the obtaining of some compensating good in the moral order. Otherwise man could put innumerable actions from which, even indirectly, God would derive no external glory. God's infinite perfection, however, requires that every action of His creatures should tend, either directly or indirectly, towards that end.

(e) *God's providential will and man's final state after death.*

Consequent on His foreknowledge of the state in which man, having the use of reason, as a result of his own deliberate choosing, will die, namely, as a friend of God, in the state of sanctifying grace, or as an enemy of God, in the state of personal grievous sin, God wills with an absolute will the eternal happiness of the former, and the eternal punishment of the latter. This eternal happiness, the end for which man was made in this world of ours, is, as we have already noted more than once, a supernatural one, consisting essentially in the Beatific Vision, the seeing of God face-to-face, and in loving Him for all eternity.

Infants and those adults who never had the use of reason, and who have received Baptism, will enjoy, as the result of God's absolute will, the Beatific Vision forever. As the result *of the same will,* however, those who have not been baptised, and who, consequently, not through their own fault, but through the carelessness in some way or other, of those who should have seen to it, die deprived of sanctifying grace and in the state of original sin, will never enjoy the Beatific Vision. Their state, however, for all eternity will not be one of punishment, but of natural happiness, knowing God with a natural knowledge and loving and praising Him for all eternity.*

It may be well to note finally, that when speaking of God's natural providence, His physical providence is called His general providence; His moral providence, His special providence. When speaking of His supernatural providence, His special providence is that which He has for the Elect.

Adversaries

Against this thesis, as direct or indirect adversaries, may be cited in addition to the Fatalists, all the Adversaries mentioned in *Thesis III.* What is said there of the Deists, who directly reject our present thesis either wholly or in part, is to be carefully noted. It may be well to mention that Evolutionists, with few exceptions, directly reject our thesis. For, denying any validity to the *Teleological Argument,* they insist that the order of this visible universe is due to chance and not to the wise planning of God. (Cf. *God and Reason, Thesis VI.*)

Proof of the Thesis

Prenote to the Proof: In proving our thesis we divide it into two parts. The question of God's providence, as it concerns man considered as an intelligent being, is treated only and solely in the second part. The first part, therefore, with its proofs, prescinds altogether from that aspect of God's providence. It may be well to note, however, that the *a priori* proof used in the first part, proves both parts of the thesis.

* For further information on this point—this whole matter strictly does not belong to philosophy—see Sasia, S.J., *The Future Life,* pp. 289ff.

PART I—*God governs all creatures, both collectively and individually taken, with a wise providence.*

He governs all creatures, taken both collectively and individually, with a wise providence, *who* for the attainment of the best possible end, ordains all creatures, collectively and individually, in a most marvelous way, and continually directs them, according to their different natures to the attainment of that end.

But God so acts. Therefore.

MAJ.—The Major is evident from the definition of providence, taken in its broad sense.

MIN. (A)—*For the attainment of the best possible end God orders all creatures collectively and individually, in a most marvelous manner.*

1—*A priori:* The end for which God, moved by His own infinite Goodness, brought creatures into existence is His own external glory—the highest possible end. His infinite wisdom ordered creatures according to their needs, collectively and individually, for the attainment of that end. It is necessarily attained, therefore, through His infinite power, not merely in a most marvelous way, but in relatively the best possible way.

2—*A posteriori:* An examination of the universal, complicated, constant action and interaction of the innumerable beings comprising the world, resulting in an order equally universal, complicated, and constant; its beauty the despair of poet and painter; its mysteries the age-old, and still enduring study of countless sciences, led us to the conclusions, in the *Teleological Argument* (*God and Reason, Thesis VI*), that its explanation was to be found only on the supposition that, before the world existed, its creator, God, in His wisdom planned most carefully the countless ways in which the beings were to compose it were to be arranged and ordered, singly and collectively, for the attainment of the various subordinate ends and the common ultimate end for which He had determined to make them. And a further examination of that order tells us what that ultimate end was. It tells us that all creatures in the world, lower than man, were made proximately to supply him with everything necessary for his bodily welfare and comfort. But above all, and ultimately, by manifesting in their bewildering perfections something of the glory of their Maker, they were to bring man to a knowledge of His existence, His transcendent perfections, His supreme lordship over the world, and man's own duty, as an utter dependent, to praise and reverence and serve Him in this life, that so doing he might possess Him in knowledge and love and glorify Him for all eternity.

In other words, a consideration of the world-order leads us to the conclusion, that—for the attainment of the best possible end, His external glory—God ordered all creatures collectively and individually in a most marvelous way.

Min. (B)—*God continually directs all creatures, collectively and individually, according to their natures to the attainment of the end for which He made them.*

Every creature because of its nature as a contingent being, necessarily depends on the immediate inflowing of God's physical causality into its very being, in order that it may begin to be; on the continual inflowing of the same causality, in order that it may continue to be; and on the immediate co-operation of that same causality, in every action it performs, no matter how small it may be. In this co-operation of God with His creatures, both God and creature as immediate, physical, efficient causes, produce each the whole act; God as Supreme, First, Universal Cause, inasmuch as the act is something; the creature as a subordinate, secondary, particular cause, inasmuch as it is *this* or *that* thing, *this* or *that* act.

In this way by His continual inflowing of existence into them and His continual physical concursus or co-operation in all their actions, God directs all creatures inferior to man, that is, all creatures not endowed with free will, and all their actions to the attainment of the several ends for which God made them. By the same physical preserving power and concursus God also directs all the necessary or non-free actions of man, and man so acting, to their ends.

How God directs man's free actions towards the end for which He created man, is considered in the following proof.

PART II—*God in a special way governs all rational creatures with a wise providence.*

If man as an intelligent and free being, essentially different from other beings in the world; is naturally exposed to a serious danger to which they are not exposed; is immeasurably superior to them in perfection, and closer and dearer to God, God in His wise providence, in a special way governs all rational creatures.

But all this is true of man. Therefore.

MAJ.—The Major appears to be immediately evident. A wise, and, *a fortiori*, an infinitely wise providence, such as God's is, proportions the means it prepares for the attainment of an end, to the objective state of those to be cared for. Wherefore, that special care, where those to be cared for—essentially different from others—are naturally exposed to a serious danger to which the others are *not* exposed; where those to be cared for are superior to others in perfection, and are closer and nearer to God.

MIN. (A)—*Man, as an intelligent and free being, is essentially different from other beings in the world.*

All creatures in the world, except man, are determined by their nature, in *all* their actions, towards the ends providentially ordered for them by God, and are directed towards those ends by God, physically and continually preserving them in being, and in their actions continuously concurring with them. Man, however, as an intelligent and free being, acts in an essentially different way. When he exercises his free will, that is, when he acts as a rational creature, his actions are not determined by his nature, nor are they determined or directed towards their ends by God physically concurring with them. For, although man, like other creatures, is preserved continually in being by God, and requires God's physical co-operation in all his free actions, still God does not, on that account determine those free actions, does not direct them to the ends for which they are put. Man, with God physically concurring, and man alone, determines them and directs them to the ends he chooses, and that, because God has given him the gift of physical freedom in his deliberate, his human actions.

God, nevertheless, does exercise over man's free actions a directive influence through His moral providence, urging him ever, and without prejudice to his physical liberty, to do good and avoid evil. This is God's special providence over man, wisely planned, as the following reasons show.

Min. (B)—*Man, by his nature, as an intelligent and free being, is exposed to a serious danger to which others are not exposed, and so needs special help from God.*

Unlike other creatures, man, by reason of the physical freedom which is his, can refuse to strive for the end for which God made him, and so make a failure of his existence. There are many forces within and without him continually urging him to do so. God, then, who wants man's free service with victory over those forces, comes to man's assistance in a special way through His moral providence, and without prejudice to man's freedom, endeavors continually in countless ways to lead him to victory. Notwithstanding these aids generously given, man, sad to say, frequently rejects them and refuses God the service due Him. How these refusals, morally evil acts, fall under God's moral providence will be considered in our *Thesis VII*, which treats of God's providence in relation to moral and physical world-evil.

Min. (C)—*Man by nature excels in perfection all other creatures in the world and so is closer and dearer to God than they are.*

Man, by reason of his spiritual soul is much closer to God in perfection than other creatures. In man's soul God is said to be made manifest as in an image. Now, though this image is most certainly but a finite, imperfect representation of God's infinite perfection, still in it God is revealed much more perfectly than in other creatures, in whom is found, it is said, but a trace of His perfections. The likeness in man's soul to God, which is a specific rather than a generic one, and which merits the name *image,* is found in this, that the soul of man is spirit, and understands and wills, and so, in a high degree, imitates, and is like to God, who is Spirit and Intellect and Will. And, what is more, as God knows and loves Himself, so man can know and love God. Again, man is the only creature in the world, of whose actions, as *his* actions, God has a providential care, and the only creature in the world who is like to God, in that he is capable of exercising providence and government. This he does not only in regard to his own actions, but also with regard to all other creatures, and even other men.

Man, moreover is the crowning glory of this visible
X creation. All other creatures are made by God for man, to aid him materially, and more than all, to lead him to a knowledge of God, of his own and of all other creatures' utter dependence on God, and, consequently, of the duty he has in this life, in thought and word and deed, to reverence and praise God, and to serve Him with a service of adoration. Though all other creatures in the world, then, are made to serve man, man it not their absolute master but only a steward in the service of God, to whom he will have to give an account of his stewardship. It is for man, therefore, by his right use of creatures to convert the objective glory that all other creatures give to God into formal glory, knowing, loving, and serving Him, and thus attaining, not here but hereafter, the end for which he was made. And that end— God Himself.

The crowning excellence, then, of man, above all other
X creatures, consists in this, that whereas all other creatures are for man, and through man for God, man is the only creature in this visible world who is made for God alone. Man is the only creature whose last end, to be freely gained, but by many lost, is to be united with God; the only creature to whom is offered the great reward of knowing and loving and being loved by God in a friendship for all eternity.

For these reasons, and for others, God has a special care of man, expressed in many ways, through His special, His moral providence. What some of these ways are has already been noted in the *Prenotes to the Thesis*.

From the doctrine of providence thus proved and explained [writes Boedder] two important corollaries are to be drawn. The first is this: God does not intend the final well-being of any individual living creature of this world except man. And man himself is to be properly happy, not here on earth but hereafter.

It is, therefore, quite intelligible that God should allow millions of irrational creatures to be sacrificed for the sake of man, to serve his internal welfare remotely or proximately. No less reconcilable is it with Divine Providence that under certain conditions mortal man should be wasted by contagious diseases, emaciated by famine, or fall in the flower of his age on the battle field. In a word: God cares more for the immortal soul that does not resist Him than for the whole material universe.

God must rule His creatures with a wise regard for their natural dignity according as that is greater or less. Now, the human soul stands by its nature in an infinitely nearer relation to God than the most perfect of dumb animals. It is an image of the Creator, whilst every other living creature of this world exhibits only some trace of His majesty. It owes its origin immediately to His creative power; whilst a dumb animal is a living erection made by secondary causes on the groundwork laid by God in the creation of matter and life. The rational soul alone is capable and destined to know and love God, and thus to be personally happy, whilst everything else is made to reveal the Creator to His rational creatures and to promote their eternal welfare during a short period of time.

The other corollary we are to derive from the great truth of Divine Providence may be thus formulated: Every man, however low his social position, ought to be treated with reverence by his fellow man, as a personal being destined for an eternal exaltation and happiness infinitely greater than all the aims of temporal ambition. (*Natural Theology*, pp. 391-393.)*

COROLLARY I—There is no such thing as absolute chance, that is, a happening which is neither intended nor foreseen by anyone. God from eternity foresees every event that has happened or will happen, and intends either positively, or, as in the case of a morally evil action, permissively, all of them. Many things, however, happen to men, which they neither intend nor foresee. Relative chance, therefore, is possible. (Cf. *God and Reason, Thesis VI*, pp. 119ff., for an explanation of the nature and properties of chance.)

COROLLARY II—The presence of evil in the world, either physical or moral, can in no way be used as an argument

* A fuller development of the above points will be found in St. Thomas, *Summa Theologica*, I, q.19, *passim; Summa Contra Gentiles*, Book 3, cc.111-120, 140, 147.

disproving our thesis. As this matter, however, is of some importance—in fact, according to some of our adversaries it is the "crux" of theism—it, and the difficulties it gives rise to, will be considered in *Thesis VII*. Accordingly, no difficulty based on the presence of evil in the world, will be found among those to follow here.

Difficulties

1. If God's providential care extends to everything, chance happenings in the world are impossible. But chance happenings in the world are impossible. Therefore.

D. Maj. Absolute chance happenings are impossible, *C.*; relative chance happenings are impossible, *N.—Cd. Min.*

2. If God has a providential care of everything, human providence is superfluous. But human providence is not superfluous. Therefore.

D. Maj. If God has a providential care of everything, which excludes man's providential direction in the order of secondary causes of his own actions, and of other creatures, human providence is superfluous, *C.*; if it does not exclude such direction, human providence is superfluous, *N.—D. Cons.*

3. If it is not fitting for a king to exercise immediate care over his subjects in all matters concerning them, even matters most trivial, it is not fitting for God to exercise an immediate providence over all things even those most trivial. But, it is not fitting for a king so to act. Therefore.

N. Maj. The Major is to be denied because of the infinite difference between an Infinite Ruler, and a finite one. The following are some of the reasons for its denial.

1. It would be impossible for a finite ruler to be busied about everything concerning his subjects, even trivial things, without neglecting matters of serious moment. This reason does not hold with regard to God, who, by one act of His Infinite Knowledge, knows everything, and by one act of His Infinite Will accomplishes everything.

2. On occasions, it is necessary for finite rulers to be represented by ministers of various kinds. These ministers, as representatives of the ruler, are supposed to have a certain amount of dignity and, consequently, to have a right to a certain amount of consideration. They would, however, be mere puppets, if the

ruler they represented insisted, if it were possible, in keeping the direction of all things in his own hands. This reason does not hold with regard to God, because His immediate care of all things still leaves finite rulers the authority of principal causes in the order of secondary causes.

3. If a finite ruler insisted on the immediate direction of all matters, even trivial ones, which concern his subjects, he would be obliged to do many things altogether beneath the dignity of a ruler. This reason does not hold with regard to God, because, by one act of His eternal, infinite, efficacious will, all things at their appointed time come into being. In their production He is an immediate, physical, efficient cause, producing with the creature the whole act, but in the case of free acts of the creatures, not making, and hence not being responsible for, the choice made.

4. If a finite cause can construct a machine which will work without his continual immediate direction, God, who is Infinite, should be able to make a world, the creatures of which would not need His continual immediate direction. But a finite cause can do that. Therefore.

D. Maj. If the reason why a finite cause can so act is because of his finiteness, God should be able to act in a similar way with regard to creatures in the world, *N.*; if the reason why a creature can so act were due, not to finiteness, that is, lack of perfection, God should be able to act in a similar way with regard to creatures in the world, *C.—Cd. Min.*

Because God is a necessary and, hence, an infinite being, it is absolutely impossible for any other being, essentially a contingent being, to exist, who is not brought into existence and continually preserved in existence either by God alone, or by God physically concurring with other contingent beings. For the same reason, it is impossible for any other being to act, unless God is also a physical, concurring cause in all its actions. Moreover, all creatures, with regard to all their actions, excepting man's free actions, are necessarily directed toward their various ends by God physically concurring in their production. With regard to man's free actions, although they too require God's physical concursus in their putting, still they are not determined by that concursus to their various ends. Man, who is physically free in his deliberate, his human actions, and man alone, God physically concurring, determines them to those ends. God, however, because He is an infinitely wise ruler, is by His very infinite perfection obliged to direct those actions towards Himself, the end for whom man is made. This God does by His moral, His special providence over man, and without prejudice to man's physical liberty. Hence, because God is an infinite being, He is obliged by His very nature to direct all creatures according to their different natures to the ends for which He created them.

5. If God providentially governs the world, its government should be eternal. But the government of the world is not eternal (the world itself is not eternal). Therefore.

D. Maj. The government of the world should be eternal, i.e., the intellectual ordering of all the creatures God intended to call into existence, to the attainment of their various proximate and their ultimate ends, and the efficacious decree of God's will, determining the existence of all things in time according to that ordering, should be eternal, *C.*; the actual direction of those creatures to the attainment of those various ends should be eternal, *N.—Cd. Min.*

6. A being which, in a given set of circumstances, can only act one way, does not require its cause to continue to direct its actions. But there are countless beings in the world of this nature. Therefore there are countless beings in the world who do not require the continual direction of their cause—God, in their actions.

D. Maj. A being, which acts necessarily, does not require a continual direction of secondary, finite causes, *Tr.;* does not require, because of its contingent, dependent nature, the directive influence of God, who of necessity must continually give it being, and continually concur with all its actions., *N.—Cd. Min.*

7. God's providence extends only to those creatures who can give Him the glory which He desired as the final end for which He created the world. But there are many creatures who cannot give Him that glory. Therefore.

D. Maj. God's providence extends only to those creatures who can give Him, directly and immediately, that formal, express glory which He desired as the final end, etc., i.e., it extends only to rational creatures, *N.*; it extends not only to rational creatures who can give God formal glory, directly and immediately, but also to all other creatures which, giving God objective, extrinsic glory, thus indirectly and mediately give Him formal glory, i.e., through rational creatures who contemplating that objective glory, are to turn it into formal, extrinsic glory, praising and reverencing, and serving God, with the praise and reverence and service of adoration, *C.—Cd. Min.*

Thesis VII

*The providence which God exercises over the world,
as a Ruler of infinite wisdom, goodness, and power,
is in no way to be impugned because of the presence
in the world of moral and physical evil.*

Prenotes to the Thesis

In the explanation and proof of *Thesis VI* no formal account was taken of the presence in the world of countless evils, or of the way in which God, in His infinite wisdom, orders them to the external manifestation of His glory. That they must manifest it, follows necessarily from the proof of that thesis, which, founded on the demonstrated infinite nature of God, shows that everything in the world, including even its evils, must fall under His providential care and in some way or other glorify Him.

But immediately the question presents itself: How can that be? How can the countless evils which are in the world because of God's will, either positive or permissive, and innumerable of them openly and directly opposed to His infinite perfections, bring about the manifestation of those perfections? If He were infinitely perfect, and, hence, infinitely wise, and infinitely good, and infinitely powerful, would He not have excluded evil from His creation?

This question we shall strive to answer in our present thesis, offering, in so doing, our solution (necessarily a limited one) to a serious difficulty. In fact, in the estimation of many thoughtful believers and non-believers, it is the most serious difficulty which confronts the Philosopher is his reasoned defense of the One God of Theism, the infinitely perfect Creator and Ruler of our Universe.

It is frequently called the *Problem of Evil,* and may be stated in this wise: Is it at all possible, in the face of the evils, not infrequently appalling, at all times and everywhere present in the world, to hold that it is ruled by one God, who is infinitely wise, and good, and powerful, or is some other explanation to be sought for?

And the difficulty is not a theoretical one only. It is deeply practical. For centuries it has harassed, and still harasses, the minds and hearts of all classes of men, learned and unlearned. It confronts everyone, and in its practical and personal visitations may be extremely dangerous, for it appeals strongly to the emotions, may easily be exaggerated, excite the passions, and when morbidly dwelt on, may almost unbalance the reason.

What modern Philosophers, Scholastic and non-Scholastic, think of it will best be gathered from the following typical quotations.

One of the most harassing questions which have ever wearied the brains of philosophers, and stimulated the zeal of Christian apologists, is as to the possibility of such an enormous amount of evil in a world created by an infinitely good God, and continually under the sway of His Providence. (*Boedder, Natural Theology,* p.393.)

At the bottom of all trial of faith this mystery of evil lies; and it remains a mystery to every man till the hour of his death. The best alleviation doubtless is to oppose mystery to mystery, and over against the mystery of iniquity (II Thess., 2:7) and pain to oppose the Mystery of the Cross (Eph. 3:9), of God Himself in human nature suffering agony and crucifixion. (Joseph Rickaby, *Oxford and Cambridge Conferences, 1900-1901,* p.139.)

The problem of evil has recently been called "the crux of theism" . . . Nowadays it is asked: How is evil in the world compatible with there being a God at all? (James Ward, *Pluralism and Theism,* p.317.)

This is the "terrible mystery of evil" which for two thousand years has been a stumbling-block to all practical religion, tried the faith of all believers, and depressed and debased all thought on the ultimate question of life, and is as "insoluble a mystery" to the theologian now as it was at the beginning. And it is perhaps likely to remain so, seeing that, as Goethe says, "a complete contradiction is alike mysterious to wise men and fools," and that no labor can ever extract any sense out of a gratuitous combination of incongruous words. Hence, it is not surprising that no attempt at reconciling the divine goodness with divine power has ever been successful; indeed the only way in which

they have ever appeared to be successful was either by covertly
limiting the divine power, or by misusing the term goodness in
some non-human sense, to show a quality shown in God's action
towards imaginary beings other than man. (F. C. Schiller, *Riddles of the Sphinx*, p.307.)

To escape pessimism is, as we all know, no easy task. Your
studies have sufficiently shown you the almost desperate difficulty
of making the notion that there is a single principle of things,
and that principle absolute perfection, rhyme together with our
daily vision of the facts of life. If perfection be the principle,
how comes there any imperfection here? If God be good, how
comes He to create—or if he did not create, how came he to
permit—the devil? The evil facts must be explained as seeming:
the devil must be white-washed: the universe must be disin-
fected, if neither God's goodness nor his unity and power are
to remain impugned. (William James, *Will to Believe*, p.166.)

Reason, nevertheless, can offer a solution of the difficulty, necessarily, however, as we said above, a limited one.
And this is true even where reason is aided by what God
has been pleased to reveal to us in the matter. For, to give a
full solution of the problem, we should see clearly how God's
goodness and love are made manifest in a world in which,
as He foresaw from eternity, man would be cruelly tried,
tortured by all kinds of pain, and poverty and anguish of
spirit, would fall into countless abominable sins, would in
millions of instances make a failure of life; when He might
have made a world in which these sufferings and sins might
have been excluded altogether, or, at least, might have been
immeasurably less, and so, countless souls predestined to
be lost for all eternity, might have been saved. To give a
full solution of the problem, we should have to know,
granted the world to have been created by God, how, in
every instance, He so orders His creation, that all the evils
in it, especially all its foul sins, and all its human wreckage
are directed to the manifestation of His infinite perfections,
and, in particular, His infinite love, and holiness, and mercy.
In other words, to solve the problem of evil fully we should
be able to penetrate into the depths of God's infinite wisdom
and see clearly why it is that He chose to manifest His infinite perfections, especially His goodness, and love, and
holiness in a world evil-laden, sorrow-laden, sin-laden, and

how it is that in such a world each particular evil would be used by Him as a factor in the manifestation of His external glory in the degree chosen by Him from all eternity. To know all these things, however, is not granted to us.

And so, after a study of the nature of evil, and of the relation in general it must bear towards God's infinite good will, though we cannot know why God chose to manifest His infinite perfections in a world so full of bodily suffering and anguish of spirit and sin; and cannot know how in every instance out of its myriads of evils God ever brings good, still we can show how, in general, and in some classes of evil more in particular, they are so subordinated to God's infinite good will, that from none of them can be drawn argument to impugn any of His infinite perfections.

Hence, though it is true, as we shall see, that Divine Revelation gives us new light on the place suffering has in God's providence, and tells us of many new and wonderful manifestations of God's love for man occasioned by the presence of sin in the world, still the problem of evil will ever remain, as Father Rickaby says, "a mystery to every man till the hour of his death."

Evil: its divisions

Before taking up the relation which evil bears to God's infinite good will, it will be necessary to get a clear grasp of the nature of evil, and its divisions.

Evil, strictly speaking, is understood to be a privation, or a defect, in a thing; a want of a perfection which should be found in it. We distinguish the defect or privation, *the evil as such*, from the thing which is evil, seeing that no privation, or want of a due perfection, can be found outside of a thing.

A thing is said to be bad or evil, inasmuch as it suffers such a privation, or brings it about.

Evil is commonly divided into *physical* or *natural* evil, and *moral*. These two kinds of evil, as we shall see, are given other names also, by Scholastic philosophers.

Physical evil, by some called natural evil, is a defect, or privation of a perfection, in a being, in the order of real, actual existence; marring it, as a consequence, in its natural integrity, or in the exercise of its normal activities, or in both.

Physical evils may affect all creatures in this visible world —of which world only we are speaking—including man, inasmuch as he has a nature in common with the lower orders of being.

They affect man also, as an intellectual being, that is, with regard to his spiritual soul as the principle of intellectual life; but not, however, as the principle of free-will actions, that is, deliberate acts of the will. Defects due to a free-will deviation from its norm, the moral law, are called *moral* evils, sins.

In fact, the physical evils which press on man most heavily and harass him are those of the spirit. The evils that he suffers in his sensitive nature derive almost all their poignancy and dread effect from the accompanying intellectual consciousness and appreciation of them. The anticipation of a long life of misery from an incurable and painful disease, with no hope of alleviation, brings the sufferings of the future into the present, with gloomy forebodings, loss of peace, and perhaps despair. What is more, man can and does in spirit go out of himself to bear the evils that afflict others. We suffer grievously when those we love are in suffering. The physical sufferings of animals, lacking this element, are immeasurably less than those of man. On this point, more, later.

As the physical evils which are principally considered in discussing the problem of evil, are those which affect, and inasmuch as they affect, living sentient beings, including man, and man as an intellectual being, but only in the sense above stated, in the remarks which follow on physical evil, we shall confine our attention practically to those alone.

Afflicting man and beast from birth to death, are countless physical evils; many nature-made, many man-made. Of these last we include here those only which are in no way sinful or the bitter fruit of sin.

The following, taken more or less at random, are some: Property-destroying, food-destroying, health-destroying, life-destroying, in many cases with long-drawn-out suffering; earthquakes, tornadoes on land and sea; pestilences, famines, droughts; diseases of all kinds, mental and bodily, including imbecility and insanity; dire poverty with all its consequences; abysmal ignorance; never-ending wars, just or unjust; the suffering in spirit in countless ways of all those caught up in the above evils, of families mourning the untimely death of father, or mother, or both; the suffering of despairing, broken-hearted, parentless children, of mothers and fathers grieving for wayward sons and daughters—and so through the catalogue endlessly. Truly this world is a vale of tears.

Moral evil is a defect in man's free-will actions, that is, in the deliberate actions of his will, inasmuch as they go counter to the law of God binding man in conscience, and so deprive them, and the external actions which may proceed from them, and at times even the free-agent himself, of their rightful direction towards God.

Here we have sins of thought, and sins both of thought and deed; man to whom God has granted a restricted lordship over this visible creation, reaching out for a freedom which is intrinsically impossible for God to grant him. Sins of thought and deed: Who can number them? Who can describe them? Who can sound the depths of their iniquity? In comparison with them physical evils are as though they were not. Why God, who is Infinite Sanctity Itself, and essentially opposed to sin, knowing, as He alone can know, their multitude and appalling magnitude, in His long-suffering mercy permits them, no one but God Himself can understand. That, in doing so, however, He forfeits none of His Infinite Perfections, our proof will show.

With regard to the number and enormity of the sins committed by man from the time of his appearance on earth up to the present, and which he will commit till the Day of Judgment, all of which are present to God in His one infinite act of knowledge, one remark will be sufficient. Considering the sins which man has committed in the open up to the present, and saying nothing of the sins of thought and hidden sins of deed—not hidden, though, from God— there is not a law of God, not a precept of God which has not been flouted, not a virtue which has not been sinned against, and all in such numbers and such wantonness, that

GOD INFINITE, THE WORLD, AND REASON

it may be said, and without exaggeration, that an appallingly large part of the human race has lived as if there were no God. It is true that numberless good men and women have at all times existed, who in season and out of season have tried to serve God; still the black cloud of sin arising from the world continually, does not on that account appear to grow less. If anything, it is on the increase. For, in these later days, in addition to the economic and moral chaos into which the world has been engulfed, through unjust wars, greed, religious persecutions, race-hatreds, and all other kinds of injustices, and which has overwhelmed, with dire and despair-breeding poverty and all its consequent evils, millions of men, women, and children; in addition, to a more open and shameless attack on the sanctity of marriage, through birth-control, trial-marriages, and divorces for the asking; in addition, to atheism openly professed in high school, college, and university societies, and Congresses of the Godless, the realm of sin has reached a culmination of wickedness which the world never saw before: Whole nations of set purpose have united to annihilate God.

Pope Pius the XI, in His encyclical, *Caritate Christi Compulsi* (May 3, 1932), witnesses to this diabolic campaign:

Urged by the charity of Christ we have invited with the Encyclical, *Nova Impendet,* of October 2 of last year, all members of the Catholic Church, indeed all men of good will, to unite in a holy crusade of love and succor, in order to alleviate in some measure the terrible consequences of the economic crisis under which the human race is struggling. . . . But distress has increased, the number of the unemployed has grown in practically all parts, and subversive elements are making use of the fact for their propaganda; hence, public order is threatened more and more, and the peril of terrorism and anarchy hangs over Society even more ominously. Such being the case, the same charity of Christ moves us to turn again . . . to the whole world, and to exhort all to unite and to resist with all their might the evils that are crushing humanity, and the still greater evils that are threatening.

If we pass in review the long and sorrowful sequence of woes that, as a sad heritage of sin, mark the stages of fallen man's earthly pilgrimage from the Flood onward, it would be hard to find spiritual and material distress so deep, so universal, as that which we are now encountering; even the greatest scourges that left indelible traces in the lives and memories of peoples struck only one nation at a time. Now, on the contrary, the whole of humanity is held bound by the financial and economic crisis, so fast, that the more it struggles, the harder appears the task of loosening its bonds; there is no people, there is no state, no society or family which, in one way or another, directly or indirectly, to a greater or less degree does not feel the repercussion. . . .

But still more deplorable is the root from which springs this condition of affairs. . . . Is it not that lust of earthly goods, . . . is it not that sordid egoism which too often regulates the mutual relations of individuals and society, is it not, in fine, greed, whatever be its species and form, that has brought the world to a pass we all see and deplore . . . ?

Profiting by so much economic distress and so much moral disorder, the enemies of all social order, be they called Communists or any other name, boldly set about breaking through every restraint. This is the most dreadful evil of our times, for they destroy every bond of law, human or divine; they engage openly and in secret in a relentless struggle against religion and against God Himself; they carry out the diabolical program of wresting from the hearts of all, even of children, all religious sentiment; for well they know that when once belief in God has been taken from the heart of mankind they will be entirely free to work out their will. Thus, we see today, what was never before seen in history, the satanical banners of war against God and against religion brazingly unfurled to the winds in the midst of all peoples and in all parts of the earth.

There were never lacking impious men, nor men who denied God; but they were relatively few, isolated and individual, and they did not care or did not think it opportune to reveal too openly their impious minds. . . . Today, on the contrary, atheism has already spread through large masses of people; well organized, it works its way even into the common schools; it appears in theatres; in order to spread, it makes use of its own cinema films, of the gramophone, and the radio; with its own printing presses it prints booklets in every language; it promotes special exhibitions and public parades; it has formed its own political parties and its own economic and military systems. This organized and militant atheism works untiringly by means of its agitators, with conferences and projections, with every means of propaganda, secret and open, among all classes, in

every street, in every hall; it secures for this nefarious activity
the moral support of its own universities. . . .

The leaders of this campaign of atheism, turning to account
the present economic crisis, inquire with diabolic reasoning into
the cause of this universal misery. The Holy Cross of Our Lord,
symbol of humility and poverty, is joined together with the
symbols of modern imperialism, as though religion were allied
with those dark powers which produce such evils among men.
. . . Now it is a lamentable fact that millions of men, under
the impression that they are struggling for existence, grasp at
such theories to the utter subversion of Faith, and cry out against
God and religion. Nor are these assaults directed only against
the Catholic religion, but against all who still recognize God.
. . . And the secret societies always ready to support war against
God and the church no matter who wages it, do not fail to in-
flame ever more this insane hatred. . . .

Thus this new form of atheism, whilst unchaining man's
most violent instincts, with cynical impudence proclaims that
there will be neither peace nor welfare on earth until the last
remnant of religion has been torn up and until its last representative has been crushed out of existence. . . .

Today, when atheism is spreading through the masses of the
people, the practical consequences of such an error become
dreadfully tangible, and realities of the saddest kind make their
appearance in the world. In place of moral laws, which disappear altogether with the loss of faith in God, brute force is
imposed, trampling on every right. Oldtime fidelity and honesty
of conduct and mutual intercourse . . . now give place to speculation in one's own affairs as in those of others, without reference to conscience. In fact, how can any contract be maintained,
and what value can any treaty have, in which every guarantee
of conscience is lacking? And how can there be talk of guaran-
tees of conscience when all faith in God and all fear of God
has vanished? Take away this basis, and with it all moral law
falls, and there is no remedy left to stop the gradual but inevi-
table destruction of peoples, families, the state, civilization itself.

The above brief presentation, without any word of ex-
tenuation, of the multiplicity, variety, intensity, and, in the
moral order, heinousness, of the evils found everywhere in
the world, gives us the dark side of the problem of evil.
The revelation of its bright side, which looks towards its
solution, will now engage our attention. It will proceed

gradually. It may be well, however, to note, as we noted before, that, when we have given our solution of the problem, namely, when we have shown that no argument impugning any of God's infinite perfections can be drawn from the presence of evil in the world, still, why God chose to make manifest those infinite perfections through a world so evil-laden, will ever remain a mystery to us.

The relation of evil to God's infinite good will.

Towards a better understanding of this relation a prior consideration of the following points will be found helpful.

1. The term of God's creative act is necessarily finite. An absolutely best world, therefore, is an impossibility. A relatively best world, that is, a world best adapted to realize the end desired by God in creating it, is possible. The present world is such a world. In fact any world that God would wish to make, would necessarily be such a world, seeing that it would be the handiwork of an infinitely wise and infinitely powerful God.

The absurd conclusion to which, consequently those would be led, who would find fault with God because He had not made a better world than the present one, will be shown later in an illuminating excerpt from Tongiori, *Natural Theology* (Bk. 3, c.5, a.3).

2. All producible being, in its very essence contingent, is essentially finite, essentially defectible. As contingent, in itself it has no reason for its existence. Without the immediate, direct, and continual physical inflowing of God's omnipotent power into its very being and every action, it can neither begin to exist, nor continue to exist, nor exercise any one, even the smallest, of its activities. If that supporting power were withdrawn, it would cease to exist, and utterly. Apart from God it is nothing, and even with God, it always remains a finite, defective something. In this intrinsic weakness of all producible being, including the human will as free, is rooted the possibility of evil, physical and moral, and, hence, of all the evils we see in the world.

Going somewhat beyond the above mere statement, namely, that in the essential defectibility of all producible being is rooted the possibility of evil, is a view advanced, "as a suggestion that may be found provisionally tenable," by Joseph Rickaby, in his *Oxford and Cambridge Conferences for 1900-1901*. It is this:

In all producible being, because of its essential defectibility, the possibility of evil is not *merely* rooted, but it is so rooted that a world without evil would be a metaphysical impossibility.

According to this view, then, any world that God would create, must, and with absolute necessity, contain evil.

It will not be necessary for us to discuss this point. For, even if it were possible to produce a world without any evil in it, still, as our thesis shows, none of God's infinite perfections would demand that He should make such a world.

Though withholding judgment on the truth or falsity of Father Rickaby's "suggestion," it will be profitable to quote the passage in which he makes it, if for no other reason then to be helped by it to a clearer appreciation of the essential next-to-nothingness of contingent, producible being. Father Rickaby writes:

At the bottom of all trial of faith this mystery of evil lies; and it remains a mystery to every man till the hour of his death. Some souls are oppressed with it more than others. The best alleviation doubtless is to oppose mystery to mystery, and over against the *mystery of iniquity* (II Thess. 2: 7) and pain to oppose *the mystery of the Cross* (Eph. 3: 9; I Tim. 3: 16), of God Himself in human nature suffering agony and crucifixion. What I have to contribute to the solution of the mystery is a philosophical suggestion, that may be found provisionally tenable. I suggest that a world all clear of evil is an intrinsic impossibility, in the nature of things; and that the reason why God never made such a world is that it is not makable, just as a world where the truths of number would not hold good is unmakable. When we try to be rid of all evil from the outset, without any effort or struggle, we are as children crying for the moon. The most that God and nature can do for us is to put us in the way of victory over evil; and to hold forth to us the prospect of a time of triumph, when evil should be relegated to a region of its own, where none shall suffer it but they who richly deserve it, and have in a manner contracted alliance with it.

I am led to conjecture the intrinsic necessity of evil, "patrolling," as Plato says, "all mortal nature and this region of earth" (*Theat.*, 176 A) not from any speculation on the nature and attributes of God, but from the consideration of the abyss of nothingness out of which every creature is drawn. This kinship with nothingness clings to all creation. The creature cannot put off the traces of its origin, and its origin is twofold. Inasmuch as it comes from God, it has whatever goodness and positive being there is in it. But inasmuch as it is drawn out of nothingness, there attaches to it from the first a certain defectibility, proneness to decay and failure—in fact, evil. The lifework of rational creatures is to prepare their own emancipation from evil. If I am right, blank nothingness, τὸ μηδέν, should hold the place which matter, τὸ ὁρατόν, held in the Platonic philosophy as the root of evil. Had you asked a Greek of Plato's school or of the Gnostic or Manichaean school in early Christianity, how evil came to be, he might have clutched a handful of sand and told you, "This is evil, all stuff of this visible sort; and consequently all being of which it goes to constitute, is beset with evil; only pure thought is good." The Buddhist will tell you that thought is evil, and only some sort of ecstasy or trance, carrying perfect rest from thought, is good. We shall not quarrel with Matter, nor with Thought, for they are both of God, A self-existent Matter, such as Plato presupposed, would have been, as the Manichaeans saw, another and a rival God. There is nothing to rival God: there is no self-existent Evil to counteract His goodness. Only one term, which we can hardly make an object of thought or language, stands out over against God, and is no creature of His: that is sheer Nothingness. If God creates a world He must raise it from zero, out of nothingness. That seems to involve the impossibility of a world without evil. Take the speculation for what it is worth: think it out and refute it, or adopt and improve upon it, or forget all about it, or (which will be my fault) fail to understand it. (*Op. cit.*, pp. 138ff.)

3. Evil in itself, as we have seen, is a privation. It cannot exist alone. It is the absence of a due perfection in a being. As a reality which manifests in its own limited way some perfection of God, the being itself is good. It has, moreover, its own proper activities, producing effects in themselves also good.

If, then, there are innumerable evils in the world, there are also innumerable good things, producing innumerable effects in themselves also good. In fact, one with an unprejudiced mind, prescinding for the time being from the world of morals and contemplating only the physical world round about us, stupendously ordered and teeming with countless beings, in themselves and in the effects they produce both beautiful and useful, would rightly say that compared with the good things of the world its physical evils, looked at in themselves, are negligible. When considered, though, in connection with the numberless positive benefits they bring in their train, of which the major part perhaps escapes our limited reckoning, they should be called, as they really are, blessings and not evils. And likewise in the world of morals, though there may be countless sins, and many of them heinous, on the other hand there are other countless good deeds, and many of them heroic, to outbalance them. And, again, when these sins are considered in connection with the overwhelmingly great number of good deeds occasioned by them, and in connection with God's reaction to them, they too, will be found to have their part in making manifest indirectly the infinite perfections of God. But of these matters, more, later.

4. The will by its very nature, when it acts, tends towards an object inasmuch as it is good. In the case of finite intelligences there may be a going-out of the will towards that which is bad for the individual, but it is always sought for under the aspect or formality of goodness. It appears here and now to be good; it is so, however, only in appearance.

God, on the other hand, who is infinite Intelligence, and essential Goodness and Holiness, moved only by the highest good, His own infinite Goodness, to share that Goodness (that is, inasmuch as it could be shared: in a finite way), with His creatures, brought them into existence as means to give Him the degree of glory He determined on in creating them. He brought them into existence, then, to show forth in a finite way, His infinite Goodness: the inferior creation in its bewilderingly ordered array of perfections giving to man, knowing his own nothingness, reasons most clear, for praising and reverencing, and serving in humble adoration the infinitely transcendent Goodness of God, his and their Creator, and so, coming to possess Him for all eternity.

All this offering up of the perfections of the world to

God, however, man was to do freely, and for this end alone freedom was given him. Most assuredly he was to exercise that freedom during life in countless ways, choosing now this, now that creature, now this, now that mode of action; but all this was so to be done that the choice of creatures was ever to be subordinated to the end for which man was made. They were to be used as means to get to God, and rejected when the choice of them meant a turning away from Him. Now, one point is here to be emphasized. It is this. If man has the power to win God, to merit by his actions to possess Him, as his reward exceeding great, he must also have the power to lose Him—the power to sin even grievously.

God, however, who is infinite Goodness, infinite Holiness, infinite Wisdom, created the world for the good that is in it, and for the good that man could merit by living in it. If there is evil in it, it cannot be willed by God for itself, as an end. It must be willed by God, however, some way. Otherwise it would not be found in the world. It can be willed by God, therefore, only inasmuch as it can in some way or other result in good. Here, then, we have in general the relation which evil says to the infinite good will of God. Since, however, moral evil says a relation to the infinitely good will of God essentially different from that said by physical evil, to understand more particularly the relation of evil to God's Will, it will be necessary to consider them separately. This we will do immediately, beginning with physical evil.

5. *Physical evil* is a privation of a finite good. To acquire a greater good, it may be necessary at times to suffer such a privation. When this happens, one may, acting according to right order, intend such a privation—not for itself, however, but as a means to the acquisition of the greater good in question. What is primarily intended is the greater good; secondarily, the privation, as a means to its acquisition.

Now, the more than wonderful order most strikingly evident everywhere in the world, and which as God intended, shows forth in a finite way His glory, is brought about by the action and interaction of innumerable beings, of widely different natures and natural tendencies, under laws which, rooted in those natures, taken singly and as here and now

combined, brings forth as a result, not a *chaos* but a *cosmos*—
that most marvelous whole which we call our Universe.

Of these laws some are universal, others less so, and so in
descending scale, till we come to the laws according to which
the well-being of individual things, and the well-being of
the higher and lower parts of one and the same thing, as in
man, are regulated.

It is quite evident, however, that, in the daily innumerable and complicated actions and interactions of the millions
of agents continually producing and carrying on the world-
order, there should arise countless occasions when one law
must prevail over another. In these cases, then, according to
right order, the more universal and higher laws should prevail over the less universal and lower ones, progressively,
till we come to the laws regulating the well-being of individual things, or parts of them.

All of this means that here, there, and everywhere in
the world, and constantly, the lower orders must give way
to, and aid in the furthering of the higher ones, and so on,
to the highest. That is the same as saying that in many
particular cases beings lose perfections, which loss, if judged
according to the laws governing the lower order, would be
called a privation, that is, are physical evils, but if, judged
according to the higher laws demanding the subordination,
are orderly happenings furthering the general plan of the
universe, and so, not evils.

These physical evils, then, since they are naturally necessary conditions for the obtaining and continuing of the
general world-order, are willed by God, who wishes that
order to prevail, not for themselves but only as means for
the obtaining of that end.

It is to be noted clearly, however, that here where we
are speaking of physical evil, we are not considering man
according to the laws which regulate his actions from the
viewpoint of morality. These laws are for man supreme, subordinate to no other. Nor are we considering physical evil
inasmuch as it is brought about by man's transgression of
these laws. Under that aspect God does not intend it. He
simply permits it, as in the case of moral evil itself. What
that means, will be explained presently.

Furthermore, it will be found that physical evils have an aspect of goodness not only as furthering the general order, but also, in many instances, as benefiting the one suffering such evil. This is true in the case of living sentient beings, and, in a special way, true of man. In fact, as the problem of evil is concerned, practically altogether, with these two classes of beings, all the examples we shall refer to as showing how physical evils, if considered in their full setting, have a beneficial aspect, will be taken from them. A few of these examples follow, others will be given later in a Scholion to the thesis.

Pain inflicted on a child is, in itself, a physical evil; considered, however, as a salutary means of correction it is everything but an evil. So, the loss of an arm is a physical evil, but the loss of an arm in order to save the life of a man is according to right order, and under that aspect, no evil. So too, sickness, which sends a man back to God, is not, if viewed adequately, an evil, but a good greater than any material good.

As physical evils, then, are naturally necessary as conditions for the preservation of the universal world-order, and in innumerable ways beneficial to the beings suffering them, God who intends the well-being of the universe as a whole, and the well-being of its parts in the measure in which they help thereto, intends those evils, not for themselves but as means to that end; and rightly so.

It may be objected, however, that God might have, and, therefore, should have, made a world with much less suffering for man and beast than is found here; a world in which many of the benefits which now come to a man through trials and sufferings, might have been obtained without them. An adequate answer to this difficulty will be given later in connection with the proof of the thesis.

6. *Moral evil* is not, like physical evil, opposed to some finite good. It is opposed to God Himself, seeing that it is man's deliberate turning away of his actions, and, at times even of his very self, from the ultimate end for which they were made—God. God, therefore, who by His very nature as Infinite Good, must be the Final Cause of everything in the world, cannot intend it. Nevertheless, though hating and

prohibiting it, He must at least permit it, otherwise it could not be found in the world at all. This permission, however, God can give only on the condition that, such evil being presupposed, He foresees that it will be the occasion for the obtaining of some good. In fact, as we shall see later, the good occasioned by sin is in many cases incalculable. It must be carefully noted, though, that the permission of moral evil is not intended by God as a means for the obtaining of that good, for in that case God would intend its happening. The opposite is true; the obtaining of good through moral evil is a necessary condition for its permission by God. This permission, which is technically called, *a simple permission,* a permission and nothing more, as we will prove, is absolutely compatible with God's infinite perfections.

It may be well, now, to note explicitly the conditions to be fulfilled in the case of a simple permission.

(a) The thing permitted is not intended, not wished for, not desired by the one permitting it. In fact, in the present case, the thing permitted, sin, is not only not intended and desired by God, it is hated and absolutely prohibited by Him. Hence, while man is physically free, he is never morally free, to commit it.

(b) The thing permitted could be prevented by the one permitting it, if he so wished. In our present case, no sin could be committed if God wished absolutely to prevent it.

(c) The one permitting is under no obligation to prevent the thing permitted. In permitting it, he incurs no responsibility, no blame, no loss of perfection. If he be, as happens in our present case, God, the preventing of the thing permitted is demanded by none of His Infinite Perfections.

That the first two conditions just noted are fulfilled in God's permission of sin, scarcely needs proof. To one who has a true concept of God it should be immediately evident. That God's infinite perfections are in no way to be impugned because of His permission of sin, is not so evident. Hence our thesis, whose principal object is to prove it.

To prepare ourselves for an easier understanding and firmer grasp of that proof, it will be well to emphasize the following truth, already more or less known to all of us.

Moral evil is due to man's deliberate misuse of the greatest gift that God has given him, namely, the gift of free will; through which, as master of his own deliberate actions, he has the power to merit the unending possession of God. Short of taking this gift away from him, God makes use of innumerable means to urge man to a right use of it. If man fails to use it properly, then man, not God, is to blame.

Man's rebellion against God, though, when he commits sin, cannot turn any of his actions or himself away from God absolutely, in such wise, namely, that from them no glory would accrue to God. That would be to frustrate the absolute and necessary will of God that all creatures without exception must in some way or other glorify Him. *"God Almighty,"* writes St. Augustine, "would in no way permit evil in His works, were He not so omnipotent and good that even out of evil He could work good." (Cf. *Enchiridion,* c.11.)

Hence, one of the conditions, already noted, necessary for God's permission of sin: it must serve as the occasion for the furthering of His own glory.

How that glory is furthered, that is, what good God in His wise providence draws from sin, in many cases is known to Him alone. In not a few cases it is also abundantly evident to us. In a Scholion to the thesis, some of these will be noted. In extreme cases, where the sinner dies at enmity with God, and, so, deliberately refuses to give Him formal glory in the enjoyment of the Beatific Vision, he will be obliged to glorify the infinite Justice of God objectively; that is, by his eternal punishment he will give others reason for formally glorifying that Justice forever.

And here we come face to face again with what might be called the very depths of the Mystery of Evil. Could not God have created a world which would give Him immeasurably greater glory than His present creation; a world in which there would be, at least, much less sin, which He hates; in which many more of His rational creatures, whom He created in love, would merit to glorify Him eternally in heaven, for which end He created them; in which at least far fewer, dying impenitent, would give tragic glory to His Justice in unending sufferings, eternally separated from Him, to possess whom was the sole reason for their creation? If

He could create such a world, and if He is infinitely wise, and loving, and holy, and powerful, why did He not do so?

Admitting that God might have fulfilled, had He so wished, all of the conditions mentioned above, nay more, that, absolutely speaking He might have created a world in general aspect like unto ours, but in which there would be no suffering, no sin, or, at least, no sin bringing with it final impenitence, our answer to the question, "Why did not God make some such world?" is: "We do not know." God, who knows, has revealed to us neither the reasons which led Him to create our present world, nor the reasons which led Him to leave uncreated the many other possible worlds He might have created. Our thesis makes no attempt to solve these mysteries.

If, however, it is urged that because God could have made a world better than the present one, with all its suffering and sin, as infinitely wise and good, He should have done so, we answer that that line of reasoning, failing to note that any world made by God infinitely wise and powerful would be necessarily the best for the end He had in making it, leads furthermore to the absurd conclusion that God could not make any world at all.

Again, if it is urged that, because in determining the creation of the present world God might have arranged so that no sinner would be summoned to judgment when in grievous sin, as infinitely merciful, He should have done so, we answer that this line of reasoning, instead of safeguarding God's infinite perfection, by practically giving to the sinner the right to dictate to God the kind of world He should create, would make Him subject to man's depraved will.

These two points will be more fully explained in the proof of the thesis, which will follow shortly. This proof, it is to be clearly understood, rests solely on arguments supplied by unaided reason, namely, on the demonstrated truths —that God is the infinitely wise and absolutely supreme Ruler of the world; that love led Him to bring it into existence to show forth through it His glory; that love led Him to create man with a soul capable of knowing and loving Him; that love led Him to give to man, ever subject to the divine and natural law with its necessary sanctions of eternal reward and eternal punishment, the precious gift of liberty for one end only, that by freely serving God he might win Him as his possession for eternity, but carrying with it the necessarily complementary, fatal power to refuse that service, and so rejecting His love, lose Him, also for eternity. When these truths are presented in our proof, the conclusions will be evident, that from the presence in the world of physical and moral evil, even that causing the eternal loss of countless souls, no argument can legitimately be drawn to impugn any of God's infinite perfections, either His absolutely supreme and omnipotent Lordship over the world, or His justice, or His love, or His holiness, or His mercy.

Now, while reason tells us that all this is so, still it is hard for the many good people in the world who in dire poverty and sickness, and weighed down by other crosses strive ceaselessly to serve God, while they see so many leading evil lives who enjoy every material comfort that the world can give; it is hard for the sinner whose whole life has been immersed in sin and now repentant but scarcely hoping for pardon; it is hard for these and countless others suffering injustices of all kinds which they cannot remedy— to bring home to themselves in a helpful way, that what reason says *must* be so, *is so* in fact, namely, that God is a just God, a loving God, a merciful God. If, however, we had God Himself telling us in so many words that these are facts, it is quite evident that that would help much to bring peace and comfort to suffering and sinful man. And we have many such testimonies which God in His supernatural providence over the world has given to man. Some of them will be found in a Scholion to the thesis; others will be referred to in our proof, not, however, as a proof of the thesis—*our proof rests on reason alone*—but solely to bring home to all of us in a way which should remove all doubt, to just and unjust, to those suffering and those without hope, that we have a God, whose providence infinitely just, infinitely loving, infinitely holy, infinitely merciful, reaches out over all His children.

ADVERSARIES

In general the adverse attitude of non-Scholastic philosophers to our solution of the problem of Evil, which vindicates for the true, only one God, all His infinite perfections, is sufficiently indicated under the following general headings. Now, though not a few of these philosophers insist, and rightly so, if properly explained, that from the evil in the world good always emerges which transcends the evil, still their impossible handling of the problem will be evident from a glance, either at their fundamental doctrines or their general solution of the problem. It will not be necessary to descend to particulars to reject them.

1. *The Atheists.* Faced by their admitted inability to find any satisfying solution of the problem, some present-day philosophers either deny or at least refuse to admit the existence of any God at all. Professor James Ward, in an excerpt cited at the beginning of our thesis, notes this trend of modern philosophy: "Nowadays it is asked: How is the evil in the world compatible with there being any God at all?"

Professor Daniel Robinson (Miami University), in *The God of the Liberal Christian,* gives confirmatory testimony. Though Professor Robinson's philosophy is fundamentally at variance with our philosophy, and the Christianity he professes is not our Christianity, still he holds that faith through Christianity is a strong support, as it must surely be in the case of true Christianity, in bearing up under the evils of life. He calls himself an ethical monotheist. In the passage from his book which we cite, however, in addition to other errors, he appears to hold some kind of Pantheism. We quote him, nevertheless, but only as a complaisant witness to the fact that the problem of evil leads some philosophers to Atheism.

Commenting favorably on the statement of Baron Von Hugel that "Christianity gave to our souls the strength and the faith to grasp life's nettle" (i.e., the problem of evil), Professor Robinson writes:

The faith to grasp life's nettle! Who dares face the fateful contingencies of human existence without such a faith? While evil retains its potency to engender in men's minds reflection upon its meaning, ethical monotheism will not perish from the earth. Yet there have always been and there probably always will be great souls who prefer agnosticism to such a faith. And it must be frankly admitted that there is something supremely admirable in the intellectual honesty and courageous self-reliance in which agnosticism is rooted. If there be a God who includes all human persons within His own infinite personality, He most certainly includes some who doubt his existence. For among the world's most illustrious persons are numbered some agnostics. How can we condemn a man who, after thinking the matter carefully through, is honest enough to write: "Whether in fact there be a personal God or not, it seems to me we have no good reason to believe in the existence of such a being"? This is the attitude of a small minority of the most distinguished philosophers of our day. (P. 180.)

Logically and practically leading to the atheistical solution of the problem of evil is another, which may be called the finite-God solution. This solution, and its atheistical implications will be explained presently.

2. *The Christian Scientists.* For the sake of completeness we refer to the solution of our problem offered by this group, which, in the strict sense of the word, is composed neither of Christians nor of Scientists. If we rightly understand their confused teaching, they practically deny the existence of all evil. They need no refutation. Evil is a stubborn fact, not to be rejected by words.

3. *The Ditheists.* Ditheism is an attempt at solving the problem of evil by postulating the existence of two eternal, self-existent, opposed principles as the source from which the world takes its origin; one, essentially good, and the author of all good in the world; the other, essentially bad, and the author of all its evils. This error was prevalent in the East for several centuries before Christ, especially in Persia, where Zoroaster gave it birth. Plato and his followers also taught it. In the third century after Christ, substantially the same error was fathered by the Manichaeans, so called from their founder Mani, or, as his name is sometimes written, Manes.

The evil principle in these systems is commonly said to be matter. According to Plato and his school, though it is difficult to understand just what Plato's *matter* was, it was not an active principle, but rather passive, thwarting the good principle, God, by its intractability. According to the Manichaeans this principle was active in its opposition to good. Whatever its nature, though, it was supposed to be a self-existent, independent, first principle, and so, to quote Father Rickaby again, "as the Manichaeans say, another and a rival God." Hence the name Ditheism.

J. S. Mill, who favors this solution of the problem, which makes God a finite being, writes:

One only form of belief in the supernatural—one only theory respecting the government of the universe—stands wholly clear of intellectual contradiction and of moral obliquity. It is that which, resigning irrevocably the idea of an omnipotent creator, regards Nature and Life not as the expression throughout of the moral character and purpose of the Deity, but as the product of a struggle between contriving goodness and an intractable material, as was believed by Plato, or a principle of evil, as was the doctrine of the Manichaeans. (*Essays on Religion*, p.116.)

Another author, A. Seth Pringle-Pattison, who is an idealistic pantheist, and, hence, rejects not only our solution of the problem of evil but also that of the Ditheists, has this to say of their system, especially as sponsored by Plato and J. S. Mill:

Orthodox theism is defined by Professor Flint as "The doctrine that the universe owes its existence to the reason and will of a self-existent Being, who is infinitely powerful, wise and good." But this world of ours, so scarred by suffering, so defaced by wickedness, so entangled, as it often seems, in the meshes of a non-rational contingency, how dare we trace such a world to the reason and will of a perfect Being as its sole explaining cause? Here Pluralism, in one or other of its many forms, is so obviously, on the surface, what James calls it, the line of least resistance, that one can hardly wonder at the welcome it receives. God is truly good, says Plato, and cannot be the cause of evil. But what, then, of these sinister and disconcerting features? Here are the ultimate difficulties of a theistic monism. When the problem is forced on us, Plato goes on to say, we must find out a theory to save the situation. In the case of suffering, for example, we must say that what God did was right and good, and that the sufferers were chastened for their profit. From the days of Job and his comforters, the devising of such Theodicies—theories to save the situation—has been the main business of Theology and Theological metaphysics. Plato himself, as we incidentally saw, has his own way of escape from the difficulty; and it consists essentially in saving goodness at the expense of omnipotence. "We must be prepared to deny that God is the cause of all things," he tells us in the same context; "What is good we must ascribe to no other cause than God, but we must seek elsewhere, and not in him, the cause of what is evil."

Put in Metaphysical terms this means that our explanation of the course of the world must take account, not only of a divine intelligence and goodness, but also of the clogging and thwarting agency of the material in which the divine Idea seeks embodiment. But this is to ascribe to matter an independent and co-eternal reality, and thus to set a principle of unreason alongside of or over against the purposive action of reason represented by the Idea of God. This way of escape is not open to ordinary Theism, which represents God as creator in the fullest sense. It is, however, as is well known, the position adopted by J. S. Mill in his posthumous *Essays on Religion*. Omnipotence is dismissed by Mill on account of the impossibility of "reconciling infinite knowledge and justice with infinite power in the Creator of such a world as this." The limitation of power he considers to be most probably due to the qualities of the material with which he had to deal; for "there is in nature no reason whatever to suppose that either matter or force or any of their properties were made by the Being who was the author of the collocations by which the world is adapted to what we consider its purposes; or that he has power to alter any of these properties." If [then] we suppose limitation of power, there is nothing to contradict the supposition of perfect knowledge and absolute wisdom. But nothing obliges us to suppose that either the knowledge or the will is infinite. (*The Idea of God*, pp.399ff.).

This system is to be rejected. There is, and can be, only one eternal, self-existent principle of the world—God, its Creator, who is infinite.

4. *The Pantheists.* The Pantheists, according to their most common doctrine, hold that there exists only one being, the Absolute, or, theologically speaking, God, and that all other beings in the world, which appear to be really

distinct from Him and one another, are but modifications of some kind or other of this Absolute. No matter what kind of Pantheism they profess, they are, owing to this absolutely impossible fundamental doctrine, in the equally absolutely impossible position of affirming that evils, both physical and moral, are included in and internally experienced by, are an integral part of, and are so willed by their Absolute, their God. They hold, nevertheless, that this God is infinitely good. How this can be, how physical evil and sin, which is essentially evil and opposed to God, can exist in Him and be willed by Him, they say is possible, because since God is infinitely good, all evil that exists in Him must exist as transcended evil, that is, as good. This juggling with words means that evil in God is not evil, sin in God is not sin—a clear contradiction.

Yet it is practically the solution of the problem of evil given by all present-day Pantheists. It is, of course, to be rejected, as their whole system is, and for reasons more fundamental.

It will be helpful, however, to allow a Pantheist to propose the problem with the solution we have just referred to, and which may be said to be typically pantheistic.

Mary Whiton Calkins, an Idealistic pantheist, does so, in this way:

A real difficulty is, however, involved in the reconciliation of the possible or probable goodness of the absolute self with the actually experienced evils of the universe. How, if the absolute self be inherently good, can the universe contain the evil we directly know?

Griefs which narrow and belittle the mind, unresisted temptations which work the ruin of the soul, contaminating vice with its entail of hopeless misery and multiplying sin—all these, it is urged, are evils of so positive a nature that they must taint the goodness of the self which, by virtue of its absoluteness, actually must have willed them, inasmuch as they exist.

Only one reply can be made to this objection. The absolute self, because complete, includes—it has been shown—all human experience, [therefore, sin] as an integral part of himself. It follows that the absolute self has all the experience that the human selves have. In a real sense, therefore, he shares our sorrows [and our sins], is afflicted in our affliction, knows our grief. In other words, the absolute self is no God afar off, no supreme Being who decrees misery that he does not share, no divinity who feasts and delights in a distant Olympus, while below him his human subjects toil and sin and suffer [no, he shares in all these, including sin]. But it is not conceivable that a self whose will constitutes reality should will his own evil, if that evil be positive and unconquered. The fact that the absolute self shares in human suffering [and sin] is, thus, a guarantee that the sorrow is neither final nor ultimate, that sin and misery, to human view irreconcilable with goodness, are none the less the elements— but the transcended elements—of the experience of an absolute and good self. . . . What has been insisted on is simply this: that the existence of evil is reconcilable, though not by us at this stage of our development, with the goodness of the absolute self. And the grounds of this conclusion are simply these: the absolute self has willed his own evil as well as ours; and would not have affirmed it save as subordinated to a wider good. (*Persistent Problems of Philosophy,* pp.430ff.)

5. *The finite-God Pluralists.* A Pluralist, as opposed to a Monist who is a Pantheist, is one who admits the existence of many beings distinct from God and from one another. A finite-God Pluralist is one who, among other things, solves the problem of evil, by admitting that God who rules the world, though he be good, and, many say, infinitely good, is not all-powerful. If He were, there would be no evil in the world. Though not all-powerful, still, according to the general run of these pluralists, He is powerful enough to triumph over evil finally. Because it denies the existence of the orthodox God of Theism, who is infinite in all His attributes, this variety of Pluralism is sometimes called non-Theistic. Among modern philosophers it counts many supporters. We have already noted some. Their opinion is to be rejected. God, as we have proved elsewhere, is absolutely Infinite.

How this solution of the problem of evil offers an easy descent to Atheism is shown by Professor Otto (Faculty of Philosophy, University of Wisconsin). After noting that those who hold it, cling to it because of their trust in the infinite goodness of God, even though they admit Him to be finite in intellect and power, he continues;

But if we insist that God may make mistakes and be defeated, like any one of us, what logical ground is there for maintaining that He can do no wrong? There would seem to be none. If similar to a human being in one respect, why not in another? The men we have been considering, as well as Mill, Harrison, James, and others who have been compelled by a sense of the reality of evil to insist on the finiteness of God, have always at the same time insisted upon, or tacitly assumed, His ideal goodness. It is not at all impossible, however, that their disciples living in an era of extraordinary self-assertion, may take the next step. Having been persuaded that God is not as wise or as powerful as He might be, they may become bold enough to add that He isn't as good as He might be, either. If the masters can retain their rationality only by concluding that God is doing the best He can with the limited wisdom and power at His disposal—and this they insist upon—the disciples may find it necessary, for the same reason, to conclude that God is as good as He can be in view of His moral limitations. And what if they then refrain (in May Sinclair's phrase) from "white-washing God"? Having proceeded in emancipation so far, what is to hinder them from going further and urging their fellows, with all the earnestness and zeal for social regeneration characteristic of their masters, to try the hypothesis that there is no supernatural being of any sort that cares to, or can, assist men in the furtherance of human desires.

Certain thinkers, to be sure, favor trying out this hypothesis, as various God-hypotheses have been tried out, and predict that happy results would follow the experiment. Obviously, however, the champions of the finite God are not in this class. They are quite as convinced as those who believe in the infinite God, that the attempt to operate without some kind of faith in a divinity that shapes our ends, can lead only to disaster. Nevertheless the very arguments they use to prove that God is finite, will go a long way towards proving either that His existence is doubtful, or that He may be left out of account. They come as voices in the wilderness, heralding a new God; it may be their fate to be received as pioneers of a new agnosticism. (*Things and Ideals,* p.268f.)

PROOF OF THE THESIS

If the presence in the world of neither physical nor moral evil implies any imperfection in God, the providence God exercises over the world, as a Ruler of infinite wisdom, goodness, and power, is in no way to be impugned because of the presence in the world of those evils.

But the presence in the world of neither physical nor moral evil implies any imperfection in God. Therefore.

MAJ.—Presupposing the truth of *Thesis VI,* which we have proved; and that of the thesis establishing the infinity of God, the Major is to be admitted as immediately evident. (*God Infinite and Reason, Thesis II.*)

MIN.—PART I.—*The presence of physical evil in the world implies no imperfection in God.*

It is certainly no imperfection in God to be possessed of the power to bring into the existence beings outside of Himself, and to exercise that power by an act of His efficacious will—His Omnipotence.

Again, as all beings other than God are by their very nature contingent, finite, defectible, it implies no limitation in power, no imperfection in God, to create such beings. Furthermore, it is no imperfection in God, if, moved by His own infinite Goodness to share His infinite perfections in a finite way—the only possible way—with His creatures, He made them not for themselves but for the highest end for which they could be made—Himself. That is, God made His creatures to manifest His own perfections through their perfections, in various ways and in various degrees. Thus, *all* creatures would give God *objective* glory; and *man,* God's highest creature, would give Him also *formal* glory; knowing, loving, and serving Him, their God—the Beginning and the End of all things.

Finally (and this has an immediate bearing on the truth of the Minor), it is no imperfection in God, having thus determined to bring about the manifestation of His glory in His creatures, to have done so in a universally-ordered world of surpassing beauty and magnificence; in a world filled with riches and with mysterious forces for man's finding, and for his aid and convenience; in a world in which order would be effected and perpetuated in countless instances through loss of perfections, through loss even of the existence of numberless of its members—in a word, through *physical evils.* For, while such physical evils considered from the viewpoint of the *individual members* and the *particular groups* to which they belong, are *evil,* they are yet *good,*

when considered in relation to the universal order, in subordination to the laws of which these physical evils came to
pass (laws, indeed, without which that universal order could
not exist). Such physical evils are *good,* also, in many cases,
even for the individual members suffering them, and benefiting by them in other ways. Such physical evils are *good,*
too, in the case of the individual man, for in the formation
of his character, trials and sufferings properly appreciated
and borne with, play a most important part.

In all this there is no imperfection in God, seeing that
it was but the exercise of His freedom, as Absolute Lord of
all things, in calling into existence one of the possible crea-
table worlds: that one in which changes (evil or good, from
different viewpoints), follow naturally upon the action and
interaction of the beings constituting it—changes without
which that world would be a chaos and not a cosmos. Furthermore, there is no imperfection in God, seeing that He
willed or permitted these physical evils not for themselves,
but for the good naturally brought about by them, or accompanying them, as well as (and especially so), for the
resulting universal good. For, herein is that grandeur and
glory of His visible creation, which reflects something of
His own infinite, eternal glory; which gives reasons in abundance to man (for whom proximately all other creatures in
the world were made), for knowing and loving the world's
Creator and his own, unto his final possession of God, forever. In all this, of a certainty, there is no imperfection in
God.

But, it may be objected: God, if all-powerful, might have
made a world giving Him glory equal to, and even greater
than the glory given Him by the present world, and with no
physical evil in it, or, at least, much less than His creatures
now suffer. Does not the fact that He did not do so, supposing Him to be all-powerful, seem to point to want either of
foresight, or of goodness, or of both?

The difficulty comes to this: God could have made a
physically better world. Therefore, if all-powerful, He should
have done so.

Our answer is, that this line of reasoning logically leads
to the absurd conclusion, that it would be impossible for

God to make any world. Tongiorgi (*Natural Theology,* Book 3, c.5, a.1), after enumerating not a few of the blessings that come to the world through physical evils, and especially to man, answers this difficulty well. The whole answer is worth quoting. We subjoin a translation.

In the first place, if the existence of physical evil, as such, were repugnant to God's goodness, there are many things surpassingly good which he could never will. Passing over the innumerable good effects that are produced through the destruction of the non-living substances, God would be shut out absolutely from willing many things which not only greatly benefit man, but are also the crown and glory of man's nature. To name but a few: the ennobling gift of fortitude in the face of danger, sublime and fearless patience in the midst of trials and troubles, persevering constancy in carrying out difficult enterprises, steadfast and manly self-reliance when evils threaten the soul, trust in God in adversity, the cheerful foregoing of even necessary things to gain self-control, punitive justice in righting wrongs, and mercy for the unfortunate, so lovable in man and in God. In a word, every heroic virtue, which is born only where hardships abound, and grows and flourishes in the midst of physical evils, would disappear from the face of the earth.

What is more, many of the industries so helpful to man, and many of the arts that bring him enjoyment and recreation, would never have come into being, seeing that, as the poets wisely have said, poverty and dire want gave them birth. Who is there, then, who would dare to say that the willing of these good gifts on the part of God would go counter to His goodness?

But most assuredly there are many other good things which are now brought about by certain physical evils, for example, the order in the world and the stability of society, which God could obtain without them. Even if that were granted, it could not be inferred that therefore God is obliged so to act by reason of His goodness. For, either it would be better to produce these good effects making use of physical evil, or better to produce them without it. I have no desire to decide the matter one way or the other. What is more, it might be very difficult to do so. It is sufficient for our purpose to have proposed the question. Now, if the first would be better, namely, to make use of physical evil, who would say that God because of His goodness could not make that choice? If the second way would be better, namely, to exclude physical evil, it would not be lawful on that account to conclude that God would be obliged to adopt it. First, because God in that event would have no freedom, and, secondly, thus to conclude would logically lead to the absurd affirmation that God could not create any world.

For he who is obliged to do the better, simply because it is better, is always obliged to do the better. As a consequence, he could never stop short of that which is absolutely the best. But in finite things there is no absolute best, for there is nothing finite than which something better cannot be found. It is evident, then, that God because of His goodness, cannot be obliged to exclude physical evil from that which He wills. He may, then, will physical evil as a means to a good end.

Min.—Part II—*The presence of moral evil in the world implies no imperfection in God.*

If, in endowing man with a free will capable of sinning, God acted in no way imperfectly; if He is in no sense the cause of sin; if, finally, His permission of sin is without imperfection; the presence of moral evil in the world implies no imperfection in God.

But, in endowing man with a free will capable of sinning, God acted in no way imperfectly; He is in no sense the cause of sin; finally, His permission of sin is without imperfection.

Therefore, the presence of moral evil in the world implies no imperfection in God.

Maj.—The fulfilling of the three conditions of the Major necessarily excludes the only way in which imperfection could possibly be found in God because of the presence of sin in the world. The Major, therefore, is to be conceded.

Min.—(A) *In endowing man with a free will capable of sinning, God acted in no way imperfectly.*

The greatest gift that God has bestowed on man is the gift of free will, by which man is able to merit the possession of God, loving, and loved by Him, for all eternity. Who will say that the giving of this gift points to any imperfection in God? Yet this gift—the power to merit the possession of God— the greatest glory of human nature, brings with it to man his greatest danger, the power to offend God, and even to lose Him forever; the power, namely, to sin grievously, and to persevere in such sin till death. God, however, gives this gift to man not that he may abuse it but that he may use it in reaching the end for which he was made, namely, to obey God's law, praising, reverencing, and serving Him in this life, and so meriting to possess Him in love forever. This is evident, first, from the fact that God by His law absolutely prohibits sin, sanctioning His law with the promise of eternal reward for all who persevere in its obedience, and with the threat of eternal punishment for those who die in revolt against it; and secondly, from the fact that He gives to man at all times sufficient help to obey His law.

Min.—(B) *God is in no sense the cause of sin.*

Sin is essentially opposed to the Infinite Goodness of God. God must, then, and does, absolutely prohibit it. It is absolutely impossible that He should be its author or cause.

It is to be carefully noted, however, that when we say that God cannot be the cause of sin, we mean sin looked at formally, that is, the sinful action considered inasmuch as it lacks conformity with the moral law, for sin formally consists in this privation. It is this privation which makes the sinful act, sinful.

Now, as no action can be put by a creature without God's concurrent action in putting it, it is evident that God is the cause with man in putting the act which *is* sinful. The act, however, *as* sinful, as deprived of conformity with, as turning away from the moral law, is put by the man, and only by the man. For in concurring with man in man's free actions, God in virtue of His will to allow man to act freely, leaves the choice of the action to man. The man only determines the choice. The man, and the man only, is responsible for it. In fact, where the choice lies in the direction of sin, it is absolutely impossible for God to make such choice. As the one who makes this choice, however, is the author or cause of the sin, as such, God cannot be its cause.

The effect [writes St. Thomas] which proceeds from the middle cause, according as it is subordinate to the first cause, is reduced to that first cause; but if it proceeds from the middle cause, according as it goes outside the order of the first cause, is not reduced to that first cause. Thus if a servant do anything contrary to his master's orders, it is not ascribed to the master as though he were the cause thereof. In like manner sin, which the free-will commits against the commandment of God, is not attributed to God as being its cause. (*Summa Theologica,* 1, 2, q.79, a.2, reply to Obj. 3.)

MIN.—(C) *God's permission of sin implies no imperfection in Him.*

Although God is in no sense the cause or author of formal sin, still He could, if He so willed, prevent it. If, then, man sins, he sins with God's permission. It remains to be shown, therefore, that God's permission of man's sin in the world is without any imperfection or defect in Him.

If such defect could be found, it would affect God with regard to some one or other of His perfections which are concerned with His providential government of man; His Supreme Dominion, His Holiness, His Mercy, His Wisdom, His Justice. God's permission of sin, however, implies no imperfection in Him with regard to any of these perfections.

The Supreme Dominion of God over His creatures is in no way lessened by His permission of sin, even of sin which brings final impenitence, for although the sinner in sinning, and dying in sin, refuses to give God formal glory, which God desires only on condition that man also desires to give it, still God will not be deprived of the degree of glory He determined on in creating the world. For, presupposing the fact of the sin, God takes occasion from it for the manifestation of His glory in many ways: on His own part, in showing His mercy in pardoning the sinner, in showing His long-suffering patience in bearing with Him, and His justice in punishing him here, and hereafter, if he perseveres in his sin; on the sinner's part, in his sorrow and consequent better life; on the part of his fellow men, in their hatred for sin, mercy for the sinner, and so on. This point will be considered again in a Scholion.

It is to be carefully noted, however, that God does not permit sin with the intention of further manifesting His glory through it. To do so would be to will the permission, and, hence, the sin, as a means to that manifestation. On the contrary, the foreseeing by God of the way in which He will further His glory by permitting sin, is an absolutely necessary condition for the giving of such permission.

Again, God's Supreme Dominion is not lessened by His permission of sin, for this permission does not, cannot, give the sinner the power to sin with impunity. The sinner is physically, but not morally, free. He must render an account of his stewardship. If he has obeyed God's law, he will be rewarded; if he has refused service, he will be punished, and, in the case of those finally impenitent, with eternal punishment.

The Holiness of God is not to be called in question because of His permission of sin. That permission in no way implies that God's essential hatred of it is any way lessened. To give man the power through the exercise of his free will to offer his love and himself to God, and to be beloved by Him forever, it was necessary that man should have the power to refuse to serve God, and, so, by sinning, to reject Him. Now, God's hatred for sin, which He thus permits, is shown in the perfect sanction of the moral law by which the unrepentant sinner is separated from God forever. On the other hand, God's desire to save all men, to join them in love with His Goodness, to sanctify them in His possession forever, if they will only will it, is shown by the innumerable aids and helps He gives man to avoid sin and save his soul.

What is more, God's permission of sin, as we saw, is in no way possible unless that permission is conditioned by the good which God will bring about through it, as the occasion. God's Holiness, then, is in no way involved in His permission of sin.

The Mercy of God is in no way to be called in question because of His permission of sin. On the contrary, that permission, and the sinner's actual sinning, are the occasion for manifestations of His mercy which are beyond our understanding. Some examples are: God's longsuffering patience with the sinner, no matter how heinous his sins; His constant calling to the sinner, through the voice of conscience, to repent of his sins; His readiness to forgive, and restore the sinner to his former place of friendship, no matter how frequent his falls; the sending of His Son, the Second Person of the Most Blessed Trinity, to become man, to live and suffer and die to redeem sinners, and save them; all the

internal, actual aids given, through the merits of Christ's
Redemption, to sinners, with the rest of mankind, to live
worthily according to the light granted them; the gift to
mankind, including sinners, of the Church of Christ with
all its Sacraments and other aids to salvation; and—also to
be attributed to God's merciful providence, and shared in
by sinners—all the prayers and good works offered by the
faithful in general, and especially those consecrated to God,
for the furthering of the kingdom of God. What is more,
God's mercy embraces all sinners even to the last moment
of their lives. It is true, that many sinners are lost; through
their own fault, however, and despite God's mercy, for God's
justice must also be served.

God's Justice does not suffer because He permits man to
sin. Man has no rights in respect of God. God, however, is
obliged by His own infinite perfection to give man all that
He needs to reach the end for which He created him, namely,
freely to praise, reverence, and serve God in this life, and
so to merit possession of Him forever. God, too, having made
man for this end, is obliged by His own infinite perfection
to reward man according to his merits and to demand satis-
faction according to his demerits. This is all that God, in
His Justice, is obliged to do; and this God does. If man, then,
despite God's absolute prohibition, wishes to misuse the
means God has given him for service, to transgress God's
laws, and, sinning, to lose God forever, man only is in fault,
not God. God, in no sense, is to be accused of injustice. God's
justice, therefore, does not suffer because He permits man
to sin.

The Wisdom of God is not to be called in question because He permits sin, if such permission, even in the case
of sinners dying in grievous sin, does not interfere with
either the primary or secondary end God had in creating
the world, for, so, the sin and the sinner are subordinated
to His providential Will.

Now, God's permission of sin does not interfere with the
primary end of creation, namely, the determined degree of
glory God willed to obtain in creating the world. For though
the sinner by sinning refused to give to God in this life the
formal glory He conditionally desires, God in His infinite

wisdom uses the sin as an occasion for obtaining compensating formal glory from others, and even from the sinner himself, now repentant. And, again, though the impenitent sinner dying in his sin will not give God for all eternity the formal glory He conditionally desired, he shall give Him objective glory, namely, by his justly deserved punishment, which gives to others a reason for eternally formally glorifying the justice of God.

Nor does God's permission of sin interfere with the secondary end for which He created the world, namely, the eternal happiness of His rational creatures. This end He achieves, notwithstanding sin in the world, since He wills it, conditioned on their free service; and that most wisely, namely, to give to His rational creatures the greatest of gifts—the means of meriting to live with Himself, their Beginning and End, in loving friendship for all eternity.

It may appear to some, however, that the foregoing proof leaves untouched one aspect of the problem of sin, from which an argument may be drawn to show that God, in permitting sin, and in particular sin bringing with it the final impenitence and eternal separation of the sinner from God, is wanting in mercy.

This is their argument: Before decreeing the existence of the present world, God foresaw everything that might possibly happen in it. He foresaw, in particular, in the case of a sinner about to die in sin, that if He gave him a greater grace than the one he was about to receive, or called him out of life a day sooner, when he was in the state of grace, he would be saved and would give formal glory to God forever. It was within God's power thus to save the sinner. His infinite love, especially for sinners seems to demand that He do so. Instead He permits the sinner to die impenitent. Is this the way that Infinite Mercy would act?

Before answering this difficulty, it must be noted, as we noted before, that it is altogether beyond us to say why it is that God, who, absolutely speaking, could give to the dying sinner a grace with which he would be saved, does not do so. God alone knows that. But to say, as is said in the difficulty, that at the risk of being called unmerciful, God is obliged to give such grace, is not to safeguard God's Mercy or any

of His infinite perfections, but to subject Him, the Absolute
Lord of all things, to the ungoverned will of the sinner. This
will be clear from the following answer to the difficulty—an
answer which does nothing more than make explicit what
our proof already implies.

   This is the answer. The Infinite Wisdom of God, who
alone knows fully the malice of sin, its essential opposition
to His own Godhead, and Goodness and Sanctity; who alone
knows the complete history of the dying sinner, demands
that in dealing with sinners, not one or another but all of
His infinite perfections are to be safeguarded. Therefore, in
dealing with the impenitent sinner, His Supreme Lordship
over all creatures, His Holiness, His Wisdom, His Justice,
are to be considered in dispensing His Mercy. *That,* we have
done in our proof, in which we have provided for the safeguarding of all these perfections of God which are concerned
with his creatures. *That,* the suggestion offered in the difficulty does not do. It safeguards, in reality, none of God's
perfections, for, to say nothing of other injustices it would
do to God, this crowning injustice results from it—it would
deprive God of His Supreme Lordship over creatures, and
would make Him subject to the rebellious will of the sinner.
The sinner would determine the time of his own death, the
sinner would determine the kind of grace to be given him at
that moment. An example, allegorically presented, will make
this clear.

   Let us take a man, who, having been assured that he will
not live beyond the next two years, determines to live them
as he pleases. Time and again he will deliberately offend God
grievously. Occasionally he will repent, only to fall soon
again. Thus, the major part of the two years will be spent
at enmity with God, in satisfying his own passions.

   This sinner thus addresses God, in words which but
faintly express what his actions more loudly proclaim: "My
Lord and My God! With a clear knowledge of the great
gifts You have given me and the love You have shown me
in forgiving the innumerable sins of my past life, I nevertheless intend during the coming two years, whenever I feel
so inclined, by my life, to profane Your Holy Name, to tram-
ple Your gifts under foot, and, as far as in my power lies,

to crucify You. I will repent at times, and for short intervals seek again Your Friendship. It is in Your power to call me out of life during those two years when You will. At the risk, however, of being called unmerciful You dare not summon me to judgment outside of those times in which You will find me in the state of grace." If God were obliged so to act, who would be master, God or the sinner?

SCHOLION I—*The good side of physical evil.*

In this Scholion, only those physical evils which affect man and other sentient beings are considered, and principally in relation to the good with which in one way or another they are connected. In some instances our knowledge of this good comes to us through Divine Revelation. In all cases it is for the good which is connected with them, and not for themselves, that these evils are intended or permitted by God. The list which follows is not to be considered in any way exhaustive.

1. It may be well to recall here, what has already been noted in more general terms and more fully, namely, that what is considered a physical evil (that is, a privation of a physical perfection), when we confine our attention to one part of a whole, or to one order in an ordered system, may, and should, be called *good,* when considered in relation to the good of the whole, or the system, for the furthering of which it is necessary. For example, the loss of a finger through a surgical operation to save the individual; the destruction of plants and animals to supply food necessary for man's physical well-being.

Father Joyce's treatment of this point is worth recording:

As we have already urged, apart from man, the end proposed by the Creator is the perfection of the system of nature as a whole, not that of any individual creature. Where a system composed of many parts is in question, the perfection of the whole must often demand the sacrifice of the constituent elements viewed as individuals. The organizer of the system does not desire or intend harm as such to any part. But he permits that individual parts should forfeit something, in order that the good of the whole may be thereby promoted. To the system of nature it is necessary that the species should be preserved. Hence the continuance of the predatory tribes [animal] is

secured by providing them with the food suitable to them, and
that of the tribes [animal] on which they prey by the enormous
reproductivity of which we have been speaking. The destruction
of a multitude of individuals is tolerated. Undoubtedly this is,
from one point of view, an evil. But the evil of one species is
compensated by the benefit done to others. Nor would it be
reasonable to urge that the system of nature should have been
so altered that the various tribes [animal] should do each other
no hurt: that the lion should eat straw like the ox, and the
spider live out its days without doing damage to the fly. This
would be to ask, not merely for a perpetual miracle, but for
an order of things far less in accordance with divine wisdom
than is the present system. Granted that the Creator has given
being to these types of perfection which we know as carnivora
and insectivora, wisdom would seem to demand that provision
should be made for them in accordance with their respective
natures and not in opposition to them.

When once it is realized, if we prescind from the case of
man, God's end is the good of the whole and not the good of
the individual, it will be readily seen that even death and corruption, which might appear to be pure evil in regard of sentient life, serve in fact as a useful and, indeed, necessary end.
Did not death remove the older generations, earth would soon
afford no room for the latest comers; nor would it be possible
for these to find food. . . . Death is thus an essential part of
nature's provision for the benefit of the species. So also the corruption of dead matter, great as is the repugnance which it ex-
cites in us, is beneficial in its results. Were it not that through
the destructive activity of germ life, the inanimate body is
resolved again into its constituent elements, earth would become
a vast collection of corpses. In the actual course of things it at
all periods affords a home adapted to the beings which the
Creator has placed in it.

The foregoing considerations suffice, we think, to show that
the physical evils of the world, so far at least as they affect lower
creatures, are in no way incompatible with the wisdom and
power of God. . . . Granted that in the exercise of His freedom,
He chose to create a universe inhabited by successive generations
of sentient beings, even our human intelligence, limited as it is,
can see that there are good reasons why He should not remove
the evil naturally incident to creatures such as those which He
made, but should allow it to remain, using it, however, as the
means to the attainment of good. (*Principles of Natural Theology*, pp. 589ff.)

2. There is a natural compensation in this, that the faculties which bring us (and what is said here is true, in due measure, of other sentient beings), sensible pain, also bring us sensible pleasure; and more than compensation, for the sensible pleasure we experience through those faculties far outweighs the sufferings we occasionally experience through them. What is more, sensible pain, in many instances, is nature's way of warning us of impending danger, and of efficaciously urging us to seek safety from it, seeing that we are moved by pain more quickly than by any other motive to seek what is good for us and avoid what is harmful. For although naturally speaking we are busied rather in striving for what is good than in flying from what is evil, still through a lazy contentment in the enjoyment of a lesser good we are loth to make the effort to seek a greater one. It is only the insistent urging of pain which finally rouses us to action. Finally, nature which usually preserves a due proportion between the intensity of the pain crying for relief and the seriousness of the threatening evil, also wisely provides, in not a few cases, that when the pain becomes too intense we lose consciousness.

3. Physical evils of all kinds, both sensible, and suprasensible, that is, those which afflict man in spirit, have other values for man which are almost beyond estimation.

In the first place, driven by a natural desire to overcome these evils, man, endowed with a most wonderful intellect by God, busies himself in season and out of season in all different kinds of investigations to find ways and means to accomplish that end. Witness to this are the countless individuals devoting their lives to research work—to mention but a few fields: in chemistry, physics, mechanics, navigation, meteorology, geology, seismology, biology, medicine, surgery, psycho-therapy, and so on endlessly. An evil threatening the well-being of man, even one causing no more than an inconvenience, has but to appear, and lo! hundreds of heads and hands are busy seeking some way to overcome it.

Another marked benefit brought to man through physical evils of all kinds, if they are properly appreciated, is the role they play in character formation and development. As Father Tongiorgi has already sufficiently elaborated this point for us, a further consideration of it here will not be necessary.

Closely allied to the two above-mentioned classes of benefits which have come to man through physical evils, is another from the same source, and one of incalculable value. It is found in the spontaneous and generous application to suffering humanity, in natural crises, of the scientifically discovered remedies for their ills, above-mentioned, and of other relief measures. And in this application, requiring frequently the practice of heroic virtue, is found another instance of the character-formation value for man, which comes through physical evil. How many are the ennobling virtues practised in the care of the sick in hospitals, homes for incurables, asylums for the mentally deranged, on battlefields; in the care of orphans, the aged poor, and of human derelicts in general! Word goes forth of the destruction of life and property, with all other kinds of accompanying evils, caused by a flood, a hurricane, an earthquake, or by some other major catastrophe, and immediately, and frequently at the sacrifice of material wealth, comfort, health, and, sometimes, of life itself, aid pours in from all sides.

Stressing the above points, and some others of prime importance and meriting our most careful consideration, Father Joyce writes:

The case of man, as we have said, differs widely from that of the lower animals. We have seen that where these latter are concerned, the fate of the individual is a matter of indifference. The species, not the particular individual, is requisite for the perfection of the natural order. And providence disposes of the individual for the benefit of the species—its own or another. With man it is not so. By reason of his immortal destiny each individual man is an end, irrespective of the race to which he belongs or even of the universe as a whole. Divine providence is concerned with him for his own sake. It is not enough to show that what is hurtful to the individual subserves the good of the whole. It must appear that though evil under one aspect, it is not really opposed to the highest good of the individual himself.

Yet, though the reasons which we have hitherto employed are inadequate to explain fully physical evil in relation to man, many of the considerations advanced retain their force. Thus,

of man, as of the animals, it is true that the balance is im-
mensely on the side of happiness. The pessimist who declares
that, in view of the suffering of life, existence is an evil, misrep-
resents the facts. There is plenty of joy in life, though to much
of it we are so habituated that we accept it as a matter of course.
Let a man be deprived, for instance, of the use of a single sense—
of hearing, or sight, or the power of speech—and he quickly
becomes aware how much pleasure has hitherto streamed in
through that avenue, though in all probability he seldom, if
ever, adverted to the delight he was experiencing. The problem
before us is certainly not to explain why the Creator has made
misery our portion. In the main, our lot is such as to bear witness to His goodness and His omnipotence. We are merely
concerned to learn why He has not removed suffering altogether
from our life.

Much light is thrown on the question by the consideration
that this life is a probation, . . . Man's true end . . . is the
possession of the Supreme Good. . . . If, then, it can be shown
that physical evil is one of the most important factors in assisting
man to the attainment of his end, it at once becomes evident
that there was ample reason why God should not interfere with
the course of nature, but should tolerate the existence of physical
suffering in view of the good which would result.

Pain is the great stimulant to action. Man, no less than the
animals, is impelled to work by the sense of hunger. Experience
shows that were it not for this motive, the majority of men would
be content to live in indolent ease. . . . Moreover, suffering
serves to call forth in man a measure of goodness which would
otherwise never be realized at all. Virtue reaches its perfection
when it is exercised at a severe cost to the agent. . . . And one
reason, plainly, why God permits pain is that man may rise to
a height of heroism which would otherwise have been altogether
beyond his scope. Nor are these the only benefits which it confers. That sympathy for others, which is one of the most precious
parts of our experience and one of the most fruitful sources
of wellbeing, has its origin in the fellow-feeling engendered by
the endurance of similar trials. Furthermore, were it not for
these trials man would think little enough of a future existence,
and of the need of striving for his last end. . . . The sufferings
of men are directed primarily to the good of the sufferer himself, while they also afford to others the opportunity for the
practice of virtue.

In the same way, we need feel no perplexity at the numerous

instances in which human life is cut short prematurely. . . . When life is viewed as above all else a probation, it seems to be of little importance whether a man live out his full tale of years or not. Indeed, the shortening of the probation may be to the individual, not a loss, but an immense gain.

The earthquake and the volcano serve a moral end which more than compensates for the physical evil they cause. The awful nature of these phenomena, the overwhelming power of the forces at work, and man's utter helplessness before them, rouse him from the religious indifference to which he is so prone. . . .

We have laid stress on the value of pain in relation to the next life, because it is in the next life, and not in this, that man must obtain his last end. But it scarcely needs to be pointed out that pain is a source of many benefits in this life also. The advance of scientific discovery, the gradual improvement of the organization of the community, the growth of material civilization—all these are due in no small degree to the stimulus afforded by pain. (*Principles of Natural Theology,* pp. 592ff.)

4. The following remarks rightly have place in this Scholion, for though they do not show formally the good side of the world's physical evils, they do so equivalently. They make clear, namely, the fatal weakness of the arguments of modern philosophers for a God of limited power, based as they are on a misunderstanding of the nature of physical evil.

An omnipotent God would be responsible for all the physical evils in the world, and, so, wanting in goodness. This is the argument of many, especially of many modern philosophers who are willing to admit the existence of a good God of some sort but not an omnipotent one. It is abundantly evident, however, and altogether apart from what we know from divine Revelation, that man, not God, is responsible for most of the physical evils, and those the most grievous ones, which afflict mankind. Not a few of these are due to man's careless or over-confident tampering with nature's forces; many, to his manifold, rank injustices especially towards the downtrodden and poor; and many more to his countless, abominable sins committed in the nature given him by God to be honored and not debased below the level of the brute beast. These sins God hates as He hates all sin. He is in no way responsible for them or for the physical evils following from them. For His own good reason He permits both, drawing from them, however, a compensating measure of good, which His infinite Wisdom alone could foresee and arrange, and His Omnipotence bring about.

Again, these same philosophers, either not admitting a future life for man, or, at least, not seriously concerned with it, insist that man's endeavors on earth should be directed mainly, if not solely, to success in this life. And a successful life, for the generality of them, means one of easy, pleasureful contentment, with riches and honor enough for its enjoyment, and a certain amount of regard for the "golden rule." They live for this life only. "Otherworldliness," as they call it, is a crime. Anything interfering with this ideal they set themselves—pain, poverty, or physical trials of any kind— they consider an unmixed evil. They are blind to its character-forming, uplifting value. Evidently, if they admit the existence of a God at all, He must be one of limited power for otherwise none of these evils which they dread would exist. These men miss altogether the purpose of life. If God made man to enjoy here below one round of pleasure after another, His work was a failure.

Altogether out of perspective, also, is the valuation these philosophers place on the physical evils of animals in arguing from them to the admission of a non-omnipotent God. They speak of the ferocity and cruelty shown by many animals in the destruction of those of other kinds to supply themselves with food. As one of them, Hermann Lotze, *Outlines of a Philosophy of Religion,* puts it: "It is incorrect to regard physical evil as something accessory and accidental. It does not come intermittently; but, on the contrary, the whole animal creation is systematically based on the extermination of one creature by another, and on a cruelty typified in their instincts." And another, F. C. Conybere, *Myth, Magic and Morals,* writes: "It might be argued that evil among men is their own fault. But let Professor . . . become a biologist and study the natural history of insects and parasitic organisms; and I question if his belief in the love and goodness of an omnipotent author of nature will not be rudely put to the test. . . . There is . . . plenty of room left in the universe for loving spirits, but not for omnipotent ones."

There is no such thing, however, as ferocity or cruelty among animals. Words such as these connote a reprehensible want of control, in the agent, of the actions to which they are applied. They may be said of man in certain cases when he acts excessively unreasonably. They may never be used rightly of animals. Animals have control of none of their actions, and, as a consequence, are never reprehensible. They always act in accord with their natures. And "the extermination of one creature by another" is but the orderly process of nature in perpetuating the countless organisms which add so much to the glory of our wonderful world, and has nothing of that cruelty which these philosophers would read into it.

What is more, these philosophers, when considering the physical evils which befall animals seem to think that the physical sufferings of animals are comparable with those of man. On the sensible side of man's physical suffering —which is the sole aspect of an animal's suffering—there is some likeness. But even here, as there are very good reasons to believe, with the exception perhaps of some of the higher species of animals, their nervous organism is not nearly as sensitive to pain as man's is. This, however, is a minor point; for no matter how intense their pains may be, their sufferings in no way approach those of man. And that, because they lack the spiritual faculties of man—those faculties which are man's glory, but which also bring him the capacity for untold sufferings. He fears; he is filled with horror; he writhes in agony of spirit; he is the victim of despair; he can bring a past life filled with pain and sorrow into the present; he can look into the future and realize the dreary length of days that lie before him in suffering from an incurable disease; he can bring the sufferings of those he loves into his own heart and suffer with them; he can compare his own sad lot with that of the more fortunate; he can realize fully with vain regrets how easily he might have avoided his present misfortune had he made the slightest of efforts—all these, and more, are what a man may suffer. An animal knows not one of them. It has no knowledge; it cannot appreciate its own sufferings or those of others; it suffers each moment only the suffering of the moment, and only its own sufferings of the moment, and only its own sufferings and nothing more. The sufferings of animals are grossly exaggerated by those who would find in them an argument against the wise providence of God.

Scholion II—*The good of which moral evil is the occasion.*

This good comprises in general the further manifestation of God's glory in His infinite power, wisdom, and justice, and, above all, in His infinite mercy, with its gift to sinners, surpassing all understanding, the source of countless other gifts: God the Son, made man for their salvation.

When rightly viewed and patiently borne in the light of this greater mystery of Divine Love for fallen man, the Mystery of Suffering and Sin becomes for the Christian a source of many blessings, through the innumerable occasions it gives him for a closer following of his triumphant Saviour, in the Way of the Cross.

This will be made clear in the course of the following brief review of the good which, through sin (which He hates, but with full right and good reason permits), God takes occasion, in His infinitely wise and omnipotent providence, to accomplish.

With sin, then, as the occasion:

1. God's infinite Wisdom and Power are glorified, by obtaining, notwithstanding man's countless rebellions, which He permits, that degree of glory from the world which, in creating it, He determined to obtain. For, though the sinner, in sinning, denies God the formal glory which is due to Him, he cannot escape giving Him objective or material glory, in suffering the penalty he must pay for his sins.

In a special way this is true of the objective glory which those souls who have died at enmity with God, will give Him for all eternity by their suffering. The blessed in heaven, acknowledging the justice of this punishment, because of it, will give formal glory to God in His Justice forever.

2. God's infinite Justice is glorified by demanding full reparation for all sins committed, punishing the sinner in

this life, and, if necessary, in the life to come, for a time, or even eternally in the case of those sinners who, refusing to co-operate with the graces given them by God, die His enemies. The objective glory which these sinners by their punishment will give to God eternally, is, as was noted above, translated into formal glory by the angels and saints in heaven, who on that account will praise God in His Justice without end.

3. God's infinite Mercy and Love are glorified in the infinite Gift He gives of Himself; God the Son, made Man to redeem sinful man and restore him to the supernatural state lost through the sin of Adam.

As the magnitude of this Gift, the offering of infinite formal glory, in the very Person of God the Son, to God the Father, in reparation for all the glory denied by sinners, is altogether beyond our comprehension, so also is the infinite Mystery of God's Love for man, which prompted it: a Love, which wrought not merely man's Redemption, but Man's divinely superabundant Redemption.

One action of the God-Man offered in atonement for all the sins of the world, would have been more than sufficient. And what *was* offered? A Saviour, born in poverty, living in poverty, preaching the Kingdom of God in the midst of trials, bitter persecution, and at the frequent risk of His life; betrayed shamelessly by one of His own disciples, deserted by the others and denied by their leader; most cruelly and unjustly tortured; though absolutely innocent, condemned to an ignominious death, and, finally, His innocence in His very condemnation acknowledged, offering His life with the outpouring of His Blood on the Cross—all for fallen man's Redemption, and to help him to apply the fruits of that Redemption, to his own soul, by bearing the trials and sufferings and sorrows and injustices of life in union with Him, and as He bore them, the glorious Victor over death and sin in the way of His cross to Calvary, and, through Calvary, to a glorious Resurrection.

And not only that, but showing us also the true value to be placed on the Cross, in sending trials and sufferings to those who were dearest and closest to Him when in this life, His own Immaculate Mother, His Foster Father, His dis-

ciples, and down through the centuries, in the trials and sufferings of countless martyrs—martyrs unto the actual shed-
ding of their lifeblood for His sake, and martyrs to long and
hidden lives of suffering and persecutions borne in imitation
of Him, with Him and for Him.

Add to this, the founding of His indestructible, infallible,
divine-truth teaching Church, with its supernatural life-
giving life-restoring, life-building Sacraments, His own Body
and Blood for our daily Food, and Himself everywhere and
continually offered in Sacrifice in the Mass for fallen man's
Redemption.

Nor must we forget, in enumerating the many ways in
which God's Love and Mercy are made manifest because of
sin, the divine tenderness with which sinners are sought and
pardoned, and their full heritage as sons of God restored to
them, time after time, and even after lives of sin, if but a
word of loving repentance is whispered; nor all the acts of
formal glory in their later life offered by repentant sinners
motivated by a saving humility and confusion at the remem-
brance of their former rebellions; nor the countless souls led
to repentance and greater love of God because of the example given by these converted sinners—a Peter, a Mary Mag-
dalen, an Augustine, and countless others known only to God
and to those saved through them.

Finally, among the many good gifts and graces that have
come to man through sin, are the never-ending prayers for
sinners and acts of reparation for sins committed, offered up
by the Church and the faithful—priests, religious, and pious
men and women, singly, and united in societies of Reparation, especially the world-wide Apostleship of Prayer.

What wonder, then, if the Church, in her liturgy, in an
ecstasy of joy, hails as happy the fault of Adam; happy not in
itself, but in that it merited for us "such and so great a
Saviour"!

SCHOLION III.—*Divine Revelation and the Problem of
Evil.*

Unaided reason is philosophy's intrinsic guide, its source
of knowledge. No appeal, then, can be made by it legitimately to Divine Revelation, as a motive for the acceptance

of any of its conclusions. We are making no such appeal in this Scholion, nor have we done so elsewhere, for the acceptance of the truth stated in our thesis. Our appeal to Divine Revelation is for another purpose altogether. It is this.

The *Problem of Evil* is not merely an intellectual one. It is also, and perhaps, more so, a deeply practical one, affecting our whole lives. Evils of all kinds, more or less numerous, beset everyone, personally, or through family ties, or through ties of friendship, or through suffering Society—the Church, one's native land—or through more than one, or even all of these sources. These evils make the problem an individual one. How it can be solved in its entirety no man knows nor can know. Only God knows why He chose to make this sin-laden, sorrow-full world. Even in individual cases, to find a solution naturally is all but impossible. Why, for instance, has God, if He is a loving God, allowed the death of a young wife, with that of her first, just-born child; a cross which has wrecked a happy home, and brought almost to despair a devoted husband? Why has a God-fearing, family-loving mother, bereft of her husband, yet struggling bravely through years of poverty and hunger to bring up her children in the way of God, had the added heart-breaking cross to bear of seeing a son or daughter give up all religious practices and enter on a life of shameless sin? How can we reconcile with the notion of an all-wise, infinitely loving God, who could have prevented them in their remote beginnings, if He so willed, the recurring wars of hate and greed between nations, bringing in their train desolation for millions and moral evils of all kinds; or the handing over of whole nations to continual, cruel, unbelievable sufferings at the hands of rulers whose sole aim is to destroy everything good and holy—God's own Church, His faithful children and even God Himself? Why? And so on without end.

To explain satisfactorily, from the viewpoint of reason alone, why these and like evils are permitted by God to be interwoven, continually interwoven, into the life of man, is, as we said above, next to impossible. To find motives, however, which will help suffering mankind to bear up under them with patient fortitude, realizing that physical evils, of whatever kind they may be, may be so borne that they will be transmuted into the greatest of blessings—that moral evil is permitted by an infinitely just yet infinitely merciful God—*that* is possible; but possible, only when we learn to view the temporal evils of the world from God's eternal viewpoint; and reason cannot help us here. The ways of God's infinite Wisdom are to worldly wisdom foolishness.

What we need, then, is God's own infallible word, reassuring us, as He has reassured us in many ways, but especially in His revelations in word and deed as God-man during His life on earth, that no matter what evils befall, they do so only with the permission of God; a God of infinite Wisdom and Justice and Love, who loves us with a love beyond our comprehension, who died for us sinners, who bore all kinds of trials and an ignominious death to redeem us, and teach us that there is only one real evil in the world, sin; and even for that, to the repentant sinner, pardon "even till seventy times seven"; that suffering and trials, when borne with Him and for Him, are the surest means of salvation—the royal road of the cross, leading to Calvary, Resurrection, and glory with Him in heaven forever.

Our appeal to Divine Revelation, then, all too briefly made in the preceding Scholion, is to give heart to afflicted mankind; to the sinner, to return in sorrow to a loving God, only too willing to receive and forgive him—He died for him; to the just, struggling bravely on though weighed down with suffering and sorrow, to go forward with renewed courage, with the firm assurance that the crosses they bear are their share of the Cross of Christ, which He bore alone and now bears with them, to certain victory. God Himself tells us:

Blessed are they that suffer persecution for justice sake, for theirs is the kingdom of heaven. Blessed are ye when they shall revile you, and persecute you, and speak all that is evil against you, for my sake: be glad and rejoice, for your reward is very great in heaven; for so they persecuted the prophets that were before you. (Matt. 5:10-13.)

Then Jesus said to his disciples: If any man will come after me, let him deny himself, and take up his cross, and follow me. For he that will save his life, shall lose it; and he that shall lose his life for my sake, shall find it. (Matt. 16:24, 25.)

Humble thy heart and endure, incline thy ear and receive the words of understanding: and make not haste in the time of clouds. Wait on God with patience, join thyself to God, and endure, that thy life may be increased in the latter end. Take all that shall be brought upon thee, and in thy sorrow endure and in thy humiliation keep patience. For gold and silver are tried in the fire, but acceptable men in the furnace of tribulation. (Eccli. 2:2-5.)

If your sins be as scarlet, they shall be made as white as snow: and if they be red as crimson they shall be white as wool. (Is. 1:18.)

I am, I am He that blot out thy iniquities for my own sake, and I will not remember thy sins. (Is. 43:23.)

Difficulties

1. If God were a just and all-powerful ruler of the world, the good and evil things of this life would be proportioned to the needs, the rights and merits of each individual. But they are not so proportioned. Therefore.

D. Maj. They would be proportioned if man's final end is to be found in this life, *C.*; if it is to be found in a life to come, *N.—Cd. Min.*

This life is a place of trial. Man's final end is in the life to come. The merits and demerits that count with God, are merits and demerits in the moral order. Man will be rewarded according to his fidelity in keeping the law of God, and punished according to his infidelity. The final reckoning will come at the end of man's life. His final reward or punishment will come then, and it will be possession of God for all eternity, or separation from Him in suffering for all eternity. It is not how much riches and pleasures you may have in this life, or how much poverty and sufferings you bear, that counts. What counts is, how, in the midst of riches and pleasures, poverty and suffering, you have lived in accordance with God's law binding you in conscience. It might be well to add that, even in this life, a man, living in poverty and suffering, whose conscience is clean before God, is in reality much happier than a rich man with all his worldly pleasures, but with a sin-laden conscience that tortures him continually.

2. If all things fall under the wise, just, and all-powerful providence of God, wicked human rulers whose government is rankly unjust must be said to fall under it. But that cannot be said of such rulers. Therefore.

D. Maj. And falling under it would mean that God in any way intends or approves their sinful actions, *N.*; it would mean that, while allowing them the exercise of physical liberty and at the same time prohibiting their sinful actions, God, for reasons, in the last analysis, appealing to, and known only by His infinite wisdom, permits those actions, taking occasion from them to bring about many good effects, one of which, is the showing forth of His infinite Justice, in demanding from such rulers a full accounting for their actions, and inflicting punishment, even eternal, *C.—Cd. Min.*

Cf. the Prenotes to the thesis, *passim*; the Proof of the thesis with regard to moral evil; Scholion II, *The good of which moral evil is the occasion.*

3. If God, the Maker and Ruler of the world, were infinitely wise, merciful, and powerful, He should have made a world, supposing that He wished to make one, the best possible, or, at least, better than the present one, so full of suffering and sin. But God, as is evident, failed to do so. Therefore.

— *Maj. Part I: God should have made the best possible world.*

D. God should have made, as He did make, relatively the best possible world, *C.*; He should have made absolutely the best possible world, *N.—Cd. Min., Part I.*

The world which God has made is relatively the best possible world, that is, the world best fitted to attain the end God intended in making it. It is not absolutely the best possible world, for the simple reason that a best possible world is an impossibility. A possible world is necessarily a finite world, a world limited in perfection, and, hence, always admitting the possibility of a better one.

Maj. Part II: God should have made a world better than the present one.

N. This part of the Major is to be denied, and for the following reasons:

(a) To insist that God should have made a better world than the present one, is an unwarranted demand to limit God's freedom. He might have refrained, and with absolute right, from making any world, or He might have made, and with the same right, in place of the present world, any one of the countless other possible ones, since in whatever world He would chose to make, His infinite Wisdom, Mercy, Justice, and Power, would necessarily be exercised as it is in the present world.

(b) If God were obliged to make a better world than the one He wished to make, merely because it would be better, He could make no world at all, for there would always be one still better than the one He wished to make.

Cf. for an explanation of these answers, *passim,* the Prenotes to the Thesis, its Proofs, and Scholions.

4. If there are, and have been, many men in the world habitually unjust and licentious, God's providence in their regard would not appear to be that of an infinitely wise, holy, merciful, and powerful ruler. But there are, and have been many men of that kind in the world. Therefore.

D. Maj. God's providence in their regard would not appear to have those qualities, if God were in any way the cause of their acts, precisely as sinful, *C.*; if God simply permitted their sinful acts, necessarily using them as occasions for the achieving of untold good, *Subd.*; God's providence in their regard would not have those qualities, if, in permitting their sins, God did not direct the sinners towards the attaining of their, and the world's, absolutely final end, *C.*; if He did not direct them towards the attaining of their relatively final end, i.e., the saving of their own souls, *Subd.*; if He did not direct them towards that end, in the sense that He did not supply them with means sufficient for its attainment, *C.*; if He did not direct them towards that end, in the sense that they failed to reach that end, *Subd.*; if such failure were in any way imputable to God, *C.*; if in no way imputable to God, but wholly imputable to the sinners themselves, *N.—Cd. Min.*

Cf. for an explanation of these answers, *passim,* the Prenotes to the Thesis, its Proofs, and Scholions.

5. If God is the cause of evil in the world, He is not infinitely perfect. But God is the cause of evil in the world. Therefore.

D. Maj. If God, acting with physical causes, is a cause of the reality which is evil, *N.*; if He is a cause of the evil, as such, i.e., of the privation of perfection, which affects that reality, *Subd.*; if He is the cause of moral evil, or of physical evil inasmuch as caused by moral evil, *C.*; If He is the cause of physical evil as such, intending the privation, not for itself, but as a means to an end, which might be the greater physical perfection of

the being suffering the evil, or of the particular order to which
the being belongs, or of a higher order, which, in the case of
man may be a spiritual good, either natural, e.g., the formation
of character, or supernatural, e.g., his conversion or his increase
in sanctity, or, finally, which evil is intended by God as a penalty for sin, original and personal—if God desires the physical
evil for any such good end, He is not infinitely perfect, N.; if
He were to desire physical for itself and not as a means to good,
He would not be infinitely perfect, C.—Cd. Min.

Moral evil, as such, and physical evil as brought about by
moral evil, are not intended by God, but simply permitted, God
necessarily making them the occasion of obtaining much good
of various kinds, of which some were mentioned in Scholion II.

In addition, it is to be noted that all physical evil, inasmuch
as it affects man, has a penal aspect, as we know from Divine
Revelation, God imposing it on man as a penalty for sin, both
original and personal.

Cf. for an explanation of these answers, passim, the Prenotes
to the Thesis, its Proofs, and Scholions.

6. God, however, in permitting sin, appears, at least in
some cases, to be wanting in mercy and love. Therefore the
solution above is not to be admitted.

N. Ant.

Prob. Ant. If a father who, foreseeing that his son would be
in great danger of losing his soul, if placed in a certain college,
still, for the sake of so-called social advantages, places him there,
would be wanting in true love for the boy, and sin gravely
against justice in his regard; so, it would appear that God, who,
foreseeing with absolute certainty that a man, if placed by Him
in certain sets of circumstances, would lead a life of sin and lose
his soul, still places him in those circumstances, though He
might have arranged for his salvation, would be wanting in love
and mercy towards him. But, the father, in the first case, would
be wanting in love and justice. Therefore, God, in the second
case, would be wanting in love and mercy.

N. Maj. The two cases are not at all alike, hence the denial
of the Major.

The absolute want of parity between the two cases rests on
the essential difference existing between God, the absolutely independent Creator and supreme and universal Ruler of all existing things, and essentially subordinate, particular human rulers,
who, as rulers, and in every way, are absolutely dependent on

God, draw all their authority from Him, and are under serious obligation to rule the various societies committed to their care according to His divine law.

The father, then, in the case described above, whose chiefest duty with regard to his children is to see that they are educated in the way of God, and to guard them, while under his care, from anything that could endanger their following that way, is gravely negligent in his duty, and deserves the severest censure.

God, on the contrary, who is the absolutely independent, supreme, universal Ruler of all creation, is bound by no law, no obligation. Figuratively, however, He may be said to be bound to act towards creatures in conformity with His own infinite perfections. To Him, and to Him alone, belongs the right to determine the end He wishes to attain in His creation, and the choice and co-ordination of means for the attainment of that end. That He has done so, and in an infinitely wise, just, holy, loving, merciful way, and hence that the presence of evil in the world, even of moral evil, and even of moral evil resulting in the loss of countless souls, can in no way be urged as a reason for impugning any of His infinite perfections, we have already abundantly explained and proved. The difficulty here urged, therefore, has been answered in as far as it is possible for us to answer it, and, what is more, even formally, in the explanation, proofs, and scholions of our thesis, *passim*. It will not be necessary to repeat the answer here.

We have said that the difficulty here urged has been previously answered, *in as far as it is possible for us to answer it.* For the final answer to the *Problem of Evil* and to this difficulty, God alone can give: Why, namely, He willed to manifest His glory externally in a world filled with suffering and sin, especially sin bringing with it the eternal loss of countless souls. We cannot answer that question, but we can show, and have shown, that, if sin is in the world, not God but man is in fault; none of God's perfections are on that account to be called into question; and, finally, to deny God the right to make the world He has made, because sinners, resisting His every effort to save them, prefer to die at enmity with Him, would be to subject God's will to the perverse will of the sinner—the dethronement of God.

CONCLUSION

Our reasoned study of God, just completed, from a consideration of produced being has developed logically a concept of God as a Being apart from the world, unproduced, existing with absolute necessity, personal, in nature one and only one, infinitely perfect, the world's Creator, its supporter in being and in action, its Absolute Ruler, infinitely powerful, infinitely wise, infinitely good—a reasoned, indirect concept of God, limited, yet accurate. It is our first step in our ordered knowledge of Him.

A second and higher concept of God may be ours, if we will. It is higher in two ways: in the motive which draws us to assent—the testimony of God Himself; and in its content—it embraces all that our reasoned concept embraces, and much more. It is the concept which is formed through Divine Revelation; and in a special way through the Revelation made by Christ, the God-Man and Second Person of the Most Blessed Trinity, our Saviour, in word and deed during His life on earth, concerning Himself; His Church, the infallible guardian of Divine Revelation, with its innumerable means of sanctification; and the consuming, incomprehensible love of God for man.

It is this concept of God, with all that it connotes, that will give us the patient courage to bear the trials and troubles of life for God's sake, and, so, victoriously solving for ourselves its dark *Problem of Evil,* win the reward promised by Him—life eternal with Him in Heaven.

Our reasoned study of God will have been fruitful, if it leads us to seek this higher knowledge of Him, and make it the moving force in all the actions of life.

How necessary it is for us to lean on this God of Faith, our loving Father, is shown quite convincingly in an article, "The Two Voices," by R. H. J. Steuart, S.J. (*The London Tablet,* October 7, 1939). It was written to exhort all God-fearing men and women, especially Christians, in the face of

pressing tribulation—the long dreaded outbreak of a second
World-war, forced on a world already heavily evil-laden, by
nations glorying in their unjust might as conquerors of the
weak, and openly bent on destroying the very foundations of
humanity, morality, religion, God—to listen to the voice of
the God of Faith, and put their trust in Him, their all-wise,
all-powerful, infinitely loving Father.

We subjoin some passages from this article. They offer
the only motives which can bring us true and lasting peace
when trials press heavily on us. *That,* we all desire.

Father Steuart writes:

Two voices are in our ears today. One, the voice of faith,
telling us that God is Almighty, that nothing is or can be independent of Him, that all is His will and all is in His hands,
that He is not constrained or conditioned nor in any way limited or encumbered by any creature, that without Him nothing
lives or moves or has its being: *telling* us that God is good, that
God is love, that for all of His creatures He has an infinite and
unvarying benevolence, "Thou lovest all things that are, and hat-
est none of the things which Thou hast made": *pointing to
Christ,* the image of the Father, who offers to our human comprehension the one authentic rendering of His incomprehensible nature by which we may securely fashion our thoughts and direct
our worship of Him, and in whom we see as the most distinctive
quality of that rendering, mercy, pity, sympathy, tenderness,
eagerness to heal and protect and restore, and not only the will
but the power, openly exercised again and again, to save man
from the consequences of his own folly and ignorance, from
the cruel hazards of life, from death itself.

And the other voice, the voice of what we call experience,
the evidence of facts, logic, common sense, asking how it can
be that a God infinitely powerful and infinitely loving can have
permitted this huge calamity of war to fall upon us, or can,
as it seems to us, stand aside while thousands upon thousands
of His creatures suffer and die in unspeakable misery and anguish, and all the consecrated values of human life begin to
crumble and our civilization seems to be hastening to bank-
ruptcy? Either He cannot save us, and then He is not all-powerful: or He will not, and then He is not all-loving: in either
case, how is He God? or is there no God? . . .

But when we have exhausted our ingenuity in finding some
sort of answer that may act as an antitoxin to the specious and

traitorous voice that in our present anxiety seeks to query within our hearts the love or the power of Him who has bidden us treat with Him as with a Father, we are still confronted with our complete inability to put into terms of our own natural ways of thought such a response as will entirely silence it. To put it shortly, the *data* are and must be lacking to us. We see, indeed, what has happened and is happening and will yet happen—death and pain and loss and all manner of misery and destruction—but we see it in a medium which conceals or distorts more than it reveals. Actual to ourselves though the reports of our reason and our senses are, faith teaches us that the reality of what they seem to tell us is known, is knowable to God alone. Saint Augustine, in a different but analogous connection, uses the simile of two men, one of whom can read and the other not: they look together at a written page: they both see precisely the same thing upon it: but while to one the lines convey information just as speech would, to the other they are nothing but an orderly arrangement of meaningless marks signifying nothing—he does not, in fact, see the writing at all.

Just such is the difference between the vision of God, of Him with whom there is no time nor number nor space, and our vision, strictly bounded as it is by the dimensions of all three. It follows, therefore, that our judgments upon what we think we see, will be as incomplete as our apprehension of it, and our reactions proportionately as unwarranted. . . .

It is, indeed, no use at all our trying to understand God's "reasons" for which He does or permits, whose "judgments are unsearchable and His ways past finding out"; as well hope to judge of a man's appearance, not to say of his character, by the shadow he casts upon the wall. The parallel is not inapt, for what we see now of the workings of God's will, is really but the shadow thrown upon our transitory world of time and change by the timeless operation of His immutable Being. To all the harrowing difficulties and perplexities and the insistent questioning, of which the course of human life is and must be full, we have in the end no better answer to give than that "It is the Lord, let Him do as seemeth good to Him."

We cannot successfully grapple with such problems if we try to meet them on the natural plane alone. We have to supernaturalize our approach, aiming less at the reasons for the mystery than at the reasons for accepting it: and everything that helps to this is of value to us. We remind ourselves, for instance, that in the life of Christ we have the certificate, so to speak, of God's intimate concern with ourselves and with all the world that surrounds us, as actually from within, and of His identification of Himself with us and His sharing in all that we are or do or endure: that by that life of labor and suffering and (as the world would judge it) of failure—a "scandal" and "a folly" to those who do not believe—we are saved: and that our Divine King, victorious over sin and death and all evil, was crowned indeed by us but crowned with thorns, robed as a fool, throned upon a scaffold, bearing all these things (as therefore we must too bear the like) that so He might enter into His glory. Indeed, when we remember that it was we (for we cannot divest ourselves of our share in the joint responsibility of our race) who rejected God's Son, thrust Him away from us and put Him to a shameful death, the very worst evil that could befall us must seem trivial by comparison.

The voice of faith does not silence that of reason and experience, though it speaks independently of it. Rather, it urges upon us that it is reasonable, and is justified by experience itself, to tighten our hold upon the certainty that it offers to us that in the least thing that happens to us as in the greatest, in the worst as in the best, we may see both God's unchangeable will and His everlasting love, "reaching from end to end mightily and ordaining all things sweetly" for it is not merely that in the *end* all *will be* well, but that even *now* all *is* well.

In this spirit of reason-founded supernatural optimism, to acquire which our natural study of God can, and should, if we will, uplift us, we may well bring our present work to a close.

APPENDIX

In the proofs of our theses and solutions of difficulties some few abbreviations occur. Those who are familiar with the use of the syllogism will have no difficulty in understanding and applying them; those who are not, will find the following explanation simple and yet sufficiently helpful. With very little practice the handling of syllogisms becomes quite easy.

The abbreviations used are those of the corresponding Latin words. This choice was made because the Latin verb, excluding as it does the separate use of the personal pronoun, is more easily abbreviated than its English equivalent. In the appended list we give the abbreviations, the corresponding Latin words, the corresponding English words, and whatever explanation is necessary.

MAJ., *Major,* the Major, i.e., the first or principal proposition, from which, in a syllogism, the conclusion is derived. When this abbreviation is used in our proofs, it is followed either by the proof of the Major in question or any other reference to it thought necessary.

MIN., *Minor,* the Minor, i.e., the second or subordinate proposition leading to the conclusion of a syllogism. In our proofs this abbreviation is used like the preceding one.

ANT., *Antecedens,* the Antecedent. The Antecedent, referred to by this abbreviation, is the *only expressed* proposition, from which, in an enthymeme, the conclusion is derived. An enthymeme is an abbreviated syllogism; a syllogism, namely, the Major or Minor of which is not expressed. In the few cases in which enthymemes take the place of syllogisms in our proofs, this abbreviation is used like the preceding ones.

CON., *Consequens,* the Consequent. The Consequent, referred to by this abbreviation, is the conclusion of a syllogism, an enthymeme, or any other form of argumentation.

C. MAJ., *Concedo Majorem,* I concede, i.e., I admit the truth of the Major.

C. MIN., *Concedo Minorem,* I concede the Minor.

N. MAJ., *Nego Majorem,* I deny, i.e., I reject as false, the Major.

N. MIN., *Nego Minorem,* I deny the Minor.

TR. MAJ., *Transmitto Majorem,* I transmit, i.e., I pass no

judgment on, the Major. For one reason or another, it may be advisable, or even necessary, at times, to pass a Major by without comment. In such cases, the Major is said to be transmitted.

TR. MIN., *Transmitto Minorem,* I transmit the Minor.

TR. ANT., *Transmitto Antecedens,* I transmit the Antecedent.

D. MAJ., *Distinguo Majorem,* I distinguish the Major. At times a Major may be understood in two different senses. When this happens, it is distinguished, or divided, according to these senses, into two propositions. If one of these is to be admitted as true, the abbreviation, *C., Concedo,* I concede, is placed after it. If one is to be denied, the abbreviation, *N., Nego,* I deny, is used. If one is to be transmitted, the abbreviation, *Tr., Transmitto,* I transmit, follows it. If, however, as not infrequently happens, one is still further to be distinguished, the abbreviation, *Subd., Subdistinguo,* I subdistinguish, is placed after it. The propositions resulting from this subdistinction, are treated in the same way as those resulting from the first distinction.

It is quite evident that a subdistinction is a distinction under (*sub*) a distinction.

D. MIN., *Distinguo Minorem,* I distinguish the Minor. When the Major *is not distinguished,* and the Minor *requires distinction,* this abbreviation is used to denote that fact. The remarks just made concerning the distinction of the Major, are to be applied here also.

CD. MIN., *Contradistinguo Minorem,* I contradistinguish the Minor. When the Major *is distinguished,* and *the same distinction is also to be applied to the Minor,* the abbreviation *Cd.* is used to denote the fact that this application is to be made *contrariwise,* i.e., in a way contrary, to that made in the Major. To make clear just what this means it will be necessary to say a few words about the terms of a syllogism, and the application of distinctions to them.

In a categorical syllogism, i.e., one whose propositions are not conditional but absolute, two terms, called extremes, are compared with a third, called the middle term, and from this comparison, which is made in the Major and Minor, is derived the Conclusion, in which one of the extremes, which is the predicate of the Conclusion, is, according to the quality of the syllogism, affirmed or denied of the other, which is the subject of the Conclusion. As is evident, the middle term appears only in the Major and Minor; one of the extremes, in the Major, the other in the Minor, both in the Conclusion. When, therefore, a Major is distinguished, and the distinction falls on one of the extremes, as this extreme appears again only in the Conclusion, the same distinction is to be applied to it there, and in the same way. In this case, the Minor is not distinguished; it is conceded or, if advisable, transmitted. Similarly, when a Minor is distinguished, and the distinction falls on one of the extremes, as this extreme appears again only in the Conclusion, the same distinction is to be applied to it there, and in the same way. In this case the Major is not distinguished; it is conceded or, if advisable, transmitted. When, however, the Major is distinguished, and the distinction falls on the middle term, as that term appears again in the Minor, the same distinction is to be applied to it there, not, however, in the same way, but, as was noted above, *contrariwise,* i.e., that term of the distinction which *was conceded* with regard to *one extreme* in the Major, is to be *denied* with regard to the *other extreme* in the Minor, and *vice versa.*

In a conditional syllogism the Major is a conditional proposition, and the Minor either affirms the antecedent *of this proposition,* in which case *its* consequent is affirmed in the Consequent, or Conclusion, *of the syllogism,* or it (the Minor) *denies* the consequent of the *conditional proposition,* in which case the antecedent *of this proposition* is denied in the Consequent *of the syllogism.* If the Major of a conditional syllogism requires distinction, the part there distinguished is to be contradistinguished in the Minor, if it appears there; if it does not appear there, it is to be distinguished in the Conclusion.

N. Con., *Nego Consequens,* I deny the Consequent. When a syllogism is distinguished, its conclusion is to be denied, according to the sense of the distinction used.

We make no use of this abbreviation, as the denial of the consequent in this case is taken for granted in our solutions of difficulties.

When the Major or Minor of a syllogism is denied, the syllogism falls. In this event nothing is said concerning the Consequent.

INDEX

Names, and Authors referred to or cited